YOUR QUESTIONS ANSWERED

YOUR QUESTIONS ANSWERED

SWAMI KRISHNANANDA

Published By

THE DIVINE LIFE SOCIETY
P.O. Shivanandanagar—249 192
Distt. Tehri-Garhwal, Uttaranchal, Himalayas, India

Price]   2001   [Rs. 100/-

First Edition : 1995
Second Edition : 2001
(2,000 Copies)

ISBN 81-7052-109-2

Published by Swami Krishnananda for The Divine Life
Society, Shivanandanagar, and printed by him at the
Yoga-Vedanta Forest Academy Press, P.O. Shivanandanagar,
Distt. Tehri-Garhwal, Uttaranchal, Himalayas, India

PUBLISHERS' PREFACE

The daily sessions which the Swamiji holds with varieties of visitors to the Ashram attract people from different parts of the country and abroad, since these occasions provide to people a homely atmosphere to express their longings, their questions, their enquiries and their difficulties which range over a wide area of human life. This book consists of the answers that Swamiji furnishes to the queries of the visitors during a period of several years, all of which have been tape-recorded, transcribed and edited for the purpose of publication, since it was the wish of everyone that a book of this kind, when it reaches the hands of seekers of knowledge, will remain as an interesting guide-book, a medium of reference, and even an entertainment on an intellectual and spiritual level.

It is hoped that this new publication, novel in its kind, will adequately bring relief to the seeking spirits who long for enlightenment.

Shivanandanagar,
17th March, 1995.   THE DIVINE LIFE SOCIETY

CONTENTS

DR. FAUST

*[Explaining the contrast between
Self and worldly existence]*

As Faust, the Doctor, longed for widest range
Of knowledge, power and of glory great,
Surpassing known limits of human ken
And sold the soul for exchange world's treasures,
So mortal wealth summons the mortgaging
Of Spirit calm and inward unbeheld.
The learned Faust sat up visaging things
And wondered at the joys that power grants,
To possess which became his passion's peak.
When mind's intent on what it craves and broods
Becomes the master, objects assume life.
There, then, the gangs of all that one renounced
On poverty's account do rise and speak
In all the sweetness thought can fathom e'r.
The love consciousness pours on its contents
Builds up the bridge across to outer forms,
And ushers in the vista Faust awaits.

A darkened shape clothed in the worst of dreads
Presented itself as the lord of gifts,
To chagrin first of Faust and his horror
Whom, then, he quoth, "Who art thou standest here?,"
"I am thy wish, the granter of all boons,
Ask now thy loves, thy greeds, thy joys, thy hopes,
In one instant thou wilt thy askings find
At once here and now in abundance."
Faust quailed in glee at omni-powers chance,
When that the awesome form did quickly quip
And said, "But thou shalt also give returned

x

Something, though that be paltry in quantum
To what I rain on thee as royalty."
Faust thought awhile and pondered what he had
To in return exchange for what he got
From Daimon dark who offered all the world
To Faust with all its colour, sound and joy.
"Why thinkest thou, thou hast thyself thy soul.
Give it to me, and all the glories take."
So quoth the Dark One to the chagrin Faust's
For knew he not if there was soul at all,
And if it is, where is it's habitat.

Musing again in thought if soul there is,
Faust offered it, if it was there at all,
For lost he none in losing soul for world,
Which lay unfolded in its variety,
As thousand heavens rolled up in one's palm.
"Take it, then, from me, whatever worth it is,
Thou sayest 'Give,' and I ask you to take,
For I see it not, this thing soul you call;
Have it from me, if thou canst see it here."

The Genie laughed and waved his magic wand,
A cracking creak tore up the standing Faust,
Who felt he lived in Death's promising land,
Where "not to be" is glory's enthronement
And "not-oneself" is oneself's achievement,
Where objects shine as Faust's own dear heart,
Whose heart departed planting itself "out,"
As hills would break and rend themselves to dust,
As peaks to splinters get reduced at once,
As earth's bowels their boiling flames vomit
To make an end of solids into gas,
As oceans lap up their own mass in glut,
As all creation swallowed its own flesh,
And danced in glee o'er that repast of self.
What happened none can envision or speak.

xi

If Death paraded as the King of kings
By drinking life and blowing up all light
In deep darkness of loss of sense and mind
That great marathon speed of void's plenum
Would scarcely touch what Faust experienced then.

When Self to not-self transformed ensouls life,
   Midnight does shine as blazing solar heat,
Movement forward is form of retrograde,
The right as left and left as right becomes,
The high is low and lowest is highest,
To be in others is to be in Self!

Such is the fate of one who runs to things,
   To what Consciousness sights as "another,"
Lo, mark, and then beware of what is wealth,—
The not-self is it,—Self is what thou art.

YOUR QUESTIONS
ANSWERED

1

ON FREE WILL

SWAMIJI: It has been well said that all the particles of our body—call them cells, or whatever they are—are concretisations, manifestations, solid forms of the cumulative force exerted upon a particular centre called the human individuality by the total action of the planets and the sun. So, you are a child of the solar system. You are not born to any father or mother and all that; these are all social interpretations of your position, but you have a larger stellar relation. You are a citizen of the solar system.

We should not be under the impression that the sun is so far away, the planets are invisible to the eyes, and the stars are still further. It is nothing of the kind. There is no distance in this electromagnetic field of the stellar region, the solar atmosphere. "Electromagnetic field" is the description we can give of the manner in which the entire atmosphere works. It is not visible to the physical eye. So forceful, so powerful is this influence that it concretises itself in certain forms which are called individualities. They may be the forms of the plant kingdom or animal kingdom, or human kingdom.

But, there is something more about it. The entire structure of space-time is the parent of how the stellar system operates. Space-time is a complex existence which far surpasses, in extent and range, the whole world that you call the solar system or the stellar region. It is the influence exerted by the very operation of this endless space-time complex that congealed itself in the form of the solar system, the Milky Way, etc., and further down to the bodies like ours, so that we are little, tiny drops in the sea of electromagnetic force generated by what you call space-time continuum. So, you are not sitting in Rishikesh, nor in Delhi, nor in any other place. There is no such thing as earth. It is only a name that we give to a concentrated form of cosmic energy, of which we are a part.

We are born into this body by the cumulative action of various forces. One of them is the food that we eat. The mother's diet has a great influence upon the formation of the child in the womb. Whatever diet you may conceive in your mind is a form of earth principle, water principle, fire principle, air principle, and space-time principle. These put together act upon a personality, and we cannot say whose children we are, to which country we belong, what our nationality is. Our Father is somewhere else, of whom we have no knowledge, and about whom we do not think one minute, as if He is redundant.

Every atom of space has eyes. There is cosmic intelligence pervading everywhere. This cosmic intelligence which is ensouling the entire physical cosmos can be interpreted as something cosmically in relation to the intelligence pervading your personality. Dr. Rao or Krishnamurty—they are not what is visible to the eyes before a photographic camera. "Dr. Rao has come." It does not mean that a six-foot physical body has come. It does not mean that. It is a significance; it is a meaning, isn't it? Or is it a fleshy, bony individual walking—because there are many such individuals in the world. The significance is what you call "yourself." There is a meaning in you; that meaning is what you are. This meaning is the creative force behind our existence, so that we exist not just because of our individual initiative which appears to be there. The so-called initiative of ours, the effort that we put forth, is an impulsion that comes from the centre of the cosmos. If that Centre does not operate, we cannot lift a finger; it will collapse. The finger does not lift, and the legs do not walk, merely because of the food that we eat or the medicines that we take. It is because of the permission that has come from the Centre. If the whole body is sick, every limb of the body also is sick.

Dr. Rao: Swamiji, is this permission only to act, or to act in a particular manner?

SWAMIJI: To exist itself.

Dr. Rao: To exist, and to act in a particular manner, too?

SWAMIJI: That also. Now, why should it permit you to act in a particular manner? That also is another question. It can permit you to act in some other way also than the way in which you are working. That is conditioned by your previous incarnations. Why do mirrors reflect different kinds of light?

Dr. Rao: I want to ask a few questions. I do intellectually comprehend the message that you have given me, because I am also capable of thinking abstract thoughts. Now, the books that I have, have helped me at least in arriving at a hypothesis—what I think is a hypothesis. And this is the very thought every day I go through. If this is meditation, I am going through that meditation. But, before I come to the next step, if you say that I am here because of the pressure given to me by an external force...

SWAMIJI: Yes, yes, yes. It has formed you and conditioned you and made you what you are, including the circumstances in which you are born and even the length of your life, and the mode of your existence, and the manner of your action. Everything is conditioned by That.

Dr. Rao: If everything is conditioned by That, I become an agent.

SWAMIJI: You are not an agent. It itself is doing it. There is no such thing as Mr. Rao or anybody. It doesn't exist. You see, when the finger is moving, the finger is not moving. It is the whole body that is ordering it to get up like that. So, we are like fingers of this cosmic force, and it orders that you move in this particular way. If the finger had, by chance, a consciousness of its own, it would think it is moving independently.

Dr. Rao: This analogy may not hold good because if I were to order from a central point this finger to move, the finger does not act on its own. The finger does exactly what I indicate. It does not have an independent existence, Swamiji.

SWAMIJI: That is what I am saying. There is no independent existence for anything.

Dr. Rao: No. If that is so, then, while I go through various births and deaths, where do I evolve separately from the messages?

SWAMIJI: The whole point is that births and deaths should not take place, really speaking, if this consciousness is already there. But, somehow or other this takes place because this consciousness has not been implanted properly in the individuality. The ego functions as if it is outside.

Dr. Rao: But who has implanted it?

SWAMIJI: That, nobody can say. It is like asking who created the world.

Dr. Rao: You said that in the Canadian lawyer Larry's questions. Exactly the same answer has been given.

SWAMIJI: Somehow the spark or the part has assumed an independence; that independence is called egoism.

Dr. Rao: But you say ultimately it has not. It appears to exist, but it does not.

SWAMIJI: It should not be there and it is not really there also. If this personality called the ego appreciates this position, it will surrender itself to the total whole, to which it belongs, of which it is a part—why a part? It itself is That. Then the whole force of the cosmos will enter it and you will feel an inner strength which cannot be compared with any other strength that you have in this world. So why I am telling all this is, in one minute you are in a state of meditation, provided you are able to collect your thoughts and put them in the proper context. It doesn't require one hour. Immediately you are That—you are just that which you are contemplating on.

Dr. Rao: Therefore, I am thinking of me being That, or That being me, or whatever the whole thing is.

SWAMIJI: And also, when you say "That," you should not imagine a distance between yourself and That. There is no distance. It is a total integration of consciousness where distance is abolished automatically.

Dr. Rao: So, you want to concentrate on the fact that there is no distance between you and That—that you are That.

SWAMIJI: Yes; there is no distance between anything. It is one Being. So this one Being is what people call God. There is no God outside.

Dr. Rao: This is where the intellectual exposition gets, in me anyhow—while I do understand the proposition that That is not divisible, I arrive at the root through different ways, but I arrive at the same proposition. I suppose this is very close to the Upanishadic principles. Now, once I come to the conclusion that It is not different from me, I am still unable, because I am still pursuing the

*logical path as to how I have to come to the separate
feeling that I come to feel that I am separate, and that is
where you say that we cannot take this enquiry beyond a
particular level. In other words, it cannot be explained as
to how we have come to feel that we are separate from
That.*

SWAMIJI: The difficulty is that we are unable to go
beyond the level of the comprehension of egoistic personality. In whatever way we think, we assume that "we"
are existing. Even the consciousness, "I am meditating,"—that also must go.

*Dr. Rao: That means you must dissolve yourself.
Now the other thing is that somebody else does this thing
and it gives the principle of life. Life itself is infused in
you because of that particular thing. Independent of That,
you are nothing. Then, also you are not allowing me to
go logically on that principle and say, "If I am not independent of That and It is controlling me, the one who is
controlling me should control anything."*

SWAMIJI: He does control everything.

*Dr. Rao: If He does, then why should I be thinking
and get blamed for anything at all?*

SWAMIJI: You will not get blamed for that, provided
you are sure that you are not doing it. But you are not
sure of it. You feel that you are doing it. If that kind of
total inseparable identity with the whole is felt by you,
your actions cannot bind you. The Bhagavad Gita is to
this effect only.

*Dr. Rao: But coming to that conclusion, I must cross
these hurdles.*

SWAMIJI: That is up to you. You can adopt any
method. The Bhagavad Gita is this much: No action can
bind you, provided that the vision of the cosmos is before
you.

Dr. Rao: It is my way of looking at it. While the pro-

position that there is a Universal Principle, and It is indi-
visible, is logically arguable (that far I am prepared to
go), the relationship between what is called individual
and the Universal I think depends upon...

SWAMIJI: You see, there is a conceptual relation, but
not a real relation. And conceptual relation is not...

Dr. Rao: It is only after you go beyond the concept
that you feel you get integrated with that principle. First
you have to go through that evolution, thinking process.

SWAMIJI: That is meditation. Again, and again,
assert that position.

Dr. Rao: Swamiji, whatever you say gets implanted
in me and I don't leave it. I keep thinking this every day,
but yet I have not evolved into That.

SWAMIJI: The very fact that you are able to understand this shows that you have evolved enough to make it
a part of your life.

Dr. Rao: I am not satisfied with that, Swamiji.

SWAMIJI: You are not giving sufficient time to think.

Dr. Rao: Either I am not giving sufficient time to
think, or I have really come to a stage where I am unable
to break through.

SWAMIJI: You are not unable to understand; you can
understand it. The only thing is that you have to assert it
in your consciousness. And you are not going to be a
loser. You are actually going to be a gainer by that. Your
dimension will be enhanced, and why should you say that
you have no time to think while it is the thing that you
are actualiy aspiring for? Don't you want to become a
larger person with a larger dimension? How can you say
that you have no time?

Dr. Rao: Otherwise, this enquiry would have been
given up.

SWAMIJI: Don't you like to be promoted? You

should not say, "I have no time to think of it like that."
You will certainly find time if you are going to ...

*Dr. Rao: I do find—it is not just physically finding
time. I have, to some extent, read all your books...*

SWAMIJI: It is not actually the question of physically
finding time. It is the quality of thought. It should just
take possession of you, as when a person is drowning in
water, for instance. Only one thought will be there at that
time. You will be thinking nothing else.

*Dr. Rao: The Canadian lawyer's questions are very
much my questions, and they will continue to be my questions. In terms of intellectual satisfaction, the Canadian
lawyer's questions, his wife's questions, still continue to
haunt me because they happen to be my own questions.*

SWAMIJI: They are everybody's questions.

*Dr. Rao: The answers you have given have not com-
pletely dissolved my doubts.*

SWAMIJI: You have to ponder over that again and
again, and the whole thought should sink into your feeling, so that you are living that thought. You are not simply thinking it, you *are* that.

*Dr. Rao: And then the environment in which I live,
as we were discussing—the Sankaracharyas and various
intellectual or religious leaders, etc.—they go about their
activities, but it doesn't generate the amount of faith that
one hopes these leaders do.*

SWAMIJI: They are unnecessarily interfering in matters which are to nobody's good. There is no benefit. No
purpose is served by that. They come so low to the segmented social level. It is not their duty also. They are
supposed to inspire you spiritually in a divine manner,
not interfere in political governance. That is not their
duty. What is the purpose? Why are they so much interested in it? Though political activity is worthwhile, there
are other people to do that. Why are these people worried

about that? If everybody becomes only a politician, then who will be there to think and impart knowledge? Everybody can become a businessman. Then, what will happen?

Sri Krishnamurty: But then, Swamiji, how about the gunas? If no two human beings are the same, and if all of them are parts of the same whole...

SWAMIJI: In that condition of your deep meditation, the *gunas* will cease to operate. The *gunas* will not operate at that time. If at all there is some *guna,* it is *sattva guna* at that time. No *rajas* and *tamas* will be there at that time. Only when you assert your individual personality, the *rajas* and *tamas* will come. *Rajas* and *tamas* are characteristics of the ego consciousness, whereas *sattva* is of divine consciousness. And gradually they will evaporate. What is the time now? We sit for meditation and you can also sit. We sit at five o'clock,— from five to six.

Dr. Rao: Reading-wise, I read practically all of your books, and I read the message directly given to me by you on each of my visits. They make a very deep impact on me. But yet, I am still a doubting Thomas you may call it—I am a person who has to be intellectually satisfied.

SWAMIJI: I think to a large extent you have been satisfied.

Dr. Rao: No, Swamiji. In other words, I am satisfied up to the stage that there is a Universal Principle, and that It is indivisible—that there is no birth and death, etc. Up to that, logically it is arguable.

SWAMIJI: But you must draw the conclusion from that.

Dr. Rao: That is the stage of the Universal and the individual. You know in Christianity, Hinduism—I think each religion tries to explain this very relationship, and they have done so in their own manner, but sometimes I feel perhaps this is only intellectually explained. So, for me, you could say I am somewhat confused.

SWAMIJI: When the intellect asserts itself in deep contemplation, it becomes feeling, and if the intellect and the feeling go together, they can create a flash of what is called intuition. Intuition is nothing but the blending together of intellect and feeling. They are generally acting separately. What we understand, we don't feel; and what we feel, we don't understand. It should not be like that. They must act together parallelly, so that it may be one action of understanding and feeling. Feeling is nearer to you than understanding. Feeling is what you are, actually speaking. Into that the understanding has to sink. This is what they call the process of *sravana, manana* and *nididhyasana.* Whatever we are discussing now is *sravana,* hearing. I hear what you say, and you hear what I say. Then you cogitate over this matter and sink these thoughts into yourself. Finally, you be that thought itself; that is called *nididhyasana.* This practice has to be carried on throughout the day, not merely for a few minutes in some *puja* room or any such thing. Even when you are working in an office, what prevents you from stopping for one minute and putting the pen down? For one minute think this, and it will inspire you. Then start the work. It requires one minute. You put the pen down.

Sri Krishnamurty: I found that in my experience in the office.

Dr. Rao: When you get that feeling, your actions differ essentially from what you do now because informed as you are by that feeling, it should reflect in your actions. If I feel I am separate, everything is separate, the feeling generates different kinds of activity in me. The way I look at things, the way I react to things, whatever I think, is going to be paramountly different from when I realise that everything is That, and I am That, you are

That, and I am no different from That. Is it not, Swamiji? In other words, it is the thought which regulates your activity, which gives character to your activity. Now, if the feeling of divisibility, that you are different from me, obtains in my mind, with part which controls my activity, my actions would be selfish.

SWAMIJI: Certainly they would be selfish if things are different.

Dr. Rao: But when the controlling thought is that the entire universe is operating through me and I am That...

SWAMIJI: Then your actions will be impartial.

Dr. Rao: Altogether impartial. Therefore, from the types of activities we engage in, you can determine the thought that is propelling you to do these things. Is it not?

SWAMIJI: Yes.

Dr. Rao: But in terms of the activities I undertake, though it gives me great relief on several occasions, or it makes me resist attempts to influence my thinking, and this I trace to the concept "Look here, I should not do this"—I have not yet stopped doing things which I would intellectually consider to be undesirable. Therefore, the controlling thought, while it intellectually appreciates, it has not really started controlling my...

SWAMIJI: Yes, yes. I understand. You will have no problem like that if you actually enter into it. You start doing it. The problems also get dissolved automatically.

Dr. Rao: I know,—provided I go through that stage.

SWAMIJI: You start it. You decide, "I have started it."

Dr. Rao: It is as though I am at the doorstep but yet not opening the door.

SWAMIJI: No, it will open; it will open. Truth always

triumphs: *Satyameva jayate.* And if these thoughts are the truth, they will succeed, and nothing else can succeed. Only, you have to have some little faith that it will work. It will certainly work. The whole atmosphere will change. All shall be well.

Dr. Rao: I am still in search of that thing, and I am hopeful that light will dawn on me.

SWAMIJI: You should not have any doubt whether it will work or not. It will work.

Dr. Rao: I am greatly reassured, Swamiji.

SWAMIJI: If you want something, you must assert that it has already come: "It is already with me." This is one of the psychological techniques people generally suggest; and it will immediately come. If you intensely want a thing, it will come.

Dr. Rao: Whatever activity I do, I never abandon it. That is why I am able to do certain things which I think ought to be done. So, I am still hopeful that this sort of pursuit will lead me to some destination which is what I am looking for.

SWAMIJI: Actually, this is the thought that has to be in your mind always. Whether you are in the motor car, or the office, or taking lunch or dinner—it is the vital thing that sustains you. You cannot keep it segregated.

Dr. Rao: I don't. It would not be correct to say that I disengage myself from this thought at any given point of time. It may be that temporarily at that particular point I am thinking of some problem...

SWAMIJI: No... Due to problems, the intensity of the thought may diminish at some time; but, nevertheless, it will be there.

Dr. Rao: It is there, Swamiji. In every day of my activity, it is there. But something is shrouded in mystery still. Some dark area is still not resolved. Some doubt is still there. I have to put a spotlight on that and see what it is.

SWAMIJI: The spotlight is the affirmation of the Universal Being. That is the light, before which no darkness can stand. And, the affirmation of the Universal Being is done by the Universal Being only. It is not done by you. You have gone into It when you think like this. Actually, who is meditating? It is not Dr. Rao who is meditating. That is meditating because you have already entered It. You have become part and parcel of It, so you are not meditating. There is no such thing at that time.

Dr. Rao: True. But, as you said, until you realise that you are That, you will continue to believe that you are meditating.

SWAMIJI: No, that duality you should not create.

Dr. Rao: I am not creating it. But it exists because the other proposition has not yet dawned on me.

SWAMIJI: It has, to some extent, dawned in you. Only, you have to assert it vigorously by repeatedly thinking it. Once you have entertained it in a clarified form in your mind, again you should not leave it afterwards, because the ego has such a power that it will immediately throw some dust over your thought and assert itself more and more than even the thought of God Himself. The ego always parades its importance and makes you feel that it is more important than anything else. We are feeling that the world is nothing to us—the world is something outside us, unconnected with us; it is taking care of itself and we mind our business. This is what we are thinking. Totally independent we are. We can walk on the road with arms thrown, and nobody can talk to us. But it is not like that, in fact.

Even the earth is controlling you. You cannot walk on the road totally independent like that. The very gravitation of the earth is controlling your movements. There is no freedom like that, except in a cosmic sense. Man's boast that he is independent of things and he can do whatever he likes is a vainglorious feeling. You cannot even walk on the road until the earth permits it. Such is the majesty of the structure of the cosmos. It is a very important thing to remember. If the earth is not to pull you adequately down by its gravitational force, you would be floating in the air. And, if the sun were not to pull you equally from above, you would be stuck to the ground; you could not lift your foot afterwards. So, they mutually collaborate and create a situation where you can move.

Dr. Rao: These are the laws of Nature; they are immutable.

SWAMIJI: And still, we are thinking, "I will go for a walk." Who is going for a walk? You tell me. Somebody else is helping you to push yourself.

Sri Krishnamurty: The mysterious thing is how thoughts are generated.

SWAMIJI: Thoughts are generated by body consciousness. You think that there is a body. The consciousness of a body is called thought. Otherwise, there is no other thing except that. Affirmation of this body is called thought, mind-consciousness concentrating itself in a particular location of space and time. That is individuality; that is the mind.

Dr. Rao: Suppose you let things happen as you wish—you don't try to control anything—you just do whatever you want, on impulse.

SWAMIJI: What is the meaning of "whatever you want"?

Dr. Rao: Whatever you want—whatever your impulse tells you.

SWAMIJI: That impulse is an egoistic impulse.

Dr. Rao: If it is egoistic, let the activity also be guided by that. What is wrong with egoistic activities?

SWAMIJI: Unless the ego has surrendered itself to the Cosmic Being, it cannot help you.

Dr. Rao: No. But why do you want to get help? Let things happen in the way they are happening.

Sri Krishnamurty: Or, to put it another way, what is the meaning of the word "help"? How do you define help?

SWAMIJI: There is a difference between impulse and knowledge. They are two different things.

Dr. Rao: Let your ego control your activities. What happens?

SWAMIJI: That is what is happening in the world. Everybody is doing that work. Then one ruins oneself. The person gets frustrated. He will have a clash with others. One ego clashes with another ego. War takes place and destruction results.

Dr. Rao: All right. Let it.

SWAMIJI: Then rebirth takes place, which will go on endlessly. There is no end for this,—the mistake that is committed once...

Dr. Rao: Let rebirth take place. Perhaps people would like to go on being born, and then get reborn, as they are against dissolving into a higher principle.

SWAMIJI: That shows the bankruptcy of education in their mind. They are spiritually a naught.

Dr. Rao: I thought at one time you also said, "Don't think that you are going to reform the universe itself, whatever is happening—good, bad or indifferent. There is no such thing called bad or good."

SWAMIJI: But It can work through your individuality also, if you are in a state of unison with That. You can be an instrument in the hands of that power, when you are in unison with that in your deep feeling. They will propel you to act. These are the incarnations and the prophets, as they are called. They are individuals but they are working under the command of a universal force. The whole universal power is concentrated in one individual; that is an incarnation—like the entire power of the sun getting concentrated through a lens and acting at a particular spot. They are called super-human beings. The individuality is there for all purposes of perception, but they are treading in the heavens, actually speaking, because they have consciousness of earth as well as of heaven at the same time. That is a peculiar state called *jivanmukti,* as they designate it—you are liberated, and yet you are conscious of the whole of creation. It is an intermediary stage between ordinary human consciousness and Absolute Consciousness. That is what is called incarnation consciousness, *jivanmukti* consciousness. It is an intermediary stage where you can become a cosmic worker, a world saviour, as they call it. All the saviours of the world, the incarnations—Krishna, Christ, Buddha, whoever they are—they were intermediaries of the Cosmic Force, which operated through the physical individuality of theirs, as visible to the eyes. They were not thinking through the body. They were thinking through a larger area, and so we call them incarnations. That is, "incarnation," which means the concentration of universal force in a particular body. And, you can also become that. You may become a world saviour, a prophet, an incarnation, if the thoughts of yours are cosmic thoughts. And, you will not think in any other manner except that way.

Dr. Rao: By your own endeavours you can improve the quality of your perception.

SWAMIJI: You may, yes.

Dr. Rao: This is the proposition. Is there a role for individual efforts?

SWAMIJI: When That operates through you, you should not call it an individual effort.

Dr. Rao: But if I want to lay down the proposition like this—because you are all the time telling us that you should improve constantly, improve and move towards that principle, ultimately realise that you are not different from That, and you are That, and there is no subject-object relationship. You are evolving from something baser to something higher. If this is the correct understanding of what you have laid down—therefore, there is a role for me in this, a role for me to evolve.

SWAMIJI: There is a role for you as a representative of that force—like an ambassador of the Cosmic Being.

Dr. Rao: Yes, but then, still it is my role. If I don't make this, the cosmic force is not going to help me. So, therefore, I have to create this...

SWAMIJI: No, "my role" means that it is not your individual role. You are not having your own personal will. You are only an instrument in the operation of it.

Dr. Rao: If I am an instrument, then let that divine force guide me. I don't make any individual effort.

SWAMIJI: When you think, you will know that It is thinking through you. You will know It. Sometimes you say, "he is possessed by divine forces." You get possessed by That, and you can know that It is working through you, somebody else is speaking through you.

Dr. Rao: Why don't I invite the divine force to enter and say, "Now let us move forward."

SWAMIJI: It will do that. It can do whatever is necessary for the evolution of the total universe. It is not doing it for the welfare of any particular individual. There are no particular individuals.

Dr. Rao: Then, why should I meditate, Swamiji?

SWAMIJI: So that you may know that it is the truth.

You are always thinking you are somewhere, in some place. You have to remove that idea. There is a peculiar habit of the mind asserting itself as located in some place, in a particular form, in a particular condition, etc. This must be removed.

Sri Krishnamurty: What Dr. Rao says is, if I am That, why not let That guide me in the proper line?

SWAMIJI: It will certainly guide you.

Sri Krishnamurty: If that is so, then why should I meditate?

SWAMIJI: It will guide you only after you become one with It. For that, you have to meditate. The government protects and guides the ambassador, but for that he has to become the ambassador first.

Dr. Rao: But, the ambassador is different from the government. He only carries out the instructions of the government. He is not the government himself. Government is a larger entity.

SWAMIJI: That is true. So, he is acting as a representative of the government itself.

Dr. Rao: Therefore, I asked at the very beginning, "Am I the agent?"

SWAMIJI: In one stage, you are the agent. There are three stages.

Dr. Rao: If I am the agent, I carry out these instructions. I can't be held accountable at all. I am not answerable to anybody.

SWAMIJI: Certainly you are not accountable, provided you are having that consciousness of alignment with the All.

Dr. Rao: Then it is conditional; you have introduced a proviso.

SWAMIJI: Otherwise, if in the middle you start thinking you are Mr. Rao talking, then it won't work.

Dr. Rao: No, if I am the ambassador, I know that if the government gives me instructions, it is as the ambassador of that country; I go and give it. And if these instructions don't fructify, if nothing comes out of it, or bad comes of it, I can't be held responsible because I merely carried out the instructions given to me by my superior.

SWAMIJI: He is responsible only if he does something contrary to the government ordinance.

Dr. Rao: Yes. But you are also saying that I cannot even act contrary to the direction. One is incapable of doing so, because it controls.

SWAMIJI: Sometimes it is possible in the intermediary stage to slip into ego consciousness. If you are continuously maintaining a universal consciousness, you are not responsible for anything. But that consciousness is not maintained always. Sometimes in the intermediary, earlier stages, the mind slips into ego consciousness and mistakes can be committed. Even Lord Krishna said, "I cannot repeat the Gita a second time." He had come down from that level of absolute universality when he spoke the Gita. When Arjuna said, "Speak to me once again," He said, "No, no. You are a foolish man; I cannot summon it now."

Dr. Rao: If you slip into it, while logically pursuing this, doggedly pursuing it, it means are you acting contrary to the instruction of... Even that slipping into that former direction—are you accountable?

SWAMIJI: You will not so slip after a certain stage. It is the force of individuality. For ages and ages we have been living in this body, and so it is having its say even when you are meditating and insists, "I am also there." To overcome that feeling of body consciousness repetition of conscious affirmation is necessary.

Dr. Rao: One can reconcile and say that it is the divine wish that it be like this.

SWAMIJI: You are not merely saying that it is a divine wish. You know that it is a divine wish and you will never feel that you are yourself doing anything at that time. It all depends upon what you deeply feel in your mind. What are you feeling? You will then feel that you are not doing anything independently.

Dr. Rao: I somehow feel that we have to say that we can't do anything independently of the divine principle. You are also saying that sometimes you can get out of it. And when you get out of it, there is a disconsonance between you and the principle and, therefore, the grief. Isn't it? That is how it is. Then the person realises if I am totally controlled—I am a puppet in the hands, as it were, of the higher principle—then, if I am a puppet, I can't go beyond that stage. I am always whatever I do, good, bad, or anything.

SWAMIJI: But, there is no good and bad at that time, in the depths of being.

Dr. Rao: No. Until that realisation comes, you will still say that he is doing something good or something bad, and it is all on account of the operation of the divine principle.

SWAMIJI: Your operations will be for the cosmic welfare. It cannot be called good or bad in a social sense.

Dr. Rao: But you should first think that you represent the higher principle.

SWAMIJI: Not merely think it—you have to be inundated with that thought and you will not think in any other manner.

Dr. Rao: So, until that state, duality is there?

SWAMIJI: Then you are responsible for what you do.

Dr. Rao: This is what you said: In other words, as long as you remain ignorant, you are the karta (doer) of your actions. You have to reap the fruits of your actions.

Is it not what you said, Swamiji—notwithstanding the basic principle that you cannot do anything independently of the divine wish?

SWAMIJI: Even then, it remains an abstract acceptance, but the body asserts itself as "me."

Dr. Rao: Asserts itself from what? From the divine wish?

SWAMIJI: No, it rejects the divine wish.

Dr. Rao: Can it?

SWAMIJI: It is doing it now in a foolish manner.

Dr. Rao: Its ability to depart from the divine wish is what makes the principle somewhat difficult for us to follow.

Narayani: But it is not against the divine wish that one is appearing to depart from it.

Dr. Rao: So, therefore, everything is on account of the operation of the divine principle?

SWAMIJI: Finally, it is that only.

Dr. Rao: If that is so, what happens is that anything that is happening in this world...

SWAMIJI: Everything is happening due to its action.

Dr. Rao: This is what I had said in the beginning because when the Lord reveals Himself in His total existence—you see, what you consider to be good, bad, indifferent, everything is as it is, the universe as it is, is seen.

SWAMIJI: No part of the universe can be regarded as either good or bad.

Dr. Rao: So, therefore, what happens is that whatever you see now is a departure from it. This is Kali Yuga. It has evolved from Treta Yuga, Dvapara Yuga—and then, the bad is more than the good here in this age. This is nothing but That.

SWAMIJI: It has its own plan, yes.

Dr. Rao: Very difficult, Swamiji, to evolve into these various things.

SWAMIJI: This is the discussion of the law commission of the universe.

2

BEAUTY AND THE PSYCHOLOGY OF DESIRE

Lyle: Swamiji, I have a question about beauty. You have written that beauty is a mild manifestation of the soul. I find myself always looking for beauty, and I want to know how I can work with that as part of my sadhana.

SWAMIJI: Beauty is the characteristic of that object which exactly fits in as a counterpart of the lack in the mind of a person. There is a kind of lacuna in the mind, and the exact counterpart of it is the beauty of the object. It is a purely psychological question.

There is a particular lacuna in the mental structure of a person which keeps that person restless, unhappy, etc. Though everyone is unhappy in some way, the cause of that unhappiness is not uniform in all cases. The restlessness and unhappiness may be caused by different factors in the case of different persons, and a corresponding object must be presented before that particular type of mind in order that it may be made to feel happy.

What looks beautiful to me may not look beautiful to you. People sometimes get attracted even to ugly things. What you may consider as ugly and uninteresting may be an attractive thing for another person, because he/she is in a different kind of mental make-up. Each one has to find out what it is that attracts. Unless you are hungry, the food will not be satisfying. Your particular kind of hunger will determine the kind of diet that you need.

Unhappiness cannot be removed by a uniform remedy or a common medicine for all people. Either you find out yourself what you are lacking, or you try to know it through the help of some person who can guide you and analyse your mind in depth. Once you know why you are unhappy, you can also know the remedy, and you will know what kind of beauty you are after.

Lyle: The curious thing about beauty is that it is undefinable.

SWAMIJI: It is not that beauty is spread out everywhere in the world so that people can go and see it. It is not visible like that. It is visible to the individual eye only, and not to the common perception.

Beauty is not independent of the observer. Actually, there is no such thing as beauty. It doesn't exist. It is like taste. There is no such thing as taste; it is only an action of a particular thing upon the working of the taste buds in our tongue. If the taste buds don't operate, nothing will be tasty. The object as such is not tasty. There is nothing sweet, nothing bitter. There is no such quality in objects, but they act upon a particular structure of our physiological operation, and they feel palatable or otherwise. The world as such has no quality. It is impersonal—neither good nor bad, neither beautiful nor ugly. We react to it due to our own unique structural make-up.

Lyle: Then, in what way were you saying that beauty is a mild manifestation of the soul?

SWAMIJI: It is a manifestation of the soul, something like a square rod entering a square hole, when, immediately there is a sense of perfection. The soul is nothing but the symmetry, completeness and harmony of consciousness. If we thrust a round rod into a square hole, there is no perfection in the act. The round rod should go into the round hole only. There is some kind of want in the mind of a person, which craves for its fulfilling counter-correlative.

The soul is not a substance. It is consciousness, a feeling of completeness. The consciousness of completeness is the soul. There is no soul outside or inside; consciousness *is* the soul. The soul is not directly acting. It has to act through the mind. So, whatever we perceive or conceive is the mental operation. The mind reflects the soul, and only then we become conscious of certain things, but we are incompletely conscious; we are not "completely" conscious of anything since the mind is rarely an undivided function.

There is no sense of completeness in any of our perceptions. Just as when the sun's rays pass through a defective set of spectacles we will not see things properly, we will also not see things properly when the soul is reflected through a defective mind. When the mind is set right, and the defect is removed by bringing before it the exact counterpart of its lacuna, it appears as if the soul is reflected entirely. That entire reflection is the feeling of satisfaction. Then we call that medium beautiful, tasty, nice. It is a deep psychological process.

The need will differ for each person. The kind of perfection that you need will be quite different from another's. And you can't love the same thing for all times, either. Even one's own wish will change according to circumstances. You can never be happy with the same thing throughout life. That is not possible. Our longings are fickle, not of a uniform type.

Lyle: Swamiji, how can we sublimate desires?

SWAMIJI: You will never be able to sublimate the desires until that which they seek is given to them. The important point is how you will give them what they want. The manner of supplying their demand is your wisdom.

You cannot suppress a desire; no desire can be buried down. If you suppress it, it will create further trouble. You have to fulfil it, but how you fulfil it is the wisdom of the seeker.

Sometimes you may supply its need even by not giving it literally what it wants. If you literally start supplying all its demands, then it will be a very difficult problem. Sublimation is different from fulfilment. Fulfilment is a direct sensual process, whereas sublimation is a spiritual integration.

The mind wants some particular things, not all things at the same time. The mind does not want the whole world to be given to it. Nobody asks for the whole world; so every desire is intriguing in its working. When you are prepared to give it the entire thing, it doesn't want it; it will want only certain particular chosen things. This is the sign of lack of wisdom behind any kind of desire.

There are simple desires, strong desires, permissible desires, depleting desires. Desires which deplete your energy should not be fulfiled. Those which are harmless, like wanting to take a cup of tea in the cold weather, will not harm you in any way; but there are other dangerous desires which may exhaust you completely and make you weak. Such desires should not be fulfiled.

From the point of view of a *sadhaka* (a spiritual seeker), gradually the mind should be educated to feel satisfied with the whole, rather than a part. If you ask for particular things, you will never have an end for these desires, because today you will get this particular thing, and you feel that you are satisfied; tomorrow the very same mind, like a dacoit, will want another thing. If you start supplying the demands of a dacoit, today he will want your purse, tomorrow your house, the next day your land and, finally, he may want your life. So, you cannot go on satisfying the highwayman.

Desires are such things, and you should educate them. Introduce educational ways of thinking, holistic thinking. Don't give just particular things to the mind, but try to give wholesome things. Finally, nothing can satisfy you, except God Himself. All other desires are futile, and they will only bind you into more and more troubles. You must educate the mind to have trust in God and feel satisfied with the beauty of God.

We were discussing about beauty. God is the most beautiful object. No object in the world can be as beautiful as God, but we have been taught by religions that God is an old man, the Creator, Father in heaven, with a long beard; how can He be beautiful?

No religion openly holds that God is beautiful. He is rather a judiciary, lawmaker, a terror sometimes, ready to dispense justice, but no religion says that He is a beautiful person. Here is a mistake of religious teachers. We go for beautiful things, rather than a judiciary.

We must accept that God is the most beautiful, and no beauty can equal that beauty. Then the heart will feel satisfied with that perception of the most beautiful thing before us. God is not merely grand or magnificent; He is also beautiful! Let the heart accept it. Then you will see the desires subside, and you will ask for nothing in the world afterwards. Any other method is not going to be successful.

Lyle: *My mind says that God can't be conceived.*

SWAMIJI: You can psychologically conceive Him by adjusting the mind in a wholesome manner. Anything that is wholesome is God. God does not mean something far away from you. It is the characteristic of wholesome thinking, total thinking, and not partial or fragmented thinking. *The object of perception should be included in the process of perception itself.* It should not stand outside you. Our perceptions are partial as long as the objects stand outside the process of perception.

We don't see things properly; we see them partially, as isolated from us. Objects are not really isolated. They don't stand outside the process of perception. You have to educate yourself into the conviction that the object of perception is included in the very process of perception. This is the holistic thinking that I am mentioning. Then you will not desire the object as an "outside" something. When the object is included in the very process of perception, how will you desire it? The desire ceases immediately. *Sadhana* is also a process of education. One must be very careful in thinking, and not think in a haphazard manner. It is a difficult art, but you will be happy if you succeed in it.

Lyle: So, we should try to include the object in the subject?

SWAMIJI: What you see with your eyes is included in yourself, in some way. We are unable to understand it because we think through a finitised form of the mind. There is a process by which we are able to know that the object exists. If you analyse that process, you will find the object does not stand outside you. If it is totally outside you, you would not be even conscious that it is there outside you. It is an integral process taking place in perception. This itself is a kind of meditation.

Lyle: Swamiji, in the process of meditation, do you suggest a sequence to draw the mind into pratyahara concentration?

SWAMIJI: This is explained in the *sutras* of Patanjali. There are two types of psychological processes dealt with in modern days, in what we call abnormal psychology and general psychology. All thinking in terms of a particularised desire for anything in the world is abnormal perception. Thinking of objects without any particular desire for anything is general perception. If I look at a wall, I don't have any particular desire for the wall; but if I see an orange, there may be a desire to eat it. So, these are two types of thinking. The mere consciousness of an object without particular emotional reaction towards it, and consciousness of an object with emotional reaction towards it, are both reactions of the mind called *vrittis*.

The emotionally charged *vrittis* are called *klishta vrittis*, by which the author means pain-giving psychoses. Pain is caused by the feeling that you have not got it, while you would like to have it. Secondly, you have pain even after getting it, from the fear that you may lose it; worse still is the pain when you have actually lost it.

So, the object of desire is always a source of pain. When does it give you pleasure? Anyway, such desires and ways of thinking are *klishta vrittis*. These have to be dealt with in the beginning. You asked me the sequence. The pain-giving ones should be dealt with first, just as in medical treatment, acute diseases are treated first, and the chronic ones later.

Suppose a person is breathless, and also has eczema. You don't treat eczema at that time; you treat the breathlessness first. So also we don't bother about general perceptions of mountains and rivers and all that, though they are also *vrittis*. We have to deal with acute conditions first (desire-charged *vrittis*), which have been classified by Patanjali briefly into objects which you like, and objects which you dislike. Both are connected with desires. The desire to have and the desire to avoid are both desires only.

Actually, you cannot desire a thing unless you do not want certain other things. You exclude certain things automatically when you go for certain chosen things, and those things which you exclude become the objects of dislike or hatred. So, love and hatred go together; they are like the obverse and reverse of the same coin. The one cannot be without the other.

These are two types of *vrittis* connected with likes and dislikes, as Patanjali mentions. There is another *vritti* which takes the form of fear of death. All struggle in life seems to be towards the maintenance of oneself towards survival. By some means or the other, one wants to survive. With all the glorious possessions of the world, one does not wish to be threatened in regard to one's life. Fear of death, love and hatred for things, and egoism, self-assertiveness, I am first and everybody else afterwards, are considered by Patanjali as pain-giving *vrittis*.

Every seeker of truth, spiritual seeker, *sadhaka*, should dispassionately analyse these psychoses. If you want things, make a list of all those things and find out the ways and means of handling them. All the other *vrittis* mentioned also have to be taken independently, one by one. They should be dealt with in such a way that they do not cause harassment in ordinary life. Very rarely do people succeed in controlling these abnormal *vrittis*.

Even if you succeed in having no such abnormal longing for things, you will have the general perception of an object outside you in the form of the world itself. That has to be dealt with as a second stage. This is more difficult than the earlier one. You may somehow withdraw your mind from desiring things in some way, but how would you withdraw the mind from being conscious of the world itself? That has to be dealt with by *samadhi* or *samapatti*. There are stages of meditation prescribed by Patanjali. I have detailed these processes in my book, "Yoga As a Universal Science."

These desires have certain peculiarities. They do not always manifest themselves openly. Often the desires have very good intelligence. They know that a frontal attack does not always succeed. They lie in ambush and, when you are unaware, suddenly pounce on you, and you will be caught by these desires even without your knowing that you have been so caught. Suddenly you will start doing something and later you will repent, because you were not circumspect about the possibility of hidden desires.

Desires can also be dormant, like a sleeping thief. Or, when you try to corner them from every side by your meditations, they may become thin, attenuated, as if they are going to die, but they can again become robust when the occasion for it comes. A starved thief also is a thief only; he may eat well and afterwards become robust.

Also the desires may appear sometimes, and disappear at other times. When they disappear, it doesn't mean they are absent; a thing that is out of sight is not necessarily non-existent. And sometimes, they openly come and face you. So, they can be sleeping, attenuated, interrupted, or directly attacking. These are the ways in which desires catch hold of a person. One has to pass through many years of struggle in order to get over them.

In case you, by your maturity of meditation, succeed in overcoming these abnormal longings, you will have the problem of the consciousness of externality itself. That is a very serious matter. The universe has to be identified with the Self in deep meditation so that the phenomenon of externality is absorbed into universality of perception. Briefly, this is the sequence of how you have to handle your mind.

Lyle: I have been thinking that in the sitting process itself to first take care of the tamasik and rajasik mind.

SWAMIJI: These abnormal desires are a mixture of *tamas* and *rajas*. The mere consciousness of an object without desire is a *sattvik guna* or quality operating. If you are conscious of a tree in the forest, it doesn't harm you in any way; yet the consciousness of it being outside you is an important matter. It is a *sattvik vritti*, but it is a *vritti*, nevertheless.

Merely because you are bound by a golden chain, it doesn't mean that you are not bound, and the *sattvik vrittis* must also be overcome. So, from *rajas* and *tamas*, you go to *sattva*, gradually.

Lyle: And after that, don't you still have to be neither in ida nor in pingala? You have to establish in sushumna.

SWAMIJI: They will take care of themselves by your meditation. You need not even think of the *ida* and *pingala*. Actually, they are effects of thought. The channel through which you breathe is a consequence of the manner of your thinking. When the thinking is corrected, the *prana* gets corrected automatically. You need not bother about it at all. You just ignore it. It will go into the *sushumna* automatically.

The first and foremost duty is to take care of the thoughts. The *prana* will be next, and it won't bother you much. The trouble is from the mind only. It has to be considered first. All yoga is a mental operation finally, an adjustment of thought integrally.

Lyle: In the process of meditation, I find the mind in a tamasik or rajasik state. What can I do at that time?

SWAMIJI: At that time when actually *tamas* and *rajas* are supervening and they are very troublesome, stop the meditation. Take a cup of tea, have a little stroll on the verandah, take deep breaths some ten or fifteen times, and sit again for meditation. After that, the mind will start concentrating once again. It has entered into *tamas* and *rajas* due to the fatigue felt in meditation. It got exhausted, like a horse pulling a cart for a long distance. After some time the horse will halt and then there is no use of simply hitting it and making it go further.

When the mind is tired or unwilling, you should not

meditate. If it is exhausted, take rest. If it is unwilling, you find out the reason for it. It wants something else other than what you are doing.

Lyle: Usually it can be worked through, can't it?

SWAMIJI: When it is turbulent, you cannot meditate. If it is a little distraction, well, just keep quiet for a few minutes and then restart. For ten or fifteen minutes don't meditate; keep quiet, take a deep breath and start again. Sometimes you can munch something, so that it may be satisfied. The mind wants satisfaction, not too much harassment. Then, afterwards, you sit for meditation. It will come down.

Sometimes, if it is very difficult and it is not coming down at all, go to sleep for a few minutes; then get up and start meditation once again. You have to employ various methods, as you treat a naughty child which will not at all listen to anything. You have to employ various methods of controlling it. Sometimes you have to fulfil its longings; sometimes you have to use educational methods; sometimes you may give a medical treatment, etc. You have to use your intelligence in understanding the problem.

Lyle: Do you suggest pranayamas?

SWAMIJI: They are useful to some extent, but not completely. You cannot control the mind merely by *pranayama*. How will you remove your desires when they are strong, merely by the breathing process? Simultaneously you must work with the mind also. *Pranayama* is necessary as a secondary aid, but is not the complete solution.

Lyle: Swamiji, how can we try to sublimate desires?

SWAMIJI: First you must find out why desires arise. Why should desires arise in the mind at all, if you conclude that they are not good things? If they are good things, there is no need of sublimating them. If they are not good things, why are you allowing them to rise? You deliberately manufacture them under the impression that they are good, and at the same time you say that they are not good. So, you have a dual attitude towards them.

Now, who creates the desires? Are you deliberately creating the desires, or are they, in spite of yourself, coming up? That you have to find out first. It is a process of self-analysis. The deep root of the desire has to be found out.

Lyle: I think they are from basic urges.

SWAMIJI: When you use the word "basic," you perhaps imply that these desires are inseparable from your very existence as a person. That is the meaning of "basic." Your existence as a person implies the existence of these desires, also. So, that would mean that they will go only when you (as a person) go, because they are inseparable from your very existence.

How will you go? The personality of yours should cease to be; then the consequence in the form of these desires also will cease, according to our analysis. When the cause goes, the effect also goes. The whole question is the very existence of the person as an individual psychophysical existence. That has to go. That has to be sublimated, not the desires. The poor desires are only henchmen of the very existence of the person. The chief culprit is the existence of the individual himself, and the desires are only offshoots of the existence of the person. That is to say, the sublimation is not of the desires, but of the personality-consciousness.

The personality-consciousness can be sublimated only by transcending it in a universal consciousness. You are conscious that you are a person named Lyle, and it is a very wrong definition of yourself. This is a nomenclature of the physical personality. As long as this physical personality persists your problems also are going to continue. If you want to get rid of these problems, you must be sincere in handling this issue. You should not just say something and forget these things afterwards. Your physical existence itself is a problem, and that has to cease.

The individual existence ceases only in Universal Existence. It cannot cease anywhere else. So, when your meditation is fixed on the consciousness of Universality of Being, the individual consciousness gets merged into It and transcended. Together with that, the desires also get sublimated at one stroke. This is the highest technique that one can think of. There is no other solution, finally. All other solutions are temporary and a make-shift. The final solution is only this deep meditation on the Universal Existence, before which no problem can stand. The whole thing vanishes like darkness before the sun.

3

ON MEDITATION AND SERVICE

Ronald: What is the purpose of meditation? What is the goal, and how do you know when you have achieved this goal?

SWAMIJI: You should answer your question yourself. What is your method of meditation?

Ronald: I try to be as quiet as I possibly can, and watch my breathing, and then slowly go to the mantra. I move from the breathing to the mantra, and then try to think it without verbalising it——in other words, hear the mantra without any physical movement or physical manifestation——and then, as the thoughts come up, try to act as a disinterested observer. I try not to identify with any one thought, to observe the thought but not cling to it, and then to allow the next thought to emerge.

SWAMIJI: You say that you are trying to go inward, but why do you want to go inward? What do you gain by it? What is the purpose that is in your mind?

Ronald: I want to go inward to appreciate my own being, unmodified by external influences. I want a greater awareness of that thing called my Self.

SWAMIJI: What is the meaning of "going inward"? Are you going inside your stomach? Where is your Self at this moment?

Ronald: My Self is right here. The whole entity encompasses the Self, but I want to become more fully con-

scious of it—*to have a more complete sense of it as op-
posed to an intimation of it.*

SWAMIJI: Do you mean to say that you are not conscious of your Self just now? When you say that you are
Ronald, is there not a consciousness of your Self?

Ronald: In a superficial way.

SWAMIJI: Why do you say it is superficial? Is it not
a reality?

*Ronald: It is a reality, but I would say that there are
stages of reality.*

SWAMIJI: I am glad to hear all these things. Very
good. Now, do you mean to say that your real Self is hidden deeper than the Ronald self? The Ronald consciousness is also a kind of self. You are saying that it is
superficial, and meaning thereby that your real Self is
deeper than the Ronald consciousness. How far deeper?

*Ronald: That I don't know. And I don't know how
one knows if one has arrived.*

SWAMIJI: Suppose you reach the deepest level of
yourself. What happens afterwards? That is the answer
to your question of what is the purpose.

*Ronald: I would say that I would be a complete per-
son.*

SWAMIJI: Will you still be conscious that you are
Ronald when you have entered the deepest level of yourself?

*Ronald: I would say yes, because if I didn't, it
would mean that in that stage I would be limited. I
wouldn't have a grasp of something that I had a grasp of
before.*

SWAMIJI: It means that when you have gone to the
deepest level of yourself, you will also be aware of all the
other levels of your self which you have transcended; so,
you will have a multiple-personality consciousness at that

time. You will not be having a unified consciousness, but a multiple consciousness of all the layers of whatever you could be. You will feel that you are many things, instead of being one thing.

Ronald: Well, I would say that it would be a sense of there being many aspects of something, but that it would be one entity there.

SWAMIJI: You mean that these aspects are conceptual, or really existing?

Ronald: Well, they are conceptual.

SWAMIJI: Then they are not really existent levels. They are only some ideas of yours.

Ronald: Well, if you operate on a concept, then it becomes a reality.

SWAMIJI: Now, here is a great question. Is thought identical with reality?

Ronald: Well, if the thought enters the world of action, then it becomes a reality.

SWAMIJI: You have a thought that the world is outside you. You think that the world is there before you. Can you say that the thought itself is the world, because thought is identical with reality? Is the thought of the world, or is thought itself the world?

Ronald: I would say that thought is of the world.

SWAMIJI: Then the concept is not identical with reality; they are two different things. Anyway, you are asking me what the purpose of doing all this is, and you answered your question yourself by saying that you feel complete when you go into the deepest level of yourself. Do you feel that you are satisfied with this answer?

Ronald: Well, I haven't achieved it.

SWAMIJI: No, but when you achieve it, you feel that you are going to be complete. A sense of completeness will supervene in your personality, and that is the purpose of meditation. This is what you think?

Ronald: Yes.

SWAMIJI: Whatever you have told me about this purpose of meditation is perfectly all right, but there is something more than that. You have reached only one stage; even if you go to the deepest level of your self in the sense that we have tried to comprehend it, this is not the end of the journey. There is something further. There is something greater than one's deepest self because the word "me" has come. As long as these "I, you, he, she, it" terms continue to persist, we have not reached the ultimate aim of life.

In the ultimate existence, there is no he, she, it, I and you. Nobody will say "my Self, your Self," etc. These ideas are empirical, tentative, relative, connected with personality-consciousness, and the Self is not a person, it is a Super-Person. I am giving a hint that there is something more for you to know than the level you have reached now by this analysis. It will take some time even to understand what this great thing is.

Knowing your deepest Self is identical with knowing God Himself. That will be a terrifying thing to hear! How will knowing the deepest level of my being be the same thing as knowing God? You have an idea of God as the comprehensive Almighty, the universal omnipresent Being. Is He planted in my own heart at the deepest level of my being? Then what is my relationship with God? After having known that in that deepest level you will have a sense of completeness, the question still persists as to what the relationship is between yourself and God. That is the next step.

Whatever we have been discussing up to this time is the first step only. We have not touched the second level.

The second level is what your relationship to the cosmos, and to God Himself, is. That is the next step.

There is a book called the Bhagavad Gita. It has eighteen chapters. The first six chapters deal with all these questions, about which we have been discussing just now—about the deepest Self and all that. The next six chapters, from the seventh to the twelfth, touch upon this other question of what your relationship to the cosmos and to the Almighty Himself is, and then there is something more about it in the last six chapters.

An in-depth study of this profundity is necessary. You cannot know the secret of things in a few minutes of discussion. That is why we say that for years you must be at the feet of a master to understand these things. Books do not always clarify these matters. It requires a divine blessing to come upon you. According to Indian tradition, this blessing comes through the *guru*, and perhaps it may come through God Himself. It is a quest that will continue throughout your life. It is not a question of a few months or years, and it will continue until you don't have a single doubt in your mind. You are asking how you will know that you have reached it. That is a question of doubt. A person who has reached it will not have any doubt.

How do you know that it is daytime and not night, and how do you know that you are a human being? How do you know that you are Ronald? This is an intuitive perception, and you will have that kind of perception there. You will never have a question afterwards of whether you have reached it or not. A person who feels a doubt whether he has reached it or not has not reached it. He is still outside it. You have to be at the feet of a *guru* for long years, and then these questions will be clarified.

We had also this humble blessing of being with a great master, Swami Sivananda. We have been with him physically for some twenty years, and whatever peace of mind we have today is due not to study, but due to being with him. The personality of the master exudes an energy and a kind of blessing that is indescribable. You don't know what this blessing means, actually. You feel energised, clarified, elevated, strengthened, and a new light enters into you by merely having a contact with him and seeing him every day, talking to him, being near him.

Study of books is not sufficient. You may read all the library, but still doubts will persist. The company of a great master is necessary. Now you are on the right path, but it is still a long journey ahead. Be happy that you are on the path, but be also sure that you have to continue on this journey for a long time.

Ronald: Having been given this gift of life, how can we increase the quality of living?

SWAMIJI: It is a very serious question. Trees, animals, insects, and human beings live. Perhaps you have observed a difference in the quality of living among these species. Though the tree lives, we seem to be living in a better way than a tree or an animal lives; but in what way are we better? We breathe, and animals and plants also breathe; we eat, and, animals and plants also eat. We sleep, and they also sleep. But apart from these phenomena, what is the speciality in a human being? Various answers have been given.

A human being can think, and argue the pros and cons of a situation, which animals and plants cannot do adequately. We can infer the future from a present condition, which prerogative is not given to the animals fully. There is also another aspect of the matter. We want to live, but why do we want to live? What is the harm if one does not live? What is the reason behind this insistence on being alive? What do we gain by being alive?

Ronald: Well, one would hope that one's life has a purpose.

SWAMIJI: Now you have touched a vital point. We feel that by being alive we will be able to fulfill the purpose for which we are alive. Now, what is that purpose?

Ronald: I would hope somehow to make the world a little better as a consequence of having been here.

SWAMIJI: Oh! You mean to say that we are alive so that the world may become better because of our being alive?

Ronald: Hopefully.

SWAMIJI: Are we here to make the world better?

Ronald: I think we are here to make a contribution to the world, and to others. How to do that effectively, and at the same time feel at peace with oneself, so that you are not making a sacrifice when you are doing it, not punishing oneself.

SWAMIJI: Now, what is it that the world is lacking which we are in a position to give to it? It appears that the world lacks something, and we have it; if we give it, the world becomes better. We have something which the world does not have. This is what you mean. What is it that the world is lacking and we have?

Ronald: The world can be an impersonal place, and we bring a certain personality and intimacy to it.

SWAMIJI: You mean personality is superior to impersonality?

Ronald: I would say so.

SWAMIJI: Here is a question we cannot answer in this crowd of people sitting here. This is a serious question being raised about whether it is correct to say that personality is superior to impersonality. This is a metaphysical question. Perhaps, it goes deep into the spiritual depths of all existence. Can we say existence is personal or impersonal? Personality perishes; and if that is the case, you cannot call it superior to impersonality. Anything that is perishable is not worth having, and if our personality is perishable, I think we should get rid of it as early as possible. What is the good of hugging that which is perishable? And the consciousness of something being perishable brings us face to face with something which is perhaps not perishable.

What is it that is not perishable in this world? If we can contribute something to make anything imperishable, that would be a great thing. Being ourselves perishable, what imperishable contribution can come from us? Who can expect anything worthwhile from us, when we ourselves are perishable? When our life itself is in danger, what contribution can we make to the world? At any moment, anything goes. The whole world is evolutionary, subject to destruction of a prevailing condition. It is in a state of flux and permanent movement, giving no indication of permanence anywhere. If every moment is a fluxation and a movement towards destruction (which includes our own selves also as personalities), where is the purpose in life? There is something imperishable either in us or in the world or in both things which we are pursuing, and if anything can be regarded as a worthwhile purpose in life, it must be something which is imperishable in nature.

· Perishable things cannot be regarded as purposes in life. Nobody will go for perishable things, because at any moment that perishability will catch hold of our necks. So, there is something imperishable which is keeping us alive, and insists that we should be alive. This desire to be alive continuously is a touch of imperishability working in us. Perishability cannot speak because every minute it dies. I cannot speak to you, and you cannot speak to me, if there is only perishability in us, because thereby every second we are demonstrating the worthlessness of our existence. But if we are alive for three minutes at least, that would show that there is something more than perishability in us. The perishable cannot exist even for three minutes; it goes in one second. But that does not happen. We are continuing to exist, which shows that there is an imperishable in us, and we must find out what that imperishable thing is.

I think the quest for the imperishable is the purpose of life, and if that can be achieved, we can make that contribution also to the world. What is the use of giving a perishable thing to the world, and imagining that we have done some great good? Everything in the world has some element of eternity behind it; otherwise, it cannot exist. When we say that evil exists, we are saying that there is a divine element also behind it. Eternity is there in the midst of the temporal things that we see in the world. First, it is necessary for you to exist in order that you may serve the world. Are you sure that you are going to exist?

Ronald: Well, I am existing.

SWAMIJI: You are existing for how long? For how many minutes? If you say that you are going to exist for another fifty years, who gave you the guarantee?

Ronald: No one.

SWAMIJI: Then why are you assuming that you will live for another fifty years? How can there be such an ungrounded assumption?

Ronald: I am not making an assumption that I will live fifty years.

SWAMIJI: It is there, implied by the statement that you are going to contribute something to the world. It is a very important question. Unless you are sure that you are going to exist for a considerable period of time, the question of contributing to the world does not meaningfully arise. If that assurance has been given, it is wonderful; but let it be there. Otherwise, it is a futile attempt to go on saying that you will contribute to the world when tomorrow the man will breathe his last. There is some flaw in this doctrine of service to the world, which has to be found out. The man himself will not be there. What contribution can be made afterwards? There is something more in life than service, unless you interpret service in a different sense altogether.

Ronald: What do you mean by "more in life"? That implies that there's an awareness of what that something is.

SWAMIJI: I am thinking that I have spoken enough now. We should postpone this subject for another time. This is a serious matter, and it should not be discussed in a slipshod manner. It is a question of life and death, as they say.

What is our future? Let the future of the world be anything. What is your future, and what is my future? Let that be clear first. We shall think of the future of the world afterwards. We have not created the world, and we are not supposed to be so much concerned with it. Let the Creator of it be responsible for it.

Who created the world? Has He any responsibility over it? Or has nobody created it? If you believe in a person who must have created this world, can we say that He has some responsibility over it, or has He shoved the entire responsibility on you, or on me? Let us think over that matter also.

Somebody created the problem of the world, and we are responsible for it? Is it a justice? If God or somebody who has created this bad world expects us to share His burden and suffer for it, He is not a very wise person, nor is He a charitable person, also. Why should God create an evil world and expect us to rectify it?

There is something serious about this question. First

of all, let us decide whether God has created such a world. Secondly, has He created an evil world so that we have to work for removing its defect? Is it true that our service is required by the world, or are we so egoistic in imagining that we have the power to redeem the world? These are important questions. Before we talk further, these questions have to be answered.

Is it the egoism of man that makes him feel that he is capable of serving, and making the world better? Or, is there some other thing behind it which makes us feel that we are to work for the world? Many have come, and many have gone, and they have left the world in the same condition that it was. Do you believe that because of the service of so many people, a world of iron has become a world of gold? Buddhas and Christs have come and gone. They have also contributed much to the world. What are you contributing further? Are you greater than Christ and Buddha?

Ronald: I think that, as we go along, the consciousness can increase and develop, but the world in a sense is neutral.

SWAMIJI: Is the world a bad world?

Ronald: No.

SWAMIJI: Then what is the contribution that you are making?

Ronald: The world is not bad, but it is men that affect the world. It is a neutral substance.

SWAMIJI: If it is a neutral substance, it is better you leave it as it is. Why are you interfering with it?

Ronald: It's the nature of man.

SWAMIJI: What is the nature of man? To interfere with things? Why should he? Why is he interfering with things which were created by somebody else?

Ronald: Just by the mere fact of acting, we have some effect on it.

SWAMIJI: What are we aiming at, finally? That should be clear first. Whether by contributing or not by contributing, what is the final aim? What are we aiming at? What is this contribution, the purpose, the final end of things?

This is a question of eternity, rather than a question connected with time. There is an endlessness behind all these processes we call service, life in the world, etc. We cannot discuss these matters in a round-table conference. We have to be sincere in this quest which is super-physical, super-social and to a large extent super-psychological. There is something in man which defies definition in terms of society and social relations. You are not merely a social unit; there is something in you which is above society, which is an eternity speaking through you, which is the reason why you feel that you are safe and secure and that you will continue to live endlessly in this world. That impulse has arisen on account of the eternity parading in the midst of temporality. We should not discuss things like this in a casual manner. They are serious things concerned with the future of humanity, and the future of the soul of the human individual. The impulse for service, for doing good, arises due to the involvement of every individual in the cosmic movement of Nature towards the Supreme Absolute. Here is the secret of all life and effort.

4

TOTAL THOUGHT AND MEDITATION

Krishna Kumar: What is meditation?

SWAMIJI: Meditation is an integration of consciousness. It is not a routine or a ritual. It is not a religious exercise belonging to some religion. It is an opening of yourself to the final realities of life. It has nothing to do with Hinduism, Christianity, Islam, or any religion. It has no connection with any scripture, also. It is an impersonal act on the part of yourself, wherein you lift up your consciousness to a recognition of the fact that you are a temporary sojourning entity into eternity.

You have come from a larger realm, and will enter into the same realm after some time, which will indicate gradually that your existence has a kind of cosmic sweep. From plane to plane you have journeyed in your millions of incarnations. How many planes of existence have you crossed, through what forms of life, what types of experience; how many parents, relations, types of work you have had! All these things you cogitate slowly in your mind so that you start thinking along these lines, and you will not think you are Krishna Kumar any more.

This is only a temporary form that the cosmic form has taken due to some *karma*, some pressure of circumstance. Neither do you belong to Jaipur, India, nor to anything. You are a travelling cosmic force, like a meteor, coming from one plane and moving to another. Your thoughts have to be oriented along this fashion. Don't think like a man or woman thinking. We are ultimately, in what we call a spiritual sense, neither human beings, nor males nor females, but only forces of Nature which have concentrated themselves in certain space-time points, looking like individuals. This is how self-analysis has to be carried on. When you think along these lines, you will find that your mind becomes "total" instead of fragmentary.

Generally, nobody thinks in a total fashion. You always think of something other than yourself. It is taken for granted by the mind that what you are thinking is something different from yourself. If it is not different from you, there is no need of thinking it. You don't go on thinking yourself. So, every thought of every person is directed towards something which is assumed to be totally different from the process of thinking. This is a mistake.

From this little introduction about your being a sojourning individual in a cosmic setup, you will appreciate that you cannot even think unless all the atmospheric conditions of the cosmic condition are involved in the very process of thinking. When you think, it looks as if you are thinking like a cosmic being, because your mind is connected to all the circumstances through which you have passed in all your various incarnations.

They say if you can remember some thousand births through which you have passed, and all the relations which you had during these thousand births, you will find today that there is nobody in this world who is not your relative. Everyone is related to you in some way or other through the circumstance of some incarnation, some birth or other. This is why they say that the world is a single family. Though it is told in a socialistic sense, it is much more than that. It is really so. Like the various branches of a tree coming forth from the root, all these manifestations and forms of existence have come out from One Root.

I was just telling you about meditating, in my own way. We don't do meditation merely for doing it; we want to get some benefit out of it. There can be benefit only if your thoughts are harmonious with reality. If you dichotomise your thought from the reality of the world and consider it as an external object, then it will be finite thinking, and finite thinking will produce only finite results. So, I am again coming to the point of total thinking, which is called meditation.

All the thoughts of everyone and of everything will be comprehended within the total grasp of your mind in this act. When you sit for meditation, what should you do? I am thinking of some object, person, situation. Your mind has to consciously, vitally, involve in itself the object which it is thinking; otherwise, you cannot even be conscious of the object. The very fact that you are conscious of some object outside you implies that it has already entered the mind. It has become part and parcel of your consciousness. Now, here is the technique of total thinking. You cannot think the object unless you accept that it is a part of your thought itself. Thus, the thinker is not Krishna Kumar. It is something in between the object and the so-called subject. It is a connecting link, transcendent.

In our ancient scriptures we use words like *adhyatma*, *adhibhuta*, *adhidaiva*, etc. *Adhyatma* is the thinking subject; *adhibhuta* is the object, but we don't know anything else. We think only two things. I am here and I am seeing and thinking something else. But you cannot think something else unless there is a connecting link of consciousness between you and the other object. The thinker is actually that connecting link. That is called *adhidaiva*, the superintending divinity. So, who is the meditator?

Now I am coming to another more advanced step.

You are not meditating, because if you consider yourself as the meditator, you cut yourself off from the object. But I mentioned to you that you cannot cut off your consciousness from any object, inasmuch as, unless it is involved in that object, thinking is not possible. So this involvement-consciousness is a transcendent consciousness which is above both you and the object. Do you understand the point? It is a very subtle thing, and very difficult to catch that little crux of the matter.

You transfer your consciousness, as it were, to the middle connection, transfer your consciousness to the centre where you contemplate both sides, as if the body is thinking of two hands. This is the subject and this is the object, but the thinker of both is the body; so you are not one person thinking of another thing. Meditation does not mean thinking of an object; it is a transference of consciousness from the subjectivity of yours and from the objectivity of the object to a central point which is transcendent to both. That is the divinity which is called *Ishtadevata.* You contemplate like this. This is what they call total thinking, and this is the essence of meditation.

Another Visitor: But Swamiji, I don't understand...

SWAMIJI: What I was telling is that your consciousness of an object implies the presence of a connecting link of consciousness between you and the object. Actually, the thinker of the object is not you. There is something else in the middle which thinks you and the object at the same time, which fact is not known to you, due to which you get stuck up with an object. You must transfer yourself to the middle point where you will also look like an object only, so that you have no attachment to yourself any more. Neither are you attached to yourself nor to the object; you are a totally impersonal, isolated, transcendent Being which is the *devata,* the controlling principle of both yourself and the other. And there are degrees of this involvement until it reaches the Absolute. This is how you have to meditate.

Visitor: But the mind gets tormented by thinking of other people.

SWAMIJI: It is tormented by any kind of thinking. Neither you should think yourself, nor the other. The torment comes either because you think yourself or the object. You must transfer yourself to another impersonal thing, which is neither you nor the object.

Visitor: Even when you are thinking of yourself?

SWAMIJI: Why are you thinking of yourself, as if you are protecting yourself? The protector is somebody else. The whole mistake is that you are representing yourself so much, as if you are the only important thing. This is not the important thing, nor the other thing. There is something else which is controlling everybody. You have to transfer your consciousness to God. God is sitting between yourself and the other thing, and He is the thinking principle. If that concentration can be done, all problems will be solved. Neither you should think yourself, nor another thing. This art is a difficult thing, but there is no other solution for it. It must be done with great effort, and there will be no problem afterwards.

Visitor: What is the difference between total thought and meditation?

SWAMIJI: They are the same thing. Total thought means a perfect form of thought, and meditation means the same thing. It is a total thought, not little bits of thinking, one thing at a time. Generally, we think little things, but that is not correct thinking because when you think something, you exclude something else. You should exclude nothing and include all things in your thought; then it becomes a total thought. It is something like God-thought. That is the perfect form of thinking. Then you will have no troubles from the mind afterwards. There

will be cooperative forces working together. If you exclude something, that something which you exclude will
not cooperate with you. That is why troubles arise.

Visitor: But, Swamiji, in our general life...

SWAMIJI: General life does not mean imperfect life.
It also should be perfect. You have been taught wrongly;
your education itself is faulty, right from the beginning.
That is why everybody is suffering. Technological education is not real education. One requires also psychological education.

Visitor: Swamiji, we have so many mantras.

SWAMIJI: That is a different matter. You may have a
mantra, or no *mantra*. If your mind is not thinking correctly, even a *mantra* cannot help. Your mind should be
adjusted perfectly, even to the *mantra*. Even the *mantra* is
a total thought; it is not only one thing that you are thinking. All things are combined in the *mantra*. The total divinity is in the *mantra*, so even the *mantra* is a total
thought. All spiritual practice is an attempt at maintaining
total thought, complete thought, which is called perfect
thought—or you may even say it is God-thought. Everyone is meant for that ultimate attainment. Nobody is excluded.

*Visitor: The people and situations that occur around
us—are they creations of our own thought?*

SWAMIJI: These situations in which you find yourself are due to some actions that you performed in the
previous birth. They react as circumstances of your present life. Present experiences are results of past actions—
a   previous   birth   or   even   a   further   birth
backwards—something you have done, good or bad. If
you have done some good, you are well placed and you
are comfortable and happy. But if you have done something opposite, you will have pin-pricks, harassments,
etc. You will get exactly what you have given to others.

Visitor: But, Swamiji, through our own experience, we always visualise; so our experience has a limit, and so our thoughts will also have a limit.

SWAMIJI: That is what I am saying. You must try to overcome that limit by learning the art of a new way of thinking, which is called the spiritual way of thinking, about which we have been discussing now. You have to forget all the old ways of thinking, and start a new way from today onwards. Then you will find a new psychological strength arising from your mind. You will feel confident in yourself; you will not feel diffident.

When you are sure that your thinking is correct, you will receive cooperation from all the forces of the world. But if you start excluding things one by one, those things will also exclude you. Then you will have difficulties. If I exclude you, you will exclude me, also. That is the law of the world. If I include you in myself, then you will also include me in yourself. This is how the world is working.

Visitor: Should we try to correct others?

SWAMIJI: Whether you are really expected to correct them or you mind your own business, that is left to your personal choice. There is nothing wrong with trying to correct others, provided you feel it is a necessity and also a possibility. Otherwise, you need not interfere with anything. But if it is an essential thing for some reason or the other, then you can, unless you are greater than those whom you are reforming, the effort may not lead to success.

Visitor: How can we know our level?

SWAMIJI: Your level is known from your desires. You can know what your desires are in one second. You don't express them, but you know them very well.

Visitor: But how can I refine them?

SWAMIJI: You cannot refine them unless you prac-

tise meditation on God. There is no other way for refin-
ing desires. Meditation, *japa*, prayer all mean the same
thing, finally. They are only various ways of expressing
one and the same thing. You cannot refine your desires
except by directing them to God; then they become purified. Ultimately, your desire must be for God only.

We were mentioning about perfect thought. Perfect
thought is God-thought, and that only is the way of puri-
fication. Desires are all selfish and they have to be converted into unselfish desires in the next stage. Then, the
unselfish desires also should cease in the Universal desire
for God. The desire by itself is not bad. It all depends
upon to what object you are directing it. If it is directed
to your personal physical gain only, it is selfish desire. If
it is directed to the welfare of all people, it is unselfish
desire. If it is directed to God Almighty, it is Universal
desire. So all are desires only, but there is a difference in
the manner in which different desires work.

There are three stages: selfish, unselfish and Universal. Gradually, you have to rise from the lower to the
higher. Nobody, truly, works for God, and nobody works
for other people, also. Each one works for oneself, and so
mostly the world is filled with selfish people only. A few
are unselfish to some extent. But Universal desire is unthinkable. Such a thought cannot arise ordinarily in the
mind of a person. A person who entertains a Universal
desire cannot be regarded as a human being. Such a one
is super-human.

When desires cause pain, you should remove them.
When desires cause pleasure, they also should be removed. There are two desires—those that bring pain and
those which bring pleasure. Both are bondages. By
stages, gradually, they have to be eliminated.

5

WHAT IS THE SELF?

Luciano: How can I know the Self?

SWAMIJI: If you know the meaning of what the Self is, then you will automatically know how to go there. If you know where Rome is, you will know how to go, also; but if you don't know where it is, it is difficult to go there. So, where is this Self sitting? If you are sure as to where It is, then you will also know how to go. Now, tell me where It is.

Luciano: The saints and sages say that the Self is everywhere.

SWAMIJI: OK. How can a person go to a thing which is everywhere? Suppose a thing is everywhere; then, where are you sitting? If It is everywhere, It is under you, also. Then, where are you sitting?

Luciano: On the Self.

SWAMIJI: Then why are you crying? You have already attained It. You are sitting on It and asking me how to attain It.

Luciano: But I don't see It.

SWAMIJI: You are not seeing It because It is everywhere. If It is only in some place, then you will see It. That is the whole problem. How can you see a thing which is everywhere, unless you also become everywhere? If you also become everywhere, then you will see that which is everywhere. You are only in one place, and the Self is everywhere, so there is a contradiction between your existence and Self's existence.

This contradiction has to be removed. Either It should be in one place, or you should be everywhere. The Self cannot become something in one place, so you have to become everywhere. Then you will "see" It. People who think alike will become friends. If you think in one way and That thinks in another way, how will you contact It? So you must think as the Self thinks, and what does the Self think? It thinks, "I am all things." Can you think like that? The essential point is here.

You are thinking that you are Luciano from Italy. This is the only idea that you have got, but this kind of thing cannot take you to the Self. As long as you are Luciano, and you are from Italy, then nothing will work.

But you are not Luciano, and you are not coming from Italy. You have not come from anywhere; you are just where you are, and you are not Luciano. You can be any other name, also. Somebody called you Luciano, and now you are saying that you are Luciano. Somebody can call you Joseph, and you will say that you are Joseph.

Luciano: So then I have all the names.

SWAMIJI: Then you have no name! So, don't say that you are Luciano. When you start going near the Self, all kinds of trouble will arise. A big storm of troubles will come up from all sides; as the Self is everywhere, the trouble also will come from all sides. If you are prepared for It and don't mind the difficulties that come, and you are bent upon It, you will get It. But if you are only experimenting with It and seeing whether you can get It or not, then It understands your mind, so It won't come. This is a very serious matter. You will get It,—no problem. But you have to pay a high price—many *liras*! But the Self cannot encash *lira*, and all that!

For travelling, for your passport and bank account,

you may call yourself Luciano, but when you are sitting alone, forget this idea. You sit alone and look at yourself and tell yourself that you have all names so you have no name. But have you a form? You have two things, name and form.

Luciano: In the book you suggest to place the consciousness outside, between the object and the subject.

SWAMIJI: When you concentrate on any object, your consciousness is transferred to that object, and then the consciousness of you body becomes less. You are thinking too much of this body; therefore, the objects are cut off. But one of the techniques of meditation is to concentrate the consciousness on another thing. It may be anything. Then immediately the attachment to this body gets loosened. That is one method which is prescribed by Patanjali in the Yoga Sutras.

That thing which you are concentrating upon can be any object. It can be a little material thing, or it can be God Himself, or all the five elements, or the sun, the moon, the stars, space, time—to anything you can transfer your consciousness. Then, the attachment to this body gets loosened and becomes less and less. Slowly you will find that your mind spreads into a Universal state. This is one method of meditation. Here, the consciousness exists between you and what is outside you! Wonder indeed!

Luciano: When I try to concentrate on one thing, often the mind goes like a monkey.

SWAMIJI: It doesn't matter; let it go. Again you sit and start. Even if it goes again and again, it will come also again and again, by practice. Every day you eat food and every day you feel hungry also. Like that, it is the same thing. The mind goes again and again, but again you sit. Keep doing it, and you will see that it comes under control. Then one day you will find that you will be able to think only in that way. You will then not think in any other way. It is a question of repeated practice.

Luciano: At the end of the third discourse, you mention that all will be clarified if people can answer the question of where the Self is. But the Atman is everywhere, so how can I discover It?

SWAMIJI: Why should you discover It, if It is everywhere? That would mean that It is not everywhere. You are saying two things. You have to discover a thing which is not near you. If It is everywhere, how will you discover It, and also, who will discover It? Luciano is not there, because Luciano has gone into that which is everywhere; so who is discovering It? This is a very subtle point. If It is everywhere, where is Luciano at that time?

Luciano: He is nowhere.

SWAMIJI: Then what problem have you? If Luciano is not there, what else is there?

Luciano: Luciano has no problem because he is not there.

SWAMIJI: Then why are you putting questions unnecessarily? You have to sit with a *guru*, and there is no use of only reading a book. You see, what I told you in two sentences is more important than the whole book. If Luciano is not there, the problem also is not there. Then who is putting a question?

Luciano: Nobody.

SWAMIJI: So you are happy!

Luciano: Yes!

SWAMIJI: With great difficulty you are happy! This point which has entered your mind just now, which has suddenly made you say reluctantly that you are happy, should be the object of your meditation. Day and night you must think this point: If the Atman is everywhere, nothing else is. The whole thing is that Atman, the pervading light everywhere, the dazzling light of the Atman which is the Universal Being, which is the Atman of everybody; there is only one Atman.

Go on telling this to the mind again and again so that the idea of Luciano and people, things and buildings and everything goes in one second. Go on thinking It again and again, and tell it also to the mind one thousand times. Don't think anything else for three hours every day and you'll see that something will happen afterwards.

Luciano: The problem is to expand my consciousness, because I think one of the problems is the separation between us and the Atman.

SWAMIJI: The separation arises because you are thinking that you are outside that Atman, but you have already said that you cannot be outside It. Your reason says that you cannot be outside It, so the feeling that you are outside It must be raised and merged into your reason. You cannot have two things, feeling something, and the reason saying another thing. They must come together.

That act of uniting the reason with the feeling is meditation. Go on driving that thought of reason into the feeling. Keep telling the feeling that you have accepted this point, that This is the only thing that you want, that This will give you whatever you want, and that you want nothing else. Tell the mind again and again, like a *mantra*. Do this meditation for three hours—in the morning, afternoon and night.

Don't create doubts in the mind. Write in your diary that you have no doubts. You have to go on telling the same thing again and again, because, otherwise, doubt will come and say, "No, you are not all right." When Buddha, the great Yogi, was meditating, some demons came to him and told him that he was a foolish man. Even Christ was told by somebody that he was wasting his time.

The reason should merge with the feeling. These should not be two different things. The feeling is very turbulent and troublesome. It will go on telling some wrong thing only. Though the reason says the right thing, the feeling will tell the wrong thing.

Luciano: Sometimes also the reason gives a wrong answer.

SWAMIJI: The reason needs to be purified by instruction from a *guru*. Everybody has a reason, but that is ordinary, lower reason. We are now speaking of the higher reason, which accepts the universality of the Absolute and thinks nothing else. That has to be driven deeply into the feeling, all which is the process called meditation. If you can do it continuously and think nothing else in the mind at all times, then within a short time you will experience some great change in your life. You must wait for that day.

Luciano: So my first object of meditation must be that I am the only one, and that I have no doubts.

SWAMIJI: Yes. You write in your diary that you have no doubts. Every day see it, in big letters: "I have no doubts." If anybody tells you from inside that you have doubts, you say *no*. This will take you a long time; it is not an easy job. You must find time for it, and it will be all right in due course. If you persist in It, It will come to you.

The secret of success is that you can get anything you want, provided you want only that thing. But if you want two things, then you will get neither this nor that. Is there anything that you want entirely? It is difficult to find something like that, where only "that" is wanted. Nobody can live like that, with only one thing. There is also another thing, second thing, third thing, etc. So many things we want! But there is one thing, by getting which, you will get other things, also. All the waters of the world you will find in one thing, which is the ocean; so, find out that ocean.

Luciano: It is difficult for me to understand your image about drops in the ocean, and the separation between the drops, and the ocean made from infinite drops.

SWAMIJI: The ocean itself is one big drop, but it is also made of small drops; many little drops put together become an ocean. But actually, in the ocean, the drops don't exist; they are one integral whole. So, you may say there are no drops in the ocean, yet you can say it is made up of drops. Both notions are correct. Actually, the drops in the ocean are only conceptual. The mind says that there are many parts. Ideas move the world.

Luciano: So, also, in the world, I am separated from others.

SWAMIJI: It is like that. You have got a conceptual feeling of difference of one from another. Really, they are connected together into a vast ocean of infinite force. The people who are sitting here look like isolated people, even as conceptually you can imagine many drops in the ocean.

You have many cells in the body, but yet you are one man. The billions of cells make one Luciano. So, even if it looks like many, it is still one only. When there are many branches in a tree, the tree will not think that it is many trees. It is one tree only, though the branches are many.

The process is to become aware that there is one consciousness pervading everything, and it itself appears as all the objects. One tree appears as many branches, but is integrated by one tree-consciousness. Similarly, you will feel the ocean of force as identical with you. All these things that you see outside you are part of that conceptually differentiated, but really united being.

Luciano: Yes, but different people have different manners.

SWAMIJI: Even if there are many varieties of branches (one is straight, one is bent, one is up or down), it makes no difference to the tree. There are people with defective limbs, yet they think that they are a complete whole. The consciousness is not of defect. The body may have some defects, but the consciousness feels that it is perfectly all right. Varieties of limbs do not make varieties in consciousness. Consciousness is one only.

Luciano: So what appears as the forms is only a question of appearance, and not substance.

SWAMIJI: Yes. There are big waves in the ocean, and small waves, yet it is still one single ocean. This requires deep thinking every day. A long time you must take for this meditation, and do study also, if you require it as a help.

6

THE HIGHER SELF

SWAMIJI: When the drop dissolves in the ocean, at that time, what does the drop think? That experience is the Higher Self. Do you understand?

Malaya: But I am thinking that I am a drop only, Swamiji.

SWAMIJI: No. Who asked you to think like that? Otherwise, what is will power? A person has feeling, understanding, and also will. Do you know what will is? Will is determination: We determine that "it" is like "this." You have sunk into the ocean, and this ocean is your Higher Self.

Malaya: The ocean cannot see itself?

SWAMIJI: Why do you want to see? How can you see what you are? You can see somebody else. How will you see yourself?

Malaya: The process of thinking is there, Swamiji.

SWAMIJI: There is no thinking. As long as you are a drop, thinking is there but the ocean doesn't think, because there is nothing to think. What is there to think? Only "itself" is there. All the drops are inside it, so what will it think? That is the Higher Self. The drop is the lower self; the ocean is the Higher Self. But it does not mean that the Higher Self is separate, just as the ocean is not separate from the drop. You are not applying your will. Perhaps you are not fully interested, also. The heart is not eager. Will is nothing but the application of interest.

Malaya: Understanding is there, but...

SWAMIJI: No, no. Interest, not understanding. There is a difference between understanding and interest. When you are interested in a thing, you will not forget it. If you are not fully interested, you will have so many excuses.

You cannot break a mountain. However much you may try, it will not break. But if you apply dynamite, it will split the mountain into pieces. That is, dynamite is the will, you have to acquire it. It will split the egoism; the whole thing will break. If you do not want it, that is a different matter. If you have a suspicion that it is perhaps not possible for you, then it will not be possible, also. But, if you say, "No, it is certainly possible for me," then it will be possible. What you feel you are, that you really are. You should not say it is difficult.

To carry yourself is not difficult; to carry another person is difficult,—Oh, he is a very heavy person; who will carry him? But you can carry yourself, whatever be the weight. Even stout people carry themselves, but they cannot carry another person. So, likewise, there is no problem in handling yourself.

Malaya: Swamiji, in practical life...

SWAMIJI: There is no such thing as practical life. You are unnecessarily creating differences. That "practical life" is an activity of the lower self, and the lower self is included in the Higher Self. Thus, the activity also is of the Higher Self only. Then, who is telling me that there is practical life? There is no such thing as isolated practical life. It is the Higher Self only doing all these things. Do you understand the implication of it?

Malaya: Yes, Swamiji.

SWAMIJI: When the Higher Self does all your Magazine Department work, it is a cosmic action taking place. The whole world will throb when you go into the office. Actually you are not going to the office; you are entering into yourself only. The office is your own self. Wherever you go, you find yourself only, just as in the ocean, wherever you go, you find the ocean. Whether you go to a station, or market place, or dining hall, you are actually entering into yourself only. You should not say that you are going to the dining hall, and all that. There is no dining hall. You are entering into yourself, in various forms.

Malaya: There is no...., Swamiji?

SWAMIJI: That is entering of the self. The self enters into the Self. It is a metaphorical way of speaking. Everything is taking place within one thing only. You have to exercise a little bit of thinking on what it actually means. Do not say that you are going to the market, etc. You are going to yourself only, even when you go to the market. The market is inside yourself.

You think over it; a wonderful experience will come, and a miracle will take place. But, if you are doubting, then nothing will happen. "God is somewhere, and daily life is something else"—this is the argument of everybody. This is a silly argument, because the mind is not catching the point. "Practical life is something else," you are telling me. There is no such thing as practical life. It does not exist. It is your own self moving within itself.

The huge ocean is there, and tremendous waves are dashing over it. The ocean will not say, "I am sitting quiet, but the waves are practical life." The waves are not the practical life of the ocean. There is no practical life for it. The ocean is itself the waves. The waves are the ocean. The Self itself is all this practical life.

There is no such thing as secular life and spiritual life. There is no distinction. People make a distinction between earth and heaven, God and world, spiritual and secular. These do not exist, really. They are all tricks played by the mind, so that you may not do anything worthwhile. "I am working in a factory every day and I have no time to think"—you should not say that. You are not working in a factory; you are working in yourself only. There is no factory outside yourself. Is your mind catching what I am saying?

Malaya: Yes. Swamiji.

SWAMIJI: You will be a different person in one day. You will not be what you are. For such a transformation to take place, it may take one day, or even less than one day. The whole earth will tremble, if you think like this.

Malaya: The mind has to ...

SWAMIJI: There is no mind there. It is consciousness. You are not a mind, nor a body, because in the state of deep sleep you have no mind, and you have no body. So, your real nature is pure consciousness, as it is in the state of deep sleep. So, don't say "mind" and all that. That is another "practical life" you are bringing in. There is no such thing. You have seen in the state of deep sleep that the body and mind are not there. Then, who was there? It was not Malaya existing there. He, also, was not there. Who was there? That thing you grasp and cogitate.

In sleep, you had no father, mother, relations,—nothing was there. Just, you were there. And, the state of sleep brought you such a joy that you would not like to have any other joy compared to it. Even a king cannot be so happy as a person who has entered into deep sleep, because he has entered the Self, the ocean of Self. And, you had no relations, no property, no friends, no body, no mind at that time. What was there? "You" were there.

This is what I call the ocean. Do not make a distinction between practical life and factory life, office life etc.

There is really no such thing. See, this is a very interesting and important point. You must be always happy, blissful,—everything is fine; nothing is wrong. Everything is good; all is well with me. Why should it not be? It must be. Nobody can create trouble for you. Who can create trouble? You are creating trouble for yourself, because you yourself are the trouble. So, why do you complain? The mind is very subtle. It cannot think like this. If it starts thinking thus, it will become giddy, and you will fall into sleep, again.

This is the highest purificatory process that I am suggesting. Your mistakes and your sins are all completely washed off by this kind of meditation. All the sins of many lives that you have lived are all cleansed, as hundreds of years of darkness vanish in one second when the sun rises. The darkness might have been there for hundreds of years, but removing that hundreds of years of thick darkness requires only one minute of the rise of the sun. So, whatever be the mistakes that you have made in many lives, they have no consequence before the light of this kind of experience. All your old *karmas* are like mountains of straw. They can be burned into ashes by one matchstick.

7

THE GOOD AND THE BAD

Malaya: How can I compare the good to the pleasant?

SWAMIJI: You have asked me this two or three times. I have already explained it to you. You have not heard what I said last time. Do you remember that you have put this question to me on what is the Higher Self and lower self? You are raising the same point in a different way. You asked me what is the Higher Self and the lower self. This is the same thing you are repeating once again,—conquering the lower self by the Higher Self. The lower self is the sensory self, the physical self, the perceptional self. The Higher Self is the Universal Self, which is the only Self. As far as the lower self is concerned, there are many lower selves.

Many people are sitting here. They are all so many lower selves. One has no connection with another, as it were. But, there is an underground current of connection of all these lower selves. That is like the ocean of Self; that is the Higher Self. Nobody knows that It exists, because the sense organs are compelling the individual self to look outside. You cannot look inside and see what is at the back. If you see the back, you will see a sea of consciousness. That is the Higher Self. On That you must meditate, and if you do that, the lower self will get absorbed into the Higher Self. That is called salvation, liberation. It is a simple matter, if you understand it. You must meditate like this.

Malaya: What is there to enjoy, Swamiji?

SWAMIJI: I have already spoken on that previously. You are not really renouncing any "thing". You are renouncing the "thing-ness" of things. You are sitting before me as a thing, but there is something in you that is not a thing. You look like a person, but you are not a person, really. The personality of yours is a condensed form of an internal urge which comes from the Universal Being. This condensed form should liquefy, melt down into the original impulse, which comes from the Universal Being. You cannot renounce anything, because, only if you possess something, can you renounce it.

Malaya: Then, there is no question of enjoying, Swamiji.

SWAMIJI: You are enjoying yourself only, finally; and, that is the highest enjoyment. It is the merging of the whole thing into yourself, which is far greater than possessing things. You are not "possessing" things, but wish them to "become" you, because that is a greater joy than possessing things.

Even when a person desires a thing, the subtle desire is to "become one" with it. That is why if you hear that your object of desire is nearby, you feel happy. When it comes near, and you can see it, the joy increases; and when it is coming nearer still, there is more joy. When you touch it, it is still more, but even that is not sufficient. You cannot, unfortunately, go beyond that. You can touch an object of desire, but you cannot enter into it. That is why there is bereavement, suffering, death, birth, and all that following desires. The ultimate desire is to make the object melt into your being. You do not want to stand outside it. You want perpetual enjoyment, but the space-time complex which is outside prevents the object from entering into you, because every object is independent; so, how can it become your property?

There is no such thing as possessing anything. It is a foolish idea, but actually, the intention is to merge yourself with the self of that object, so that the two selves become one self of a bigger size. If all the selves melt together, it becomes a larger self. There, all the objects become the Self; then, who can compare that joy to anything else? It is incomparable bliss because the object has not been "possessed," it has "become" you. Can you imagine what kind of condition it is? You will never lose it afterwards, because you are "that" only. Can you catch this point?

It is a wonderful thing to hear it. Even to hear it is a wonder. Go on thinking like this every day, and see what happens to you. Some miracle will take place. Every day you must think like this continuously, and go on brooding, asserting it: "It is like that, it is like that." Then, you will see that some mystery will open up before your eyes. You will not be an ordinary person afterwards. Tremendous joy, power, happiness, everything will well up from inside. Daily you must go on thinking like this, and do deep meditation.

Malaya: Swamiji, what things are good?

SWAMIJI: Some things are good because other things are bad; but why are other things bad, and this is good? This is not an easy question to answer. What is the meaning of being good? When you say something is good, what do you mean by that? It is pleasing to you; is it like that? So, does it mean that whatever pleases you is good? Can you say that? What pleases you may not be good, and what is good may not please you;—this is also possible. So, how do you know what is good? What standard will you apply for knowing what is good?

Finally, without going into details, if you want a quick and brief answer. That is good, which is good to your soul. Anything that is good to your soul can be called good; but, what is good to the soul? That is good to the soul, which will satisfy the soul.

What will satisfy the soul? Who will satisfy you? A person who is like you will satisfy you. If a person is different from you, he will not like you. So, what will satisfy the soul? That which is like the soul will satisfy it. What is there which is like the soul? What is the nature of the soul?

First of all, you must know that a soul is an all-pervading presence. So, anything that has the quality of all-pervading presence will satisfy it. Is there anything in this world which is an all-pervading presence? There is no such thing. Everything is in some place only. Nothing can be regarded as being everywhere. So, in that sense, nothing in the world can satisfy the soul. Even if you become the king of the whole earth, it will not satisfy you because the earth is not all-pervading.

So, anything that has a tendency to become universal will satisfy the soul. Though nothing is universal completely, there may be a tendency towards the universal in certain things. Anything that is attempting to be universal also will satisfy the soul. And, incidentally, that which is intending to be satisfying the soul must be imperishable, because the soul is not perishable. Perishable things cannot satisfy the soul. So, what satisfies the soul is an imperishable character in anything. The perishable character will not satisfy. There is nothing imperishable in the world; everything is perishable. Only the quality which I mentioned as a tendency to become universal is satisfying.

A good person is that person who aspires for the Universal Being. He may not be himself a Universal Being; he has not yet reached that state, but he longs for it. A person who longs for the Universal Being can be called

a good being. Ultimately, God only is good; and anything that is trying to approach that state also is good.

Anyone who enters the educational field is a person
going for education. He may be in the kindergarten
stage, or the primary level, or elementary stage, or whatever it is. Any step taken in the direction of education is
education, whatever the degree of it. In the same way,
anything that is having a quality of aspiring for that
which is deathless and imperishable is good. So, only a
spiritual seeker can be called a really good person. The
other people have selfishness. Since you want nothing
but what is imperishable,—and the soul is imperishable,—it will be satisfied in the company of those people
who are seeking the Universal. The people may be perishable, but the soul in the person is not perishable.

Thus, all saints and sages are supposed to be good
people in the sense that they are aspiring for the Universal. That is why you want *satsanga* with such people.
You are not having *satsanga* with the body of the saint.
You are having *satsanga* with the aspiration and longing
that the saint has within. Actually, your soul is aspiring to
be in company with the soul which is also aspiring. That
is why you like saints and sages.

*Malaya: Those who are not seeking God are not
good people?*

SWAMIJI: They will have some selfishness.

Malaya: They are not good?

SWAMIJI: No. Anything that is contradictory to universality cannot be regarded as good. It will perish. All
the kings and emperors also will die, because they are
searching for that which is perishable. The emperor will
die like a miserable man; the king will die like a beggar.
When he dies, he is like a beggar only. Nothing will
come with him. The ownership of property, all wealth
and greatness in this world, is ephemeral as anything else

is. But, the aspiration will not die, because aspiration is the function of the soul. It will not die because it is connected with the soul.

Only a God-man is a good man; and, anyone who tries to be a God-man also is a good man. Even if he is only in the initial stage, taking only one step, he should be called good. He may not be a God-man, but he is trying to be a God-man. So, anything that has a tendency to universality is that which pleases the soul. Nothing else can satisfy it.

That is why you cannot be a real friend of anything,—not even of your father and mother. One day you would not like them, for some behaviour of theirs. Parents do not like children, and children do not like parents. The liking is only conditional. Only under some conditions they like you; if the condition is broken, they will never look at your face. Suppose you behave in a funny manner with the parents; they will think that you are no good, and will not want to talk to you. Similarly, in your case also, if they behave in a strange manner, you would not like to see them. The love of parents and son and daughter, husband and wife, is a conditioned, perishable longing.

Nothing can survive in this world except the soul, because that is the character of universality. Other things in the world, any friendships you have, are perishable because they are located in the body only. Every love is perishable, because it is connected with the body of a person. But, if it is a love born of the soul, it will have a universal tendency, and it is a love of soul by soul,—which is difficult to conceive.

Everything has a soul, but you must recognise the soul in it. You should not see that which is covering it. When you look at a person, are you seeing the body or the soul? What are you seeing? When you are talking to a person, to whom are you speaking? You are talking to the intention, the wish, the longing, the aspiration, the operation of the mind of the person. You are not loving the body of the person. His intention, his longing, his way of thinking, his vision,—that is what you are attracted to. That is the point. It is idea that loves idea. It is not body that loves the body. Ideas attract ideas. Finally, the whole world is Idea only. You may call it spirit, or consciousness. Soul likes soul; God loves Himself.

8

WHERE IS THE SOUL?

(Addressed to Roger, an Italian visitor)

SWAMIJI: Where have you kept the soul? Is it in your bag, or where have you kept it? Many people keep the soul somewhere, and then search for it elsewhere. They lose it elsewhere. By mistake, they keep it somewhere; in the railway station, or bank, or office, or somewhere they keep it. Then afterwards, they cannot know where it has gone. So, they are searching for it in Sivananda Ashram, but they can't find it so easily like that.

There was an old lady who could not see properly. She was almost blind. She was living in a small house without light, in a village with no electricity. She was poor and was living by sewing cloth with a needle. That was her profession. One day she lost that needle. It fell inside somewhere, and because it was dark, she could not see, as the eyes also were not good. She went outside into the bright sun, and started searching for the needle. Some people who came that way asked her what she was searching. She said that she was searching for the needle that she dropped somewhere. "Where did you drop it?" they asked.

"I dropped it inside," she said.

"But why are you searching for it outside, in the sun?"

"Because inside there is no light. Outside there is light, so I am searching for it here," she answered.

This is the story of the soul. It is lost somewhere, but the searching is elsewhere. Where do we search? We look for it in enjoyments of life: in living a comfortable existence; in trying to lengthen our physical life; in making more and more money; in increasing name, fame, authority, and power; in becoming king, minister, dictator, Duce, and all that. This is the way we try to find the soul, but we have lost it somewhere else. It is not sitting in the Duce, and all that. A Duce has no soul; he is like anybody else. You know what is Duce? But people want to become a Duce because they think the soul is there.

This whole world of perception is the light of the sun, and we are searching for the soul by moving from place to place, here and there, like the old lady who searched for the needle in the light of the sun; but the needle is inside, in the dark corner of one's own heart. This is the story of the soul. What do you say?

But, we are not finding it in the dark corner. It is dark; there is no light inside. In the heart, there is no light. The light is outside in the sense world. We have got electric light, sunlight, moonlight and starlight. So, why not enjoy the light that is already there, and search for the soul outside? Thus, you go everywhere, travel the whole world twenty times, and try to find the soul, like the lady searching for the needle outside, but it is in the dark corner of the heart. You can meditate on the soul.

9

THE ABSOLUTE

SWAMIJI: What will you sacrifice?

Visitor: All, if I can.

SWAMIJI: No. The Absolute wants you. It does not want anything else *from* you, it wants *you* only. You cannot give anything to the Absolute, because nothing actually belongs to you. You are alone in the world. There is no such thing as property; it is an illusion. Nobody can own anything. Each thing is independent, so you cannot give anything to God; you can give only yourself. That is the final thing, the sacrifice.

Visitor: Is meditation the only way, or are there other ways to reach It?

SWAMIJI: There are other ways also, but they all finally lead to meditation only. The final thing is meditation.

Visitor: What kind of initial way can we take to have good meditation?

SWAMIJI: Where is the Absolute at present?

Visitor: I feel that It is everywhere.

SWAMIJI: If so, is there anything outside the Absolute, or does only the Absolute exist? What about all these people sitting here? Are they inside the Absolute?

Visitor: Yes, surely, they are all inside the Absolute.

SWAMIJI: Then what is your attitude towards all things in the world? When you see a thing, what do you feel at that time?

Visitor: I respect everyone.

SWAMIJI: There is no "everyone." You said there is only one Absolute, so why do you say "everyone"? Everyone has gone into the Absolute.

Visitor: Yes, I see the Absolute in everyone and everything.

SWAMIJI: If this thought can continue always, that is the highest meditation on the Absolute. But, sometimes if you start feeling that there are many things other than the Absolute, then the meditation will not be complete. The eyes which see things always say that there are many things outside the Absolute, so you cannot trust the perception. If you can convince your deep feeling that whatever you see is inside that Supreme (including yourself and everybody), that is the meditation. Then you can reach the Absolute.

Visitor: Is the Absolute like the infinite,—that is, the more you approach the Absolute, the more It seems to go away?

SWAMIJI: No. You will go more and more near to It. It is not the infinite of arithmatic. It is the Infinite that is yourself, Itself. It is not like the horizon which, the more you go near it, the further it recedes. Here, the Infinite does not mean an endless thing, but an inclusive thing. It is not mathematical, it is spiritual. The Absolute is Pure Being.

Visitor: There are many doctrines. How can they put a limit on the Infinite, saying that It is only one way?

SWAMIJI: You cannot put a limitation on the Absolute. It includes all the doctrines. All the doctrines go inside It. Every doctrine can be accommodated into It. It cannot be limited to any particular doctrine. It is not an empirical concept. Pure Being is impossible to think in the mind, because It cannot be thought. You are thinking that you are outside the Absolute. If you are inside the Absolute, how will you raise a question?

Visitor: Is it true that only one truth exists, or several truths exist?

SWAMIJI: Only one truth is there, not several truths. There are several degrees of truth, but finally it is one only. It is now daytime. It is a truth, but it is not daytime everywhere in the world. So one truth can be here, and in another place it is not truth, also. It is true that you are a human being, but that is one degree of truth. Actually, you are a little pressure point in the cosmic sea; that is a higher truth. That is an example of degrees of truth. Finally, there is only one truth.

Visitor: We are always trying to find truth.

SWAMIJI: You have no other duty except to find truth. That is the highest duty.

Visitor: Some people don't believe that truth is here in our universe; it's in heaven.

SWAMIJI: Are they saying that this world is not true?

Visitor: We all have our own truth; it will lead to sects, or different religions which don't agree with each other.

SWAMIJI: That is a mistake of the human being. It is not the mistake of the world. The world has no religion. It is only human beings who have religions.

Visitor: Is it possible not to try to find truth, but only to live here, and only try to integrate oneself with the cosmos——to just feel a point in the cosmos?

SWAMIJI: That is a very great thing. If you can do that, there is no need to do anything else. That is the highest. Then there is no problem afterwards.

Visitor: How can we reach truth while we are involved in the materialistic society?

SWAMIJI: When your mind is saying that you must

transcend this social involvement, you have already taken one step above society by the very idea that you have to go above it. And by deeper meditations, the consciousness will withdraw itself from social involvements, and you will go to the meditation state. Even in this world, you can do this meditation. In spite of human society and modern materialism, you must find at least one hour every day to keep yourself alone and think like this. An hour's correct thinking will set right all the other troubles of the other hours of the day.

Visitor: While trying to find truth, I feel that there is only one thing to do, which is to love.

SWAMIJI: Love whom?

Visitor: All of creation.

SWAMIJI: That is the same as truth. Loving the whole creation is loving God Himself.

Visitor: Is it true that all actions in the world originate from the will of God?

SWAMIJI: It is true and not true, both, because as long as you feel that it is not true, it is not true. Even if it is true, you are not going to be benefited by that because your heart is not accepting it. If God does eveything, you would not speak to me at all. You would keep quiet. Everything would be fine.

Visitor: I kept quiet for two days, sir, and today I am leaving.

SWAMIJI: The third day it has become false. You tell God, "For two days I waited for You, and the third day I don't agree with You." Everything is done by the will of God in a perfect manner. The whole cosmos is the Body of God. Just as this body is a manifestation of your soul, the entire universe is a manifestation of the Almighty Absolute consciousness; therefore, nothing can move without the central will operating. You cannot lift your finger, a hair cannot grow on your body, you cannot say anything, your breathing will stop, your heart cannot function, unless that will is there.

But (and the but is the important thing), no individual in the world may feel that this is so. You are saying that you have come from Delhi: you didn't say that God has come. The consciousness of your being a human being immediately creates other associations like being a man or woman, this action, that action, etc. How can these ideas arise in the mind of a person when no such action is really taking place, and the universe is acting simultaneously? It is incomplete knowledge of the total comprehension of the cosmos that makes us feel that "we" are doing the action. If your mind is able to switch itself on to the cosmic setup, you will have no problem any more.

Visitor: If every action is the will of God directly or indirectly and, therefore, manifests itself, then that doesn't leave any room for free will of man.

SWAMIJI: Ultimately, what you call free will is nothing but the will of God operating.

Visitor: So, how can you blame someone for his past samskaras?

SWAMIJI: He feels that he has done it. If you ask him, he will say that it is his cow, land, property. Is there anybody who will say that this building belongs to God? We are bound and we are free in accordance with the feeling that we have in our hearts. If you say that you have done it, then you bear the consequences. But who will say that he has not done it? Every person who has body consciousness will feel that he has done it.

Your actions and your very existence are included in the cosmic action. So, whatever you do is part of that. But don't make the mistake of bringing your consciousness separately, as if you are doing it.

Visitor: But it affects me.

SWAMIJI: It affects you because your practical life is different from what you are saying or thinking in your mind.

Visitor: I can't help it.

SWAMIJI: Then there is no use of discussion. You should not talk on this subject, because practically it doesn't affect you. God cannot help you unless you believe in God entirely.

You have to go slowly, step by step, by detachment, unselfishness, charitableness, non-interference, by goodness of feeling in your heart and an ideal behaviour. That is the beginning of good conduct and the first step towards God. Then, afterwards, you do a little prayer, contemplation on these things that we have been discussing. Later on, actual meditation will start. God will take care of you.

Visitor: If the aim of man is to realise himself and finally be liberated, how does he explain this whole exercise, the cycle of predestination of man?

SWAMIJI: The whole thing that you have mentioned is included in the cosmic scheme, as all the waves and all the bubbles and ripples in the ocean are included in the ocean. You will find everything, at once, in that, and you will not raise a question thereafter.

10

TAPAS OR AUSTERITY

Carlos: What is tapas?

SWAMIJI: *Tapas* is energy and heat, a force generated in the personality by preventing the sense organs from diverting energy outside in the direction of objects. The consciousness, the total quantum of your energy, is diverted by the sense organs outside towards objects of sense when you see a thing, hear, smell, taste, touch, or even think a thing. If you prevent the consciousness from seeing, hearing, smelling, tasting, touching or even thinking an externality of any kind, the energy will not go out of your personality. It will be retained inside. Then you will feel strong, energetic, forceful. This process is called *tapas,* an inwardisation of power.

For the beginner, this much understanding about *tapas* is sufficient, but the highest *tapas* is to think like God Himself. When you can think as God thinks, that is the greatest *tapas.* You can imagine how God thinks; He will think in one Thought the whole cosmos directly, without the use of any sense organs (eyes, ears, nose, etc.). His very Being is His Thought; His Thought and His Being are identical. In the case of human beings, thought is of an object, but in the case of God, Thought is of Being Itself. This highest *tapas* you must reach one day, but in the beginning it is the withdrawal of sense organs, and creating energy in the system. Thus, *tapas* has an initial meaning, and also a higher meaning. Both these are applicable to the word *tapas.*

Tapas is conservation of energy; an increase of power in the system by sense control; withdrawal of sense organs; preventing consciousness from diffusing itself towards external things; and centreing it, fixing it, in the Universality of Being which is God-Thought. This is the highest *tapas*. So, there is nothing mysterious about it. It is a simple matter, if you can analyse it carefully. Yoga is not a mysterious thing; it is a simple process.

Tapas is nothing but what you ought to do in this life. You are not supposed to waste your energy, make yourself weak, and think of things which are not really there. We are mostly thinking about things which are illusions. The world is not outside you, nor are you outside the world; yet, you look as if you are outside the world, and as if the world is outside you. This is the problem before everybody. If you can remove this misconception that the world is outside you and that you are outside the world, then you will find that you are protected by the world.

Now the world is kicking you out as if you are an unwanted person, and you also want to kick it out as if it is something unwanted. It wants to maintain itself, and you want to maintain yourself. You are two contending parties. The subjective side and the objective side are opposing and warring. This is actually the *Mahabharata,* as they call it, the conflict between the subject and the object, yourself and the world. This is the *Mahabharata,* the *Trojan War,* the *Iliad*, the *Odyssey*, the *Ramayana*; this is any epic of the world symbolically described by poets and authors, and here is the conflict between yourself and the world described as epics. If this conflict continues, there is no way out of it. The *tapas* that I mentioned to you is a simple process of removing this conflict and establishing harmony between yourself and the world outside (between the subject and the object) by introducing a transcendent unifying force in between.

This process is yoga, *tapas*, spirituality; this is religion, this is your duty in life, and this itself is the way to God-realisation. The whole of life is summed up in this little intricacy of human operation. There is no need of reading too many books. The matter is simple, if you go deep into it.

The world will flock around you if you are one with the world. You need not run after things; things will come to you. You will not be a slave of anybody afterwards, you will be a master. Now you have cut off the world from your consciousness, and so you look like a small, tiny, helpless person, but really you are not so. You are not a tiny, helpless person. Everything potential, great and grand is inside you. It has to be brought out by this process which is called *tapas*. The only duty in life, finally, is *tapas*, austerity, self-control. Without that, you can't succeed even in ordinary life. Even in ordinary work-a-day business life, some kind of self-control is necessary. You cannot diffuse your energy completely outside and be happy.

Try to think "all" things. Don't think only one thing. Why do you think only a particular thing? Why do you bestow special attention on some particular thing while all other things are equally good? Let the thought be an inclusive one, in which you and the world are both included. Then it is a thought of transcendence. This is the highest *tapas*.

Visitor: What is the special kind of relation (if there is a relation) between the knower and what is to be known?

SWAMIJI: Between the knower and the known there is a knowledge process. Finally, the Atman is the knower, and what It considers as outside is the known. By "knowing," you mean that you become aware of something other than what you are. Generally, when people say that they know something, they don't mean they are knowing themselves. The idea generally in the minds of people when they say they know something is that they know something other than themselves; the knower is different from the known in the ordinary process of knowledge. But if you analyse this whole process, you will realise that the knower and the known are connected by an intelligence, a consciousness; otherwise, the knower cannot come in contact with the object of knowledge. You can know even a mountain in front of you; the mountain is far away from you, yet you know that the mountain is there. How do you know that the object is there in front of you when there is actually no visible connection between you and the object?

If the mind that knows a thing is inside your body, then it is locked up inside the body and cannot know anything outside, beyond its own body. You cannot know another person sitting in front of you if your mind is only inside the body. How do you know?

The mind which appears to be inside your body for all practical purposes is basically a universal pervading intelligence. Your so-called individual mind gets connected with that universal mind in the process of knowledge, as in a broadcasting process, for example. In a broadcasting station, somebody speaks and a sound is made. This sound gets converted into an ethereal universal medium. What travels in space is not sound; it is a mysterious energy content that travels in space and is received by a receiver set somewhere else, where this ethereal thing gets reconverted into sound, and then you hear a sound here. It doesn't mean that the sound is travelling in space. There is a universal principle connecting two terms of relation (the receiver set on one side, and the broadcasting station on another side).

In a similar manner, there is an unknown medium

between the subject and the object. You can see the broadcasting station, you can see the receiver set, but you cannot see what is happening in between; it is invisible. In a similar manner, you can see yourself, you can see a mountain, but you cannot know what is happening between them. That "between" is a very important item. The mind that is universal operates between you and the object outside, and connects the individual mind with the object outside through the medium of its universality. If that universal principle is not to operate, you will never know anything outside your body. You would be locked up inside yourself only.

So, there is a universal mind operating everywhere, of which you are a part, of which the object also is a part. Finally, you must say that only one thing exists, which is the Universal Mind. If you can deeply concentrate on this essential fact, you will be thinking like a cosmic man and will no longer be thinking like an individual person. You will become a superman. This is how a yogi or God-man thinks.

Your problem is yourself only; you have no other problem. You require to be saved from yourself. The greatest problem is one's own self. Nobody else gives you trouble. Your ignorance, your foolishness, your individuality, your finitude, these are the problems, and they constitute what you really are. So, you have to be saved from that. One has to be saved from one's lower self, for the sake of attaining the higher Self. In the Bhagavad Gita's sixth chapter, the higher Self is said to save the lower self.

11

UNIVERSAL ACTION AND DUTY TOWARDS OTHERS

Visitor: I have a question about your book Problems of Spiritual Life, *about Hitler's action,—if it was his action or not his action. You said:*

"Ultimately it was not Hitler's action but yet he felt it was his, and so he paid for it. It is your feeling that binds you or frees you. It is not the action that you do that is important. Your feeling that is connected with that action is important, your feeling that you are doing it. When you feel that you are doing it, you are responsible for it. Your consciousness is your bondage; your action is not the point."

I don't understand when you say that your action is not the point.

SWAMIJI: The whole universe is acting perpetually for the purpose of the evolution of the lower categories into the higher ones. Actually, there is only one action taking place in the universe. This is why some people say that God is doing everything. The idea behind it is something like the action that the physical body does. For example, whether you lift your hand, walk with your feet, see with your eyes, eat with your mouth, digest with your stomach,—whatever be the diversity of these actions, you will agree that it is one action being done by the whole body. In a similar manner, the universe, being a large organism (sometimes in religion they call it the body of God), all these diversities of action which differ one from the other are actions of the central force which is the will of God or the Centre of the cosmos.

There are not many actions taking place in the universe; only one action is taking place, regardless of who is appearing to do it. The problem is that each individual part imagines that it is doing it. It is something like the legs not agreeing with the eyes. You can imagine that they can assert and not give any credit for the cooperation received from the other limbs. Each one could say that it is independent.

The different limbs of the body do not quarrel among themselves. Each one performs its function, one totally different from the other, yet it is a total action of the body. In the same way, it is a total action of the Universal Centre that is operating the cosmos. But the parts of the cosmos, which are like limbs of the body of the Universal Whole, due to the egoism of their nature, appropriate everything to themselves: "I am doing it." This is a dangerous thing, because the doing by the "I"-individually is always motivated by selfish ends for the pleasure of the body, ego, feelings and emotions, and then that action becomes either good or bad. If it is done only for the pleasure of the individual outlook, irrespective of what consideration it has on other people, it becomes a destructive activity. But the same person can do a good action also by taking into account the welfare of other people, all things.

There are people in this world who do bad actions and good actions. Really, neither good actions nor bad actions exist in themselves. These are names that we give by segregating different aspects of nature, like saying that seeing is better than walking.

From the spiritual point of view, real action is not anybody's action. It is one action that is taking place, and anything that you do is supposed to be thus offered to the Almighty. But be careful to see that you don't do it with feeling of egoism or any selfish motive. That is the commentary on this little recipe.

Visitor: So, the answer is from the spiritual view, but then in daily life there is this problem...

SWAMIJI: In daily life always we make the mistake of appropriating action to ourselves, and if you are a little *sattvik* in your nature, you may be doing it for the welfare of people; but if you are *rajasik* or *tamasik*, you may do it only for your pleasure. Then it becomes destructive. There are only two kinds of activity in this world:— constructive or destructive. In daily life, this is the drama of action. Individuals do either constructive work or destructive work, but really it is a transcendent action taking place, if you see it from a wider point of view.

Visitor A: What is the responsibility of a seeker towards others,—the relationship between the responsibility of the individuals towards his or her own growth, and the responsibility towards other people?

SWAMIJI: What is the conflict? You have a duty to everybody. I cannot see any conflict. You have a duty to family members, the nation, society, God, your *guru*. Now, in what way are they self-contradictory? They are only different forms of your obligation which you call duty, but they cannot be regarded as contradicting themselves.

Visitor A: But all these duties take time.

SWAMIJI: Let them take time. What is the objection?

Visitor A: But the amount of time that you devote to one as against the other...

SWAMIJI: No, you can do all of them, if you are wise enough. You can harmonise all these duties in a systematised manner, and you will find time. It is not true that you have no time. You have enough time; the only thing is that you have to organise these duties in a proper manner. It is not possible to have a duty and then have no time to do it; that is not possible. It ceases to be a duty if there is no time for it. If you consider it as a duty you have time for it. You will find time; otherwise, it is not a duty.

Visitor A: At the beginning, when one starts, does one start by working on oneself (focusing down on oneself, increasing self-awareness), in the hope that spiritual growth will take place, or does one serve others at the same time?

SWAMIJI: Yes, do it. What is the problem now? Self-help is the first help. Why do you consider it as a problem? Unless you are alive, you cannot make others alive. You must be alive first. So what is the difficulty? You see that you are safe first; if you are not safe, how will you make others safe? So, you are right. Take care of yourself, and then you gain strength enough to take care of other people. If you yourself are not there, then what is your problem? Understanding oneself is primary. Duty towards others is secondary; it comes afterwards.

Visitor A: May I give an example of what I was thinking? We all want a peaceful world; we all want inner peace, but we see a separation between the two.

SWAMIJI: It is not necessary that there should be any such conflict between outer peace and inner peace. You have to strike a harmony between these two, also. If you want to live in human society, you have to be in harmony with human society. If you say that you cannot be in harmony with human society for reasons of your own, then you should not live in human society. Isolate yourself from society completely, if it is true that you cannot get along with human society. But be sure that it is so. Don't come to hasty conclusions.

Is it possible for a person to live in the world dissociating oneself totally from human society? If you say it is possible, your problem is solved. But if you say that it is not possible,—that you have to gain sustenance of some kind from human society, that your life is social, not merely personal and individual, then it is your duty to make the sacrifice necessary for the purpose of your living in society.

You cannot have everything that you want. A little bit of sacrifice also is called for. If society needs something from you, you have to give it, as a sacrifice. Society also will make a sacrifice for your sustenance.

The government protects you, but also takes a tax from you. You cannot say that you will not pay any tax, but still the government should take care of you. There is a mutual collaboration between government and individual, society and the person, etc. I don't think any conflict is there, and it is necessary for you to strike a harmony between the two, the inner and the outer, the personality and the human society.

Visitor B: Swamiji, I feel that taking care of my family pulls me away from my sadhana.

SWAMIJI: You cannot call a duty as a problem. You should not complain against your duty. Don't you want to take care of your family? Who asked you to marry, and then complain afterwards? You deliberately enter into marriage, and afterwards say that a problem has come. You should not complain like that.

When you have done something, the consequence also is yours. You cannot have only fifty percent of it, and except the other fifty percent to go to somebody else. You have married with a specific rationality behind it. You have done it with a good purpose; what that purpose is, you know very well. When the consequence follows from that, you must take care of it also. How can you consider the family as a bondage?

Everything is a part of *sadhana*. Your walking, sitting, talking, any necessary unavoidable thing cannot be regarded as outside *sadhana*. If it is an unnecessary thing, you need not do it, and it is up to you to find out which things are necessary. You must use your reason there.

Free yourself from doing unnecessary things. You waste your time on things which are not connected with you. Keep yourself free from them. But if it is unavoidable, why do you complain? The word "unavoidable" explains the whole situation, and you should not say anything further afterwards. You must bear it without complaint. Bearing it with complaint is no good. You must bear it without complaint; only then it becomes *sadhana*. If you curse and cry and then bear it, then it is not *sadhana*.

You should bear the troubles of life without complaining. If you ask for a thing, that is your responsibility. Suppose you are employed in some office and have to do hard work. It is not a very pleasant thing to go on doing hard work in an office for eight or ten hours. But you find out whether it is necessary to do that work or not. If you don't do it, what happens? You may be in a worse condition. So you stop your complaints; you do the work.

If you say that it is not necessary, then, you can give it up. It is up to you. Nobody forced you to go into the office and work, but you want to do it because you know the beneficial consequences are there, also. Pain and pleasure are mixed together in life. Even to eat a meal, have your lunch, somebody has to work hard in the field, plow the earth and grow the crop, thrash the husk, grind it, cook it. It is also a painful thing. So much work you have to do for a little meal. Now, is sweating and toiling in a field an unnecessary activity? Nobody likes to do such a painful thing, but if it is not done, food will not go into the mouth.

You cannot have only one side of the matter, so don't complain. Bear life for what it is. Even if you complain, who will listen to you? What is the use of complaining? It is called crying in the wilderness. It is no use, so don't waste your time in unnecessarily saying things.

Visitor C: Swamiji, I want to do some service in the hospital. Is it beneficial for my sadhana?

SWAMIJI: Now you are alive. Suppose you, yourself, are not alive, then who will serve? If you destroy yourself by illness, then who will do the service? You serve yourself first so that you may be alive, at least. If you don't exist, then who will do the service? The person must exist first. Suppose one defeats the very purpose of one's existence, then who will serve? Service is necessary, but the person who serves must be existing, and he will not exist if he engages himself in self-destructive activities.

Visitor C: What do you mean by self-destructive?

SWAMIJI: Anything that ruins bodily health, disturbs the mind, and obstructs aspiration for God. These three things are the self-ruining things. That which obstructs the realisation of God, that which disturbs the mind, and that which spoils the health of the body,—these three things must be avoided. Otherwise, suppose there is bodily ill health, then you will be in the hospital, and who will do the service?

The body, mind and soul should be intact first; then you can go ahead with service. But if that is not assured, then it is dangerous. Somebody else has to serve you afterwards, instead of your serving others. The boot is then on the other leg.

Visitor C: But sometimes when you serve others, you are also doing good to yourself.

SWAMIJI: It will not be good to yourself, unless you know the reason why you are doing service. You may be doing it for some selfish motive, or some egoistic satisfaction like name or fame. These are all important matters. Why are you doing service? Some subtle motive may be there inside. If the motive is not unselfish, service will not bring any benefit. Politicians also are doing a lot of good service, while they are doing it for their subtle benefit. It is not easy to do service with no motive whatsoever.

If you expect something in return, that is selfish action. Let anyone analyse this matter. Is this work done with the expectation of return of some kind, or do you expect nothing? If you expect nothing,—wonderful; go ahead, but you should not expect even thanks. If you think that you have done so much and people should thank you, then it is no good. Why should anybody thank you? You have done your duty. They may not thank you, they may even insult you after you do service. You may receive a stone instead of thanks.

Visitor C: Swamiji, it is very difficult.

SWAMIJI: Then you must bear it. People who did a lot of service to humanity were killed by the very people who received the service.

Visitor C: How can you bear it?

SWAMIJI: It depends upon your motive. Who asked you to do the service? Do you want a stone on your head in return for the service that you did? If you are prepared for that, do it. Or do you want something else worse than that? There are people who did a lot of social service, and got a bullet in their head in return. Why did it happen? How is it that people who receive service react in such a negative manner to the person who did service? What is the reason? Each one should find this out. There is some irregularity in the handling of things.

Something is rotten in the state of Denmark, as Shakespeare says. Some little trouble thing is there. One little sand particle in the eye is sufficient to cause irritation.

The particle will look like a mountain sitting. You will be worrying the whole day because one little dust particle is sitting in the eye. Likewise is *karma yoga*. A little small dot of irregularity will spoil the entire structure, and it will collapse.

Visitor C: So we must perfect ourselves first?

SWAMIJI: Your motive should be clear. And also, you must know if the people whom you serve are deserving your help.

Visitor C: Everybody is deserving.

SWAMIJI: No, that is why they thrust a bullet in return. When you handle a lion, you don't go and put your hand into its mouth. There is a way of handling it. Each thing must be handled in the proper manner. Some people go to excesses, extremes, and they lose their lives. Each thing has to be handled in the proper manner. If there is a snake caught in a wildfire, you may like to save it. Will you go and touch it with hand, or will you handle it in a different way? It can also strike you for the service you have done. Each thing has to be handled in the manner necessary, with care.

12

HOW TO LET GOD INTO THE HEART

Visitor: How can I let God open my heart?

SWAMIJI: You have to open your heart. You open it, and He will enter. Your mind is filled with thoughts which are other than God's.

"Empty thyself and I shall fill thee," is an old saying from the Bible. If you want to fill a basket with the fragrance of flowers, the rubbish and dust that is inside it must go first. Is the mind thinking of God, or is it thinking something else? That "something else" is the obstruction. You have closed the gates, and you want God to enter in.

There was a painter in England who painted a picture of a beautiful house. He called all the artists to see if there was any defect in the painting. Everybody admired it, saying that it was beautiful. Finally, one man said that he had forgotten to put a latch on the outside of the door. The painter said that the latch is inside, it is always open from the outside. That is, God's doors are always open, and you put the latch inside so that He may not enter.

The idea is that our thoughts are our bondages; our thoughts also are our friends. They can act in two ways, like a double-edged sword. When you develop integrated thought, harmonious thought, inclusive cosmically oriented thought, God will enter, because God is another name for integrated, harmonious, Absolute Consciousness. That cannot enter the little pinhole which is constricted on account of an abundance of other earthly desires.

Desires connected with this body, society, property, money, relations, psychobiological impulses, all hamper the opening of the heart. For this purpose, finally the only remedy is to sit quiet for as much time as possible, and deeply tell the mind that you are part and parcel of the universal inclusiveness. You have come from God and, therefore, you have to go back to the same place. You have come down by restricting your operations more and more, until you have restricted yourself to such an extent that you have become a little body. Now you have to follow the reverse order of ascent.

As you have come down little by little to greater and greater limitations, go back by expanding yourself into greater and greater expansions of delimitations by intense affirmation of God's universality. This is meditation. It is not a difficult thing, provided that you have determination.

Even if you have many desires, they may be fulfilled by God, so you need not have any suspicions about it. The fear is that you will lose all the wealth and glories of the world if you go there. All the glories here are only shadows and they will be found in the original there. When you have the original, why do you want a shadow? When you have the whole, why do you want a part? Give this kind of teaching to the mind and sit for prayer and meditation. You will see that some miracle will take place.

The devotional path is one way of diverting human affection to God. But before that, you must know what human affection is; then only you will know how to divert it to God as a divine affection. What is affection, and why does it arise in the mind of a person? Why do people love others?

If you think deeply, it becomes difficult to answer this question. Is it because someone gives something to you which you don't have? No, you can love something even if nothing comes from it. Actually, love is not love if you expect retribution. If you expect something back, it is a merchandise; it becomes a commerce, a business, not love.

Why does love arise like that in the mind? The reason for the arising of love must be known; only then you will know why it is humanly conditioned and how you can make it flower into that divine universal love.

This is purely a psychological question. The spiritual effort is finally a kind of internal psychology. When you eat food, it is not that you want *chappati,* rice, and all that. You want to create an internal chemical reaction. These instruments like rice, etc., are only instruments that stimulate certain conditions in the system which rejuvenate your personality chemically and make you feel strong and healthy; what you want is the satisfaction, not the thing as such. If the satisfaction doesn't come, the thing will not be loved. The cooperation from your side is important, apart from the thing that goes inside.

So is the case with spiritual life. It is a pure impersonal movement of your psyche, your mind and your consciousness towards a larger impersonality, You take as instruments in this process a symbol like Krishna, Radha, etc. They are all symbols, like articles of diet. They have a value only to the extent that they bring about that satisfaction and transformation in you.

The important point is what happens to you when you think of it. If you are feeling elated, in what manner has that thing evoked this joy? Why not another thing? Your mental makeup at that time is conditioned in such a way that only that particular object can satisfy this mental condition, just as in one particular condition of your body, only one particular kind of diet is best. Sometimes fasting is better than eating; sometimes fasting is bad and eating is good.

So, what it means is that external conditions are only instruments used in producing certain transformations in your personality, and that is what is important, more than the thing itself. No thing in the world has any meaning in itself. Its meaning is only in the capacity it has to bring about inner transformation in you. If that transformation takes place, you can take anything as your *guru*. Sage Dattatreya had twenty-four *gurus*. Anything can be a *guru*, provided it helps you. But if you don't know why you are feeling happy, you may get caught by it.

How can you divert the affection to God? The diverting of emotion to God is the most difficult art. It is a movement of the finite to the Infinite. In ordinary loves, the finite moves towards the finite only; therefore, it is brittle and breaks. But here in divine devotion, the finite moves towards the Infinite,—so they are very different things. You feel happiness when the finite moves towards the finite also, because you think that two finites make a little larger finite; therefore, you feel a little happy. That is why people want to accumulate quantities. Many finites look like the Infinite, but it is not so. Many finites do not make the Infinite. They are also a bundle of finites only.

Many thieves put together do not make a saint. They are all thieves only. So, devotion to God is not a movement of the finite to finite, but of the finite to the Infinite. It is a complete transformation. It is something unthinkable, because ordinarily nobody will (as a finite being) think of the Infinite. How many people think of the Infinite in the mind? They always think of something which is finite and small, it may be property, relations, money, etc. All are finite things. With that, we want to be happy.

We accumulate a huge bundle of finites and think that we are having an artificial Infinite, but the artificial Infinite is finite only. That is why the world is suffering in spite of accumulations. To completely bring about a transvaluation of values and transmute the finite into the Infinite is a Herculean task. It has to be done, with great effort, under the guidance of a master.

13

WANTING ONLY GOD

Priest: Now, officially, I am a priest, but I am aspiring for God-realisation.

SWAMIJI: So, being a God-man is an unofficial designation. There is no contradiction between the two. There is nothing wrong with being a priest. You can be. The only thing is that it has to be divinely oriented. The priest has an official function to perform, under the dictates of the Pope, finally. It is a systematised organization of Christianity which expects the priest to give sermons either in the church or in public. What sermons he gives depends upon the instruction that he is given.

Priest: The message has to be conveyed, but the main thing is from within.

SWAMIJI: The priest also has a duty to proselytise. Is it a duty on your part?

Priest: The witnessing of his own faith is expected, but trying to convert others is not.

SWAMIJI: Proselytising is not a duty on his part?

Priest: If it is, I would not agree with it.

SWAMIJI: If a priest lives a good Christian life but he would not convert anybody, don't you find fault with him for being a priest without doing that duty?

Priest: No. That is the way I try to live.

SWAMIJI: Some Christians have the feeling that converting also is a duty, because of the fact that Christianity is the true religion, and everyone else who follows another religion is following a lesser religion or perhaps a false religion, and so converting is an essential duty. This is one of the doctrines which has been inculcated to the priests. You are saying that it is not a necessity.

If a Christian feels that his religion is the true and best religion, it follows from that feeling that others are inferior. If the idea that others are inferior is simultaneous with the feeling of one's own superiority, there is a third corollary following from it that it would be good to transform people into the true religion. This follows automatically. So, if the priest does not do that, he is not doing his duty properly.

Priest: But he may not agree with the first and second. Then the third doesn't follow. I don't believe in the first; otherwise, I wouldn't have been here.

SWAMIJI: I have met many good Christians, and they are honest people. One priest from Italy likes me very much. He used to tell people that I am a very nice person, and I am on the right path, and one day I will become a Christian!

De Smet is a very scholarly Christian. I had all sorts of philosophical discussions with him, especially on the concept of trinity, the existence of sin, and all that. Many of these people get caught up in the concept of sin. Where is sin existing? Is it existing somewhere, or is it existing nowhere? Such questions arise and we used to discuss them. Finally, we draw a truce and go happily.

You are a spiritual man. You are aspiring for the realisation of God. Is it true that finally you want God, and you want nothing else? Or, sometimes does the heart and the feeling say that there is something else also that you would like to have? This question has to be answered. Is it a hundred percent true that your heart is seeking God only, and nothing else?

Priest: In principle and in desire, but not always in reality.

SWAMIJI: Now, you are using the word desire. Desire is a want for something. Is it a desire for God, or is it a desire for something other than God? Let this question be answered by one's own heart. If the desire is for God only, you cannot call it a desire at all. It is a holy longing, an aspiration, and, therefore, there is nothing wrong with it. Everybody should desire God; if that desire is the only desire and there is no other desire, it is a wonderful thing. But if the desire implies the longing for something other than God, one must put a question to one's own self: What is it that one wants, other than God?

Now, can you tell me if there is anything in the world, in this creation as a whole, which the one seeking God would like to have? Is there anything in this world which you would like to have as something other than God? Or there is nothing outside God?

Priest: In principle, no, and in the mind, no. But in reality, yes.

SWAMIJI: What is not a reality then? The reality is something else?

Priest: In real life, there is that strong longing for God.

SWAMIJI: Let us concede that the world is real, and God is not so real. Shall we come to that conclusion?

Priest: God is very real.

SWAMIJI: How real? More real than the world, or equally real, or less real?

Priest: In principle, He is the only real, but in practice...

SWAMIJI: No, don't bring practice and all such things. There is no such thing as practice. Either the

mind is thinking honestly, or it is not thinking honestly.
You cannot say *A* is *A* and there is nothing more than *A*,
and practically in life say, "No". *A* is *A* only in a profes-
sorial classroom but in the heart of hearts, *A* is not *A*.
There is also *B* outside *A*. How can you live a dual life
like that? Which is your real life? Is your real life the
reality that you are speaking of, or the classroom life?
Which is the real life?

Priest: There is a conflict.

SWAMIJI: Now who is going to guide you in this
conflict? I am only analysing the situation, not talking to
you as a *guru* or mentor. A conflict can only be between
two realities; there cannot be a conflict between reality
and unreality. That is not possible, and you have con-
ceded reality to both things. There is some reality in
God, and there is also reality in the world.

*Priest: There is a conflict between reality and the
unreality that appears as reality.*

SWAMIJI: No. When it appears as reality, it is reality only. A thing that you call as reality, because it appears as reality, you have accepted as reality. If you
don't accept it, you can tell the reality, "I don't accept it,
because it is an appearance."

You may say, "No, no. I don't regard it as an appearance. It is a reality. It affects me very seriously." If
that is the case, to the extent that it is real for you, you
must handle it in an intelligent manner. Now, you must
find out what realities of the world are affecting you.
How many things?

If you want something in the world, it need not necessarily be a source of conflict. If you get that thing
which you want, do you think the conflict will cease? If
you want a thing and you get it, the conflict ceases?

*Priest: Only temporarily. Then something else
comes.*

SWAMIJI: Then you get the other thing also. If you have that second thing also, are you satisfied? No. The third comes. So, why does this happen? Why does the mind operate in this manner, that it moves from one object to another, not getting satisfied with anything? This is a philosophical question, not merely a theological one. There is a reason why the mind wants something, and yet cannot be satisfied with that thing. Why does it feel like that?

Priest: Ultimately, it is seeking God, but it doesn't go straight.

SWAMIJI: If you feel like that, then your problem ceases. Do you also believe that God will protect you and save you from your problems, or do you think that He has no powers? Why don't you resort to Him? If you really have the faith in God, and say that your problems will be solved by God Himself, and if you resort to Him, He will be your mentor finally, will you be able to resort to Him? You can't do that because the other thing will pull, that which you call the desire for the world. Is it so?

Priest: Partly, but that is the best answer I have received.

SWAMIJI: There is one prayer of Christians: "Our Father who art in heaven, hallowed be Thy name. Thy kingdom come... Thine is the Kingdom, the Power and the Glory for ever and ever." This is one of the best prayers ever. Do you think this prayer has no effect?

Priest: It has. I need to renew my faith in it.

SWAMIJI: Don't you have faith in it?

Priest: I have.

SWAMIJI: Then it will work. It must work. I don't think you should have any problem. This is a kind of self-created confusion. One cannot call it a problem, it is a kind of chaos in the way of thinking, which must be handled by yourself or your mentor, or by God. God will solve it, if your heart is really in it. What do you say? Be happy.

14

THE INADEQUACIES OF SCIENCE

Address to Dr. Saklani:

SWAMIJI: Modern subatomic science is not measurable in terms of ordinary mathematical calculations. All the values of life get negatived in a realm where mathematics and logic do not operate. In this condition, science also will not operate. When you cross that limit, it becomes metaphysics. It is not physics any more; it is not geology. It becomes meta-geology afterwards, because any kind of measurement, observation and calculation cannot apply in certain realms.

You are feeling that you are sitting here as a whole person, but how should you feel that you are one whole total being when you are made up of little parts? You have got ears and eyes and nose and bone and flesh, heart and lungs. Why don't you feel that you are an assemblage of so many little things? Who is sitting here? You should not say that you are sitting here; you should say that here is a bundle of little particles. Why don't you feel like that?

Here you yourself are something behind science. Your very existence as so and so defeats the calculative process of science. Otherwise, if it is an observable, measurable thing that you are, then you have to describe yourself as an anatomical and physiological entity, and not Mr. Saklani. Who is Mr. Saklani? Is it a nose or eyes or ears? None of them is Mr. Saklani. Who are you then,—not the nose nor ears nor brain nor lungs, and not even an aggregate. When you call yourself Mr. Saklani, are you calling yourself an aggregate of little things? No, you are something which is beyond description in physiological terms. So it is said, "Know thyself and be free." You have not succeeded even in knowing who you are.

How is it that you feel that you are one total compact whole, in spite of the fact that you don't seem to be that? Anatomically, physiologically, X-ray-wise, you are not that. The X-ray will never show Mr. Saklani there. Where is Mr. Saklani, then? How did the conviction arise in your mind that you are Mr. Saklani? When no scientific instrument can prove it, why should you say something contrary to it? Here science fails. You will say that what you are feeling is much better than science,—let the X-ray say anything, but you are not that.

So, you are a mystery, a mystery that eludes every other mystery. To understand this requires concentration of mind. It is not a question of time. Even if you go on thinking in a shallow way for years, it won't work. If you dig only one foot down, even if it is for years, it won't show water inside.

The entire earth also is a mystery. You must have observed that all the great cultures of the world have thrived in the northern hemisphere. In South America, Africa and Australia you don't find these cultures as you have in North America, Europe and Eastern Asia. Why should the earth be differently constituted in the northern and southern hemispheres? Why should there be a difference?

And, why are there physiognomically different structures of body? The Mongolian, Caucasian, Red Indian, and Negroid all have different faces. Generally, people say there are four types of human structure. Why should it be like that? How is it that if you go north from here into Nepal, to the Chinese and Japanese side, the face changes, and if you go to Africa, it is another? The impact of the structure of the earth on human beings should not really vary, because everywhere the earth is the same, but it does not seem to be the same.

We say the entire earth is a ball of mud, and everywhere it must be the same, but it is not so. It has produced varieties of cultures. If you go to the Middle East, people think in one way; if you go the Far East, they think in another way. In the West, they think in a third way. Why should they think differently? Who told them to think differently?

The very atmosphere of the earth generates the personality, the psycho-physical individuality, and has such an impact upon them that they start thinking differently. Otherwise, why should there be so many different cultures?

The whole earth is made like a human being; it is one person. Sometimes we say it is Mother Earth, sometimes we say the Father in Heaven, whatever. The human personality will, to some extent, explain the difference in the structure of the earth and the whole solar system, also.

The sun is the brain of the solar system, and the moon is the mind. Scientifically you can't understand this. Though the head, heart, lungs, stomach, thighs and legs are all parts of one particular person, they don't operate in the same way. You revere the head much more than the feet. It is not that the feet are unimportant, but they are not so important as the head.

You have certain very valuable parts of the body like the head and heart. The brain and the heart may constitute the positive and negative sides of action, like electricity's positive and negative current. You cannot say which is more important or less important, yet they act differently like sun and moon, yin and yang, etc. But as you go down, the importance becomes less and less. The most important thing is above the neck and the trunk; if any part fails there, the lower parts will not help you much. The whole human being is valueless if one cell in the brain is not working properly. And when you go further down to the thighs and the feet, you would not mind even amputating them, if necessity arises, as long as the upper part is safe. But you won't like any upper part to be removed. There, even a little of it should not go.

Why I am saying this is that the earth also is made in that way only. The upper part, the northern hemisphere, the Arctic region, has some effect, something like the brain of the earth, from where the electric current flows. A peculiar electric current flows from the north to the south. There is one saying that when you sleep at night, you don't keep your head to the north; otherwise, the current will pass through the brain and go through the legs and it will have some adverse effect.

Some people say Lord Siva cut off the head of a little child whom Parvati created from her own body; afterwards it became Ganesha. Parvati said, "How is it that you have cut off the head of my little child?" Siva said that he didn't know and that he would make it all right. He told his retinue to bring the head of somebody who was sleeping with the head towards the north. Nobody was sleeping with the head towards the north except one elephant. So they took the head of the elephant and put it, on the sacred trunk, and Ganesha became elephant-headed. So what is the fate of the elephant? His head went off! In the future, don't sleep with the head towards the north. But actually, the story has arisen on account of this magnetic current passing.

In the same way, the Vedas say that the whole universe is considered as one cosmical human being. You need not call it human; call it super-human. In the *Pu-*

rusha-Sukta the universe is compared to the body of the Supreme Creator. The whole universe is One Person. We say many *purushas* are there in the world, but they are all like cells in the body of that Universal Purusha.

Thus, everywhere this logic of the structure of the human personality applies, and that is the reason why we say the human body is a miniature cosmos. It is called *pindanda*, and the other one is called *brahmanda*. This is the microcosm, that is the macrocosm. So, you are the cross-section of the universe. As the different parts of the body are evaluated by you in different ways, in the structure of the earth also the northern part has one effect, the southern part another effect—and beyond that, in the whole solar system also, says the Veda.

The Sun is the soul of the solar system; the moon is the mind, and all the planets constitute the other limbs of the body. You can go to the galaxies, and beyond the galaxies to the entire space-time structure. Finally, you will find that the universe of creation is one organic living being. That is why they say there is only one God. Just as you say you are one person inspite of your being made of little parts, there is only one Creator, one God, inspite of your seeing many things in the world.

You are seeing millions of things, just as you are seeing millions of parts of the body, but you are one person. In a similar way, there is only One Person in the whole universe. You unite yourself with that One Person. Then, you will have no problems. This is called Yoga, spirituality, religion, or meditation, and that is the aim of life.

15

SEXUAL IMPULSE VERSUS MEDITATION

Miyazawa: During the practice of my meditation, some strong desire, especially lust, is coming in my mind, so I cannot continue my meditation.

SWAMIJI: That is the same thing I was telling this lady in the assembly. What is your desire?

Miyazawa: Lust.

SWAMIJI: Have you got a father, mother, and all that?

Miyazawa: Yes.

SWAMIJI: What is your father or mother doing?

Miyazawa: Now he is maybe retired.

SWAMIJI: What are you doing in Japan?

Miyazawa: I have no job.

SWAMIJI: How is it? Is it difficult to get a job?

Miyazawa: No, it is very easy.

SWAMIJI: Then, why don't you get a job?

Miyazawa: No, my purpose is to continue my study and meditation.

SWAMIJI: Are you under the impression that people who are working in the office cannot do meditation? Is this what you are thinking? Do you think a meditation man simply sits quiet, and for the whole life he will meditate only?

Miyazawa: No, not like that.

SWAMIJI: Then, why don't you do some work?

Miyazawa: Yes, to get a job or not is not so important for me.

SWAMIJI: No, it is important. I am not talking some unnecessary thing. Work also has a connection with life.

Miyazawa: Yes, yes. I know. So, whatever I work, I try to meditate maybe in the working state, also.

SWAMIJI: No, you answer my question. Why are you not doing any work? About meditation, we shall think afterwards. First, you tell me why you are not wanting to do any work. Work and meditation should go together. Otherwise, if you emphasise one side only, the other side will trouble you.

Miyazawa: Yes. The working is only to get some money to maintain myself.

SWAMIJI: No, it is not for money only. It is a necessity of the human personality. Action and thought are two aspects of the human personality. You cannot only think, without doing anything.

Miyazawa: Yes, yes, yes.

SWAMIJI: So, one answer of mine is that you must do some work.

Miyazawa: Yes.

SWAMIJI: Another question is,—what is your age?

Miyazawa: Thirty five.

SWAMIJI: You don't want to marry? You have no desire?

Miyazawa: Not so intensely.

SWAMIJI: Anyhow, mildly, at least, it is there. The desire to marry is there.

Miyazawa: Not so strong.

SWAMIJI: Not at all? No, it will become strong afterwards. Why do you want to wait until it becomes strong? That is why it is harassing your mind. If you live continuously at the feet of a great *guru*, and do whatever he says, then this problem may not arise. If you have no *guru*, and you yourself are starting to do some meditation, this problem cannot be avoided. The *guru* has some method of freeing the seeker from troubles of this kind, which is a secret technique known to the *guru* only, and it is not meant for public demonstration or lecture.

But if that is not possible, you have to follow the normal course of life. You must be living an active life, and there is nothing wrong with living a married life. Married life is not against spirituality, because it is one aspect of the requirement of personality, in the same way as meditation is also a requirement. It is not absolutely necessary that one should marry. You can be without marriage, also; but then, when the trouble arises, you must know how to handle it. So, now you are having only the trouble, without the method of handling it.

Spiritual life does not mean escapism. You escape from the responsibilities of life, and then go to God. That is not possible. The human personality is a structure that is approved by God, and that structure has certain requirements. Inasmuch as you have to pass through this structural pattern of your personality, all the needs of the personalty also have to be taken care of. You do not want to marry, and then you need not eat food, also, afterwards. Why do you want to eat? If one thing need not be done, the other thing also need not be done. So, you want to eat, but not marry. These are two sides of the pressure of human personality.

But, as I mentioned to you, if you have a great master under whose protection you are living, then this problem will not arise. But now you have no *guru*. There is no master under whom you are sitting and receiving the blessing. Independently you have started some meditation.

I have told you two things; now the third thing: If you are persisting in this meditation, the problem will slowly evaporate, after a long time. Do you understand me?

Miyazawa: Yes.

SWAMIJI: Either you marry, or you have a master, or you wait for the grace of God, and one day the trouble will evaporate. And, don't eat too much. You should eat only once a day. When the body is very robust, it creates all sorts of further desires. Eat once a day only. Don't take dinner in the night, and don't take breakfast, also. But, don't go to extremes in that, also.

Miyazawa: So, my meditation method is...

SWAMIJI: What is your meditation? Tell me how you are meditating.

Miyazawa: It is a conceptual one, but I am sitting and thinking that the whole universe itself is meditating. Like that.

SWAMIJI: It is very good, beautiful. This method is wonderful. Continue this meditation. If you don't want to marry, don't marry. I am not compelling you, but you must work and have friends around you, so that you may have a social life also. If you don't have any social life, you cut off your connection with people, and don't do any work, also, and say, "I will meditate," then it will not be very successful. You have no friends to chat. The chatting also is a necessary thing. It is one food,—it is a food for the mind, sometimes. If marriage is a bondage, you need not marry. But, if it is an unavoidability, you can go for it. Or, you wait for the grace from above coming to you. If you are sincere in your meditation, it will take care of itself. How long are you meditating every day?

Miyazawa: Every day, one hour in the morning.

SWAMIJI: And, what are you doing for twenty-three hours? There are twenty-four hours in the day. One hour you are meditating; for twenty-three hours, what are you doing?

Miyazawa: Now?

SWAMIJI: Yes.

Miyazawa: One hour meditating, then some asana and pranayama, then come here and attend darshan, then go back...

SWAMIJI: In Japan, when you go, you will do meditation for one hour?

Miyazawa: Yes.

SWAMIJI: And, for twenty-three hours what do you do in Japan?

Miyazawa: In the morning, the same way,—medita- tion, and a little asana and pranayama, and then some temporary working.

SWAMIJI: Are you doing some work in Japan?

Miyazawa: Yes, but temporary.

SWAMIJI: But even if it is temporary, it is daily work?

Miyazawa: Yes.

SWAMIJI: How many hours do you work?

Miyazawa: About seven hours.

SWAMIJI: It is all right. Even five hours is good. Five hours you work. Have you got friends?

Miyazawa: Yes.

SWAMIJI: Be friendly with people. Go for a walk. Be open and free in your behaviour. Don't be restricted. Many spiritual seekers think that spiritual seeking means that you should not talk also. You will simply sit brood- ing. That is not proper. You should not put any pressure on your personality, in any way. Anyway, the final word for you is that you go on with this meditation; be a normal man, happy inside, very sociable, friendly with people; do some work; then, finally, everything will be all right in due course of time.

Miyazawa: Yes.

SWAMIJI: This is my answer to you. What is your goal, finally?

Miyazawa: Immersion in the Absolute.

SWAMIJI: You are a great man. I am glad to hear this. If you are really wanting it, you will get it. Are there other people here sitting who want to merge in the Absolute?

Other Visitors: Yes! [laughter]

SWAMIJI: Who is that lady? Janaki? Do you know English language?

Janaki: Yes, Swamiji. I can understand, but I cannot speak anything.

SWAMIJI: You want to merge in the Absolute?

Janaki: Yes, no doubt. Bless me, Swamiji.

SWAMIJI: Yes, it has to come one day.

Janaki: Thank you, Swamiji.

SWAMIJI: Listen, you are saying that you have lust, and all that. Actually, lust means wanting a counterpart, a woman. Do you know that the Absolute includes woman, also? Do you know that?

Miyazawa: Yes.

SWAMIJI: Hundreds of millions of women are there inside the Absolute. [*group laughter*] What is the problem? Unnecessarily you are worrying! Inside the Absolute there are millions of women, so why are you worrying unnecessarily? I think there should be no problem.

Miyazawa: Yes. The problem, maybe, is confined to one lady, or... [group laughter]

SWAMIJI: No, why one lady? The Absolute will give you millions of ladies. Why do you want one? [*group laughter*] This is also another trouble. When somebody is going to give you too much, you don't want it. You want only a little.

Miyazawa: No, no. [laughter]

SWAMIJI: You are a very funny boy. Somebody says, "I am a poor man; I want money." "A hundred million dollars I am giving to you. Take." You say, "No, no, I don't want it. I want only ten dollars." Like that if you think, what can I do? You want only ten dollars. That is what you are asking. But the Absolute says It will give you a hundred million dollars or more. You say, "I don't want it. I want only ten." Is it all right?

Miyazawa: No.

SWAMIJI: Your problem is an unnecessary creation. Millions of women will come to you. Do you want? [*group laughter*] No, I am not joking. It is a serious matter. The whole world will melt into what you want, if you so wish. You are thinking that it is a funny thing. It is not so funny as that. The entire earth, heaven, everything will melt into liquid and pour nectar on your body, and nothing will stand before you. Everything that you want will immediately manifest from inside your consciousness. You have some foolish ideas of women and such things, which has no meaning, truly speaking. There is no man, no woman,—nothing is there in the Absolute. It is Supreme Perfection, which you want to have by company with somebody outside. It is a psychological defect in the mind. Wanting something outside is due to a defect in the process of thinking. While there, in the Absolute, everything is there at once, the whole heaven and earth will melt down and come to you. Men

and women,—everything will be there, whatever you
want. Do you want it or not? What do you say?

Miyazawa: Yes.

SWAMIJI: Then, meditate more, and don't complain
that you want to marry a woman, and all that. These
ideas are stupid crotchets. You should remove these
ideas from your mind. When you are going to get the
whole universe of perfection, why do you want some little thing? All right?

Miyazawa: Yes.

SWAMIJI: Don't have any problem in the future. It
is gone. Say "it is gone."

Miyazawa: Gone.

SWAMIJI: Be happy.

16

DIAGNOSE THE ILLNESS OF LIFE AND GO BEYOND

SWAMIJI: No medicine can be considered as appropriate unless the diagnosis of the case is done properly. You cannot prescribe any medicine unless you know what the illness is. You may do *vipassana*, *japa* yoga, *asana*, *pranayama*, *karma* yoga, *bhakti* yoga, *jnana* yoga, *raja* yoga, pilgrimage to holy places, *satsanga* with *mahatmas*, etc., but this is like eating all kinds of medicines from a chemist shop. All right, take it, but what is your illness? Unless you know what your illness is, these medicines will not be of any utility. Thus, each one who meditates must be clear about what the trouble is; if the nature of the trouble is clear, you also know what to do for that. You may do *vipassana*, you may stand on your head; do what you like, but don't unnecessarily do a thing without knowing what your problem is.

What is your problem? What is wrong with you that you are running about in search of *gurus* and yogas and meditations and all that? Let anybody be clear to one's own self.

Sean: I think the problem is separation from the universe.

SWAMIJI: All right, if your problem is separation from the universe, how will you unite yourself with the universe? How are you going to rectify this mistake? What is the method that you are adopting?

Sean: To find the common thread. Everything must be connected.

SWAMIJI: In your meditation, you are thinking something; that is your method. What is it that you are thinking?

Sean: I am thinking in very slow steps. I start thinking of the common connection,—first feeling that everyone and everything here in the room are connected in some way. Then, I try to expand outside the walls and feel the connection with the river and the mountains. Then, I try to take it further to include the planet; then, higher and higher.

SWAMIJI: Higher and higher, up to what point?

Sean: As far as I can go.

SWAMIJI: You must go up to that point beyond which you feel there is nothing. If you feel there is something beyond that point, then you have not reached the highest point.

Sean: It is just a visualisation.

SWAMIJI: Yes. Visualisation, not merely like a theoretical concept,—it is a strong sense of being That, from which you seem to be separated. It is not just an ordinary kind of identification of uniting two different things. You are not uniting yourself with some other thing which is different from you; you are identifying yourself, affirming your being with that whose being is your being. It is feeling a sense of being with that which has been apparently isolated from you. You are not thinking it, you are *being* it. You are the very thing from which you seem to be separated. Then, they say, it is available at once. The Kingdom of God is not merely within you, it is just you. You meditate like that. This "within" and "without" idea also should be given up. That also is a limitation of thought.

Sean: Swamiji, sometimes one can feel from outside, then one shrinks back down into this.

SWAMIJI: That is because of the old habit of thinking in the old way right from childhood. Everyone is brought up in a family, in a community, in a cultural background, in an atmosphere of thinking which is influencing one even now to some extent. There are certain basic prejudices which die hard. You are a Westerner; you will never think that you are an Indian. It is impossible for you to think like that, though it is not wholly correct to imagine that you are only a Westerner. You are a human being and you think like a human being. Are you thinking like a Westerner, or thinking like a human being?

You boil down your essence a little more. For some practical social outer purposes, you may think like a Westerner, and it may not be identical with Eastern thinking; but as a human being, you will think like any other human being. You have the same emotions, same feelings, same sense of heat and cold, hunger and thirst, and sense of self-respect. This is not peculiar to a Westerner only, it is in any human being.

A Christian cannot think that he is Hindu, though he may study Hinduism. Whatever may be the extent of his knowledge of Hinduism, a Christian can never say that he is a Hindu; a Hindu can never think that he is a Christian. This is a kind of prejudice which must be given up.

When you were manifested out of the cosmic substance as an individual, you didn't come out as a Christian or a Hindu; neither did you come as an Easterner or a Westerner. You came as a little piece of matter ejected out of the cosmic stuff; to that condition you will return in your meditation. You don't go to God as a Christian or a Muslim going to God, not even as a man or a woman going to God. Even that is a prejudice from the cosmic point of view.

This is a moot point, which is interestingly delineated in the different sections of the Bhagavad Gita. The first six chapters deal with one issue; the next six chapters deal with another issue and the last six deal with a third type of problem,—the Individual, Cosmological and the Absolute. When you reach the Absolute point of view, even the cosmological prejudice of being a created something would drop. You are not a created entity, also. That idea also must go.

This is a very difficult thing, and this exercise you must do in your meditation daily, as if you are going to God today. You may say that you will do it slowly after fifty years, and reach God in the next birth. These ideas also are obstacles, because you may get it today by a miracle of Providence. All great things happen suddenly,— birth or death, rise or fall, they take place in one instant. Suddenly you become big, suddenly you become small. Suddenly you come, and suddenly you go. Everything consequential is a sudden thing in this world.

When you meditate, you must go through these exercises that I have indicated with great intensity, as if you are going to reach God today, under the hope that it is possible. You should not start thinking that it is not a possibility. "It may be or may not be!" Again the Gita comes in, saying that you should not expect the fruit of an action. The possibility or impossibility of it is like expecting the fruit of an action. That idea also should be given up. Do your duty. Again, here, in meditation also that *karma* yoga principle comes in: do your duty, but expect not the fruit. Meditate in this manner of practising the exercise, *without bringing* the idea of possibility or impossibility; else, it would spoil the whole thing. You should never think of the future. "Act, act in the living present", "heart within and God overhead" as is the poem of H. W. Longfellow.

ENERGY CONSERVATION

Visitor (Italian): How can I conserve my energy?

SWAMIJI: Your energy becomes less and less as you desire things more and more. Whoever wants things, loses energy; whoever is one with things, becomes filled with energy. One who is united with things has no desire for things; this is the way one becomes filled with energy.

When things stand outside us, they take away our energy; if they are one with us, they give us energy. This is the secret of Yoga. Nothing should stand outside us; everything should be one with us. You cannot be a friend of anybody when that person is outside you. A person has to be one with you in thought and being; then he is a real friend. This is how you can be a friend of all things, even God Himself.

When you become the very things that you want, all energy comes in. This the secret behind success. You have to intensely feel that *you already have what you want*. Then things will really come to you, without your asking for them. This is how energy increases. Yoga is the technique by which you do not run after things, but things, by themselves, will come to you. You have not only to *know* a thing but also *be* it.

LOOKING FOR HAPPINESS

SWAMIJI: What is your final aim?

An American Visitor: I think, speaking philosophically, joy or peace is what we all want, whether we seek it in business, or love, or religion.

SWAMIJI: In a life which is characterised by momentariness and fluxation, with temporality reigning supreme everywhere, and nothing permanent worth the while, with no control finally over anything, what kind of happiness are you expecting in this world? Perhaps happiness that is going to be enduring and not merely fleeting cannot be had in a world which is fleeting by its nature.

Nobody can be happy in this world, yet it is happiness that we seek. It looks like a contradiction in our approach. Being involved in a world of fluxation and temporality, how do you expect permanent happiness? Yet our heart seems to be yearning for permanent happiness. It doesn't want a joy for one moment, and destruction the next moment.

Actually, the joy that we seek is super-physical, super-terrestrial; it is transcendent. All that we empirically experience, sensorially perceive or contact, what we feel psychologically in terms of sense perception is not the joy that we seek, finally. There is a transcendent superphysical element operating in us, and if you can contact that transcendent element in your own self or in the world, you may be contacting the source of your joy. This is the work of religion.

Religion is nothing but the art of contacting the source of real happiness which, as we have in this little analysis found, is not to be had in this world. When I say "in this world," I mean anything that is sensorially perceptible. Even this body is not a reliable source of happiness, because it comes and goes.

This body was given birth to, and it also will pass away some day. Would you like to connect your happiness to a bodily existence which comes and goes? Would you like to have a joy which comes and goes? You have already decided that you don't want such a kind of joy. We want a joy which is always there and shall not leave us, but the body has come, and it shall leave us. Our relations, property, the world, this body, will all leave us. Where are we going to be finally? *That* you have to contact, by an inner vision and an in-depth analysis of one's own self, and a meditation which is called yoga, religion, metaphysics.

Direct action is necessary in this connection; something has to be done about it. Meditation is a practice of concentrating the consciousness on some thing, but what is that something? In *kriya* yoga there is a breathing process prescribed on which you concentrate; that is one method. Meditation is the art of contacting reality, and for that you have to first be sure what reality is. You cannot concentrate on something which is not clear to the mind.

What are you wanting, finally? On that you have to fix your attention. Whether you call it *hatha* yoga or *kriya* yoga or anything else is not important. Fix your consciousness on your concept of final reality, and it shall bless you. You have to decide yourself what is ultimately real, in yourself or in the world; then fix your attention and attune your consciousness with it. This is meditation. It has no particular name.

When you adopt certain preparatory techniques which vary according to different schools, you call them *karma* yoga, *bhakti* yoga, *raja* yoga, *kriya* yoga, *kundalini* yoga, etc. These names are given only to the preparatory stages, but the final end is the same in all cases. It is a plunge into reality. What is reality? This requires a knowledge which is obtained from the teacher. Everyone has to approach a teacher for this purpose. A *guru* is necessary.

Each one has a concept of the Ultimate Being; on that you concentrate. The word "ultimate" implies the finality of it, and there is nothing above it. When you ask for it, you need not ask for anything else. On that you fix your mind. This is the whole of religion, philosophy, and yoga.

19

SPIRITUAL ATMOSPHERE & GOD-WORLD RELATION

Carlos: Why is it that when we meditate here in this place we can go deeper than in other places?

SWAMIJI: It is because of the influence of the atmosphere. That is the reason behind it. If you are in a different atmosphere, the thought gets diluted. Circumstances and the atmosphere around you have a great influence. If you are alone, you think in one way; if you are in the midst of many people as in a railway compartment, you will think in a different way. If you are inside a church or a temple, you will think in one way; if you are in a marketplace, you will think in a different way altogether. If you are in the presence of a holy man or a great soul, you will think in one way; if you are in the presence of a thief, you will think in a different way. This is to give an example of how circumstances and the atmosphere around have an influence upon oneself. That is why it is said that the most important requisite for a spiritual seeker is company of good people, called *satsanga*. Nothing is equal to *satsanga*. The company of noble persons is the best remedy for every kind of problem in spiritual life.

The books that you read and the company that you keep will tell something about you. You find out what books the person is reading and what company that person is keeping; from that you can know something about that person himself. It is an old saying or proverb: "Tell me the books you read and the company you keep; I shall tell you what you are".

Devote some time to reading elevating literature, generating noble thoughts, and don't keep company with people who will distract your mind. In modern days people have company of television, cinema and clubs. This is the company that people keep, and you can know how dissipated the mind can be after having such company.

Carlos: How can we live a more spiritual life in the West? Sometimes it looks like the world doesn't want God.

SWAMIJI: The object does not want the subject merely because it is the object. What you call the world is the object of consciousness. As long as it is considered as an object, it will want nothing except itself, and nobody will want it, also. But it is a wrong notion which dubs a thing as an object. When the object becomes the subject, then it will cease to be troubling you. If the world has become the subject itself, there is no need of renouncing it. You are renouncing only the wrong notion about it.

Carlos: But Swamiji, how can you live in the world without being distracted by cinemas and clubs, and so on? The distractive forces are like an antithesis. They are there. They have an attraction.

SWAMIJI: You need not go to cinemas or clubs, and don't go to bars. Who asked you to go? Let them be there, but you need not go there. Why are you interested in them?

Carlos: I am not interested in them, but they have a pressure. The social atmosphere has an influence on the spiritual seeker.

SWAMIJI: It cannot influence you, unless your mind is weak. A weak mind can be influenced by any devil, and everywhere there are devils in the world ready to jump on you.

Carlos: But Swamiji, we say that there is just God.

SWAMIJI: But the devil is also there. You can say anything, but your mind does not believe it. The mind says that there is a club, but by theory you say that God only is there. So what is the use of such theoretical talking, when your feelings say that there is a club? Tell me what your heart says. Does the heart say that the club does not exist? If it does not exist, I have no objection; but you are saying one thing and feeling another. That is a contradiction.

Carlos: Then how should I act, practically?

SWAMIJI: You become that trouble itself; then it will cease to act, and won't affect you afterwards. It becomes your very self, which cannot trouble you. The question will not arise. You become the question itself, yourself.

Carlos: People will think I am crazy if I talk like that.

SWAMIJI: You become those people also yourself. Then who will think about you? If you become those people, there are no people to think of you. Again, you are thinking that somebody is there outside.

Carlos: It is a gradual process, Swamiji.

SWAMIJI: If you don't want to do a thing, you start talking like that; otherwise, you can do it in one minute. It doesn't take a gradual course and all that. When the time comes for us to depart from this world, it has to be done instantaneously. You cannot say "tomorrow we will do it."

Visitor: Swamiji, when we are not accepted by other people, what should we do?

SWAMIJI: Why are you worried about it? In what way are you affected by the other person not accepting?

He may not understand you and, therefore, he is not accepting. How do you expect everybody to understand you? The world is so big. Many will not understand, and if they don't understand, leave it there. Why are you worrying? What is the problem? You are unnecessarily creating problems for yourself. It is mainly a psychological problem.

Visitor: If really someone doesn't accept me when I would like to do something for them, what should I do?

SWAMIJI: Then you don't do anything. Keep quiet.

Visitor: There are two ways for our life. One is to attach to the world around us and perform our works perfectly, and the second is to attach to the Almighty only. Which is the better one?

SWAMIJI: You tell me whether God is better, or the world is better. If you think the world is better, you need not think of God. Forget Him. But if a doubt is there, then think a second time. There are people who think that there is no God at all, that they need not bother about Him, that the world is perfectly all right, and that they can get on without Him. If there are people who think in that manner, let them please themselves. But if there is a doubt that it is not so and there is something else, then it is worth knowing what that something is.

God created the world. How can He have a clash with His own creation? You are imagining that there is a clash, but there is no such thing. God is embodied in this world, so how will He clash with Himself? That is not possible. The clash is only in our mind; it is not in God, nor in the world. We have not understood what God is or what the world is. So, both ways we are having imperfect ideas 'bout things. The world is an appearance of God; so, now can there be a conflict?

20

CONCEPTS OF GOD

Swedish Visitor A: Are not intelligence and good-ness narrow human concepts? How do we know that God is a person or a personality,—that He has personal qualities?

SWAMIJI: Whether God is a person or not,—this is your question? You see, this is a fairly important question in the study of theologies everywhere, in all religions. All the Semitic religions (Judaism, Zoroastrianism, Christianity, and Islam) consider God as a Supreme Person, almost identifying Him with the concept of a Supreme Father. "Father in heaven, hallowed be Thy name,"—that is how the prayer goes. All these descriptions of God imply that He is a large inclusive universal personality. You are asking me whether He is really a personality.

Personality is a human concept. When we talk of personality, we always think of the pattern of human personality. We don't think of the personality of a lion, or an elephant, and all that. Our thoughts are conditioned by the human way of thinking. Now, is it true that the human way of thinking is the only way of thinking, and there is no other way? A frog also thinks, a reptile thinks, a cow thinks, an elephant thinks. Do you think that their thinking is wrong?

Visitor A: No, I think they are personalities, too.

SWAMIJI: They are personalities, but we don't think that God is a huge lion. We generally think that God is a huge human form, as big as this universe. The first point about this is that we are thinking like human beings, and it is not necessary that this is the only way of thinking. It may be subject to modification when we evolve further in the process of evolution. Man thinks in one way, a super-man thinks in another way, and it is believed that man has to become a super-man, until he becomes a God-man.

The other point is: what is personality, be it human or otherwise? A person exists in space and time. If space and time are not there, there cannot be personality. A person exists in space; there is space around him, and time also is there. Now, we believe that space and time were created by God, and they were not there prior to God's existence. We always say that God is first, not that space and time are first. "God created the heaven and the earth," says the scripture, which means to say He created space and time. If that is the case, God cannot be said to be conditioned by space and time. In other words, He is not in space and time. If He is not in space and time, how will you see Him as a person?

God, thus, is not really a person. He is not in heaven only. We say God is in heaven, but God created the heaven; so, before He created the heaven, where was He? Neither can we say that He is a person, nor can we say that He is in heaven. God is universal, all-comprehensive, infinite Existence. That seems to be the only conclusion we can draw by going deep into the question of the nature of God.

But, for the purpose of devotion, you see otherwise. Man cannot think of infinitude always. The mind is not made up of such potential. We want affection, love, and also response to our affection. An infinite all-pervading, non-spatial, non-temporal Existence cannot evoke our affection so much, just as logic and mathematics cannot evoke our affection. Logic and mathematics are perfect sciences; we accept that, but we cannot love them. Our heart does not go for them, our heart goes to a painting, music, architecture, sculpture, literature, etc. Where our heart is, there our love and our happiness also is. To manifest our love, we require an object. We cannot love the Infinite for obvious reasons. So, we have to consider God as a Supreme Father. Sometimes, in India, people consider Him also as a Supreme Mother.

From our point of view, from the requirement of human nature, there is nothing wrong in thinking that God is a Person, because the Infinite can also appear as a Person, in the same way as a block of stone can appear as a statue by carving. The block of stone does not contain the statue, but it contains a statue potentially. God can be a Person, and yet we need not limit Him to personality. He is rather a Super-Person. This is what I think God must be. What do you say?

Visitor A: I say thank you very much for an excellent answer.

Visitor B: May I ask a question?

SWAMIJI: What is your question, sir?

Visitor B: I agree with you on this description of the nature of God, but I must confess that I find it a little alien to see this multitude of idols which appear in Hindu temples. How does that go together with this idea of God?

SWAMIJI: This question has been put to me one hundred times. This is the one-hundred-and-first question. This is a difficult thing for a Western mind to understand; they are not accustomed to see these things. You must go deep into the psychology of this kind of religious behavior. One who worships an idol is not worshipping that particular thing.

There is a person called the President or Prime Minister of a country. You say, "The President has come, the

Prime Minister has come," but really, only a human being has come, who is just like you. The President of the country is just like you, just like a shopkeeper, a person who drives a car or a railway engine, or a hotel keeper. He is the same human being as anybody else, but you don't think him to be so. When the President of the country comes, you do not say that a Mr. Guy is coming. Then, who is coming, actually? Is it a human being that is coming, or the President that is coming? Tell me. You are seeing the President in that human being, which is to say, the President is a concept of an all-inclusive authority and power in the jurisdiction of the country. You respect the President because he has all the country concentrated in him. But really he is only a Mr. x y z. Is it not?

The person is an idol, and you need not have any concern for him. Are you concerned with everybody in the world? So many people are walking on the street, but when the President comes, you will immediately get up and receive him with honour. Then, whom are you adoring? You are worshipping "something" that you see "through" this idol of a human being. Do you understand my point? Likewise, the idol in the shrine is not actually an idol but a representation of what it stands for, beyond its visible shape or form.

The whole universe is one integral being. Nature is not made up of little parts. Just as I can touch any little part of your body, and it is equal to touching the whole body, if I touch your finger, you will say, "You are touching me," so, a little part that I touch is equal to the touch of the whole to which it belongs. In view of the fact that Nature is an integral all-comprehensive whole, every part of it also is Nature. Every part, you may say, is even God Himself.

This "part" concept is only notional. There is no

part in God; there is no part in Nature also. There is no part in your personality; you are a whole person. When you come here, you don't come like a jumble of many parts of your body, though it is so in fact. You are a conglomeration of many limbs, and yet you don't say that the limbs are coming. You say, "I am coming." In the same way, Nature is one whole person, and any part of it is as good as any other part. Because of the fact that it is difficult to conceive the total whole at once, due to our immature notion of reality, we symbolise it in an idol. We reach the ocean through a river. We cannot go to the ocean immediately. I will catch hold of a boat and sit on the Ganga, and it will take me to the ocean. All the rivers are like idols, through which you can see the ocean behind. In a similar manner, you touch any part of the world, and you are touching the entire world.

The worship of idols is not worship of any particular thing. It is symbolic as a part of the total which is hidden in that little thing, even as the President is present in one single individual.

Another example is that there are officials in the government,—there are police, collectors, magistrates, and varieties of powers. Every person here represents the government, which is the total whole. If you want to see the government, you cannot go and see it physically anywhere; you cannot see the government where it exactly is. You rather go to a person who represents the government, such as a magistrate, a collector, or a commissioner. When I want to see the government, I go to a person. The total whole is represented in that person, which is the administrative authority of the government, which is impersonal in itself.

In a similar manner, any part of the world can represent the whole universe, and so, when a person worships the so-called idol, he sees the whole cosmos represented in it. Remember the examples I have cited to you. Thus, there are not many gods, just as there are not many governments, though there are many officials.

Visitor B: You are in good shape this morning! Thank you very much.

SWAMIJI: So, I have many friends now.

21

THE WORLD'S MOVEMENT FROM MATERIALITY TO SPIRITUALITY

Visitor: It seems that the world is moving away from spirituality, towards materialism. Do you think we will be able to reverse that trend?

SWAMIJI: What are the causative factors? Why has it become like that? Unless you know the cause of this situation, you would not be able to handle it. You said something which requires proper handling. But why did it happen at all? Is it due to historical reasons, or ethnic, anthropological, educational, or geographical problems? Something is there at the back which has brought about this condition, and which has to be set right.

If you have thought over this matter, and if the cause is clear to the mind, the treatment also will be easy. It is like diagnosing a case, like a medical operation. Diagnose the case first, and then you see what you can do. What you have pointed out is a disease, and there is a diagnosis. Why do you think this has happened?

Visitor: It has happened because people both in the West and the East have looked in other directions besides spirit.

SWAMIJI: Why should they look in another direction beside the spirit? Why do they feel the need for such a behaviour?

Visitor: I think maya is very attractive.

SWAMIJI: No, that is not a good answer. The answer

should be scientific and precise. *Maya* is a word which finally has no meaning. Forget that. You should not use such words. Something is happening to their minds that has propelled them to move in that direction. What has happened to them? This question has arisen in the minds of many people in India also, but very few people have given thought to it. The answer is not a palatable one, so they don't want to give the answer at all.

The need for material prosperity and acquisition, when it is overemphasised, takes a person in the direction that we have been mentioning just now. Does it mean then, at least from the point of view of these people who are in this condition, that working for material comfort and acquisition is more important than working for the spirit? If anyone thinks like that, then there is something basically wrong in the very outlook of that person. His illness is deep-rooted. He is totally misconstruing the very structure of life. To put it shortly, he requires a fresh education altogether. So you mean to say that people require new education? I am not against that project. Let them all be newly educated. Now, who will bell the cat? Who will start this work?

Visitor: That is something that has been started by people like Swami Sivananda and Swami Chinmayananda.

SWAMIJI: Yes, they have helped, and many other great souls like Sri Aurobindo, also. Sri Aurobindo was positively engaged in the resuscitation of the original values of the country which he emphasised in all his writings. He has written a book called *Foundations of Indian Culture*, a treatise every person should read. His understanding of India is superb,—a mighty appreciation it is.

India has the blessing of God, somehow. It has not died like other nations, and it does not appear that it is going to die easily. India has suffered due to one mistake that it has committed. It lost its independence for some centuries because it discredited the value of earthly existence, and gave too much credit to a transcendental existence. That is, your love for God was not equally commensurate with your duty to the world. This is what he says, and so the worldly forces attacked, and God did not come to help because people segmented God Himself into two parts,—the Creator and the created. The country suffered economically, militarily, and even in its concept of spirituality. Yet, in its aspiration for the transcendent, though it was not conceived properly in an integral fashion (it was segmented because it was separated from world's existence), the intensity of the longing for the transcendent was such that its soul is still surviving, though economically, and from the point of view of defense forces, it is not possessed of much that can be admired.

Most of the religious people in India asserted the importance of the transcendent Creator, and it was not so easy to bring together into a state of harmony the world and God. The two always appeared to be different things, and, they will appear to be so always, as long as the mortal brain thinks in a mortal manner. The total thought of the integration of Being, wherein the Creator and the created become one,—that was the true spirituality of the Upanishads and the Bhagavad Gita. But nobody in India lives in the spirit of the Upanishads or the Bhagavad Gita. People have only rituals and some gods of their own which they have imbibed from the Puranas, the Epics, the Agamas and Tantras.

Who lives like the Bhagavad Gita in India? Who lives like the Upanishads? Who lives like the Vedas? All that you call Hinduism today is conditioned by the dictates of the Puranas and the Epics, with a lot of ritual and mythology. The One God has become the many gods, and we worship all the gods, not necessarily knowing that all these gods are aspects of the One God. The concept of the One Absolute cannot easily enter the mind of the human being because of the dichotomy created in the mind between man and the world, and between world and God.

Now, the tables have turned. Economically, India is strong. Militarily, also, it is very strong. But, something is missing still. A very strong body we have, and a lot of wealth too we have, but we seem to be slowly losing the soul. At one time, only the extra-cosmic Soul was emphasised, and the body was neglected. Now, we are taking care of the body very well. We have all the requirements for it. But, the soul is perhaps going under the cloud, which we hope will not be for all time to come. We are passing through a temporary period of transition. We are barely fifty years old. Fifty years is a small thing in the history of the universe. A day will come when the world will see India rising up with its might and main.

There is a belief also that culture moves from the East to the West. China and India were highly cultured nations once upon a time. Then, slowly, culture moved to Greece, then to Rome, then to Europe and England. They became mightier than the East. Then it went to America, which is now supposed to be the strongest country. Now, further, it is moving the other way to Japan, which is coming up mightily. And then, the Sun will come back to the East, and India will again have the same status as during the time of the Vedas and the Upanishads. The cycle will be then complete. So, we are hoping for the very good day to dawn with all its brightness and glory. "God is in heaven, and all is well with the world," thus may we sing with the poet.

Visitor: What is the unique contribution that the Divine Life Society is making to bringing the spirit more alive,—to bringing people more alive to the spiritual side?

SWAMIJI: Swami Sivananda's dream was the integration of the human personality for the purpose of social integration, and finally, what you may regard as cosmic integration,—which is virtually the realisation of God Almighty. From a lower level, the human personality has to be taken up to the higher level, and then the highest integration, which is universal. He worked for that, and the entire mission of the Divine Life Society is centred in that noble objective.

Visitor: For people in India who have mistakenly chased western material values...

SWAMIJI: I do not say that every Indian does like that. Mostly, people who are not properly oriented are enamuored of the external facilities available by contact with a Western way of thinking. This overemphasis that they are laying in their life is due to a misconstruing of the nature of the aim of life which should not happen, especially in an Indian, who is supposed to be living in the cradle of ancient culture.

Externals cannot make a human being. It is the total that makes you what you are. I do not say that external facilities and comforts are unnecessary, but you are not made up of mere externals. Though externals are necessary, they are only an appendage to your total personality. Emphasis excessively laid on one aspect of the personality alone will be like thinking of one side of human nature and completely ignoring the other side.

You are a physical body, a social unit, a political individual, a biological structure, a psychic entity, an intellect, a reason, a spirit. All these aspects of the human personality have to be fed properly with their own required diet by what we call real education. Any aspect which is ignored will set up a reaction and make life miserable.

Education, which is actually the way in which you live in this world, should be the procedure that you adopt every day, every minute, every moment of time, taking into consideration every aspect of your relationship to the world. This is to see that you are integrally growing from the lower level of your personality to the higher dimensions of it, until you reach the highest dimension of your being, which is Universal Existence. This is my concept of real education, and of the aim of all life.

Visitor: So, at a human practical level, how do you go about educating people at all these levels at once?

SWAMIJI: That is the technology of education, which has to be properly tabulated by a competent teacher. Just as you have educational institutions, schools and colleges, we have Ashrams where there are mentors, guides, teachers. Sometimes they are called *gurus*. The study of life along these lines is to be carried on under a competent master in an institution something like the Divine Life Society. It is purely a personal matter. If a student goes to a professor in a college, he must follow the curriculum set forth for the purpose of this kind of education, attend the classes, and be with the teacher throughout the career of the education.

So, we have a syllabus of the very process of thinking itself, into which the student is introduced gradually, by practical guidance in his day-to-day life. This is what is propagated by Swami Sivananda by his personal example of living, much more than by what he spoke and wrote in his books. Example, they say, is better than precept. The life of the teacher, the manner in which he lives, his personal outlook of the structure of existence, will be an object of observation and study more beneficial to the student than the books that he wrote or the words that he uttered. This is the method we are adopting here in this little closed Ashram called the Divine Life Society. There are many other such Ashrams also in India. I am just mentioning this as one example.

Visitor: What message would you give to someone in the West about what they can do in their life to become closer to the spirit, and to make spirit more alive in the world around them?

SWAMIJI: They have to learn the art of thinking in a holistic manner. That is the first thing that one has to do. You have to know how to think in a manner which is complete, not fractional. Holistic thinking is thinking of everything at the same time.

The art of thinking in a holistic manner means thinking in terms of the spirit of the cosmos. That is holistic thinking, which includes every aspect of life, because spirit includes all things. The total comprehensiveness of the structure of existence is the object of this holistic thinking. This is Yoga, finally. This is spirituality, this is real religion, and this is the duty of every person in one's day-to-day existence. This is what we practise and teach, to the extent possible for us, under the conditions prevailing.

Visitor: What are the steps by which an individual can learn to think holistically?

SWAMIJI: You have to take a person from the lowest to the highest, gradually. The involvements of a person have to be understood first. There are political involvements, social, financial, biological, family involvements. These have to be taken care of first. You should not speak anything other than these things in the earlier stages. People are worried about these things very much, and other things do not so much carry weight. When these things are cleared, you can take up the question of the psychological involvements,—how the mind, emotions, intellect, *prana,* and body are working. From outward considerations, you come to the inward ones, which are psychoanalytical and psychological.

Then, the third stage would be to set the personality in tune with Nature as a whole, the entire cosmos of astronomy, as you may say, with which also you have to be in harmony. You cannot be at loggerheads with the sun, the moon, the stars, and the planets. They also determine your life in some way. When that also is taken care of adequately, you centre your soul in the Spirit of the cosmos, which is God Almighty. Thus, from outside, you have come inside. From inside, you have gone to the whole of Nature, which is all creation; then, you have embraced the Absolute. This is how you proceed slowly from the lower wholes to the higher wholes, the highest one being the Absolute, God.

22

THE PHENOMENON AND THE NOUMENON

SWAMIJI: You must be affectionate, kind and compassionate, serviceful, and charitable, they say. All this is very, very important indeed, but there is something more important than all these things, which is the destiny of the soul of the human individual,—what happens, finally.

This world shall vanish one day, with all its humanity. If it had a beginning, it shall have an end, also. Even the solar system may not survive eternally. It would not be a wise complacence on the part of anyone to imagine that everything is fine, as it appears on the surface to the sense organs. Things come, and things go. People are born, and people die. Empires rise, and empires fall. Caesars and Napoleons have come, and many have gone, also, at the same time. Nothing remains. What is this drama?

In this mysterious presentation of the history of the universe, the history of humanity, nothing seems to be enduring, and even when something appears to be enduring for some time, we do not know for how long it will endure. None of us knows how many minutes more we will be in this world, let alone years. There may be only a few minutes, for some reason. We have to learn by past experience, and by history.

What is the aim behind all this pageantry, this drama, this enactment of humanity? Why are we busy? What are we busy about? What for are we working and running about, having projects and embarking upon all kinds of activities, as if everything is milk and honey in this world?

Now we come to what we generally call the philosophical implication of human culture, and human history. There is something super-physical, super-sensory, super-perceptional, super-social, and super-personal. There must be something towards which the whole universe seems to be gravitating, without the acceptance of which, all that we do in this world would look meaningless.

If there is meaning in life, it cannot be on the basis of what we see with our eyes, because it is passing. It is a transition, a fluxation; it is finally unreliable. We cannot rely even on our own security for a long time. There is no security anywhere. Everything is dubious; yet, we live and work as if we are immortals. Nobody believes that tomorrow is the end, though it can be. How is it that there is a contradiction in human thought so that every one of us seems to be under the impression that we shall be living for eternity, though we know very well that this is a false assumption? How is it possible for us to entertain a false assumption, which is entertained by everybody in the world?

We think in total opposition to the facts. While the vanishing of all things is a fact, the disbelief in the vanishing of all things also seems to be a fact. Everybody has to accept that at any moment anything can happen. But, at the same time, we have a hope that nothing will happen, everything shall be fine, and tomorrow shall be a better day. We never think that tomorrow may be a worse day, though there is no argument against it.

On the one hand, something tells us that everything is insecure, and no one can say what will happen the next moment. At the same time, we feel that nothing will happen,—everything is OK; tomorrow is a better day, and I shall live for another fifty years, at least. Though I know that I shall die, I will not die tomorrow. Nobody will believe that he will die tomorrow.

Now, here are certain points for us to consider. There is eternity masquerading in this mortal frame of the human individual, the great fact of the universe which is peeping through every pore of our perceptional faculties. We belong to two worlds at the same time, as it were,— the mortal and the immortal. Our involvement in the body, in the space-time complex, in causation, in human society, in anything that is external, is the mortal aspect of our personality. Everything shall perish, that which is spatio-temporal, that which is causally bound, involved in cause and effect relation, yet, there is something in us which is not so bound. We are not mortals basically, essentially, in our roots. The immortal in us summons us every moment of time. That is why we cannot be satisfied with all the treasures of the world if they are to be offered to us.

If the whole earth is to be presented to us, we shall not feel secure. If all the sky also is under our possession, we cannot be secure. Endless is our longing. We want endless wealth, endless possessions, and endless duration of life in this world. Infinity is our asking, eternity is our desire. Nobody wants anything less than eternal duration, eternal continuance. Even if one is an emperor of the whole world, taking for granted that such a thing is practicable, would that person like to live for only three minutes more? No. Even if I have all the treasures of the whole world, infinity is in my grasp, if it is only for a few minutes, that is of no use.

So, it has to also be eternal. Our infinitude should go together with eternity, also. Space and time should blend together, embrace each other in a fullness. You may call this the Absolute, if you like.

The realisation of this in actual life, the attainment of cosmic universality, which is identical with spiritual Self-hood, is the ultimate aim of life, for which purpose we are finally busy in this world. We are not busy for any extraneous purpose. We are active in this world from morning to evening, not because the earth can give us anything or offer us anything worth the while; all these services that we are rendering, all the work that we do, in any capacity whatsoever, is a preparatory process for the realisation of this universal· Selfhood,—you may call it God-realisation. This is, in brief, the aim and object of this ashram of Swami Sivananda, which is also, I believe, your own institution's aim and object. I would like to hear something from you because I know you are a great man, and a little message from you to the audience would be a blessing to us.

Roy Eugene Davis: Well, our people already know what I say. Our philosophy is the same, rooted in the Vedas, so our teaching is essentially the same. And our emphasis is essentially the same.

SWAMIJI: You also teach some meditation?

Mr. Davis: Yes.

SWAMIJI: Do you have any special techniques of meditation?

Mr. Davis: For new students we teach mantra, and then we move on.

SWAMIJI: You chant a *mantra*?

Mr. Davis: We use hamsa mantra, or so-ham mantra. And then, sound-light contemplation, then certain kriya processes taught by Yogananda, bringing the current through the sushumna.

SWAMIJI: *Kriya* processes. And a little bit of the Patanjali technique also may be there?

Mr. Davis: We emphasise it; our basic text is the Patanjali Yoga Sutras.

SWAMIJI: Patanjali mentioned so many things in his *sutras*, but for our daily practice, a few of them will suffice.

Mr. Davis: Yamas, niyamas would be the guidelines.

SWAMIJI: *Yamas, niyamas, asanas, pranayamas, pratyahara, dharana, dhyana.* We may go up to that; we need not think of *samadhi* just now. *Samadhi* is intriguing, isn't it,—very intriguing? We won't easily understand what it actually means, and what will happen to us in that state. We cannot even imagine what will happen to us in case we realise God. Suppose you have attained God. What will happen to you there? What is your position in that status? Even such questions we cannot answer easily. We bypass these things. Everything will be OK.

23

THE TRUE HEART

Visitor: When we meditate, Swamiji, we generally concentrate at trikuti but sometimes the mind wanders. It keeps on wandering. We say "OK," and go to the heart centre...

SWAMIJI: Meditational techniques are learned through initiation by a *guru*. It is not done of one's own accord. Have you been initiated by any teacher who has suggested that you should meditate on some spot of the body?

Visitor: Yes. It was suggested.

SWAMIJI: What did they suggest?

Visitor: I follow the Yogananda system of meditation. They said to concentrate at the trikuti, but in my own experience I prefer to concentrate at the heart centre.

SWAMIJI: Why are you having an experience different from what the *guru* has told? The *guru* must have told something very right and proper. What is the problem that you have?

Visitor: I find it easier to concentrate at the heart centre than the trikuti.

SWAMIJI: In what way is it easier?

Visitor: I feel a feeling of peace and joy.

SWAMIJI: All right. There is no objection. You can concentrate on the heart centre if you feel peace and joy. But a question has to be raised here. What actually do you mean by the "heart"? When you say that you are concentrating on the heart, what do you mean by the "heart"? That fleshy substance which pumps blood,—that is the heart?

Visitor: That is the place where the heart centre Anahata chakra is.

SWAMIJI: So, you are not meditating on the physical heart.

Visitor: No.

SWAMIJI: You are meditating on a conceptual centre, not physical. Is it so? What do you say?

Visitor: Yes. I prefer to concentrate on the heart chakra, visualize the petals.

SWAMIJI: It has no connection with the actual physical heart?

Visitor: No.

SWAMIJI: OK. Since how long are you doing this kind of concentration?

Visitor: Three or four years I have been following this Yogananda.

SWAMIJI: But you have modified it by concentrating on the heart.

Visitor: No, I concentrate at kutastha also, but whenever I find that my mind keeps on wandering...

SWAMIJI: What actually is your aim in concentrating like this?

Visitor: To go deeper into the heart.

SWAMIJI: You are using some word. What are you wanting to achieve, finally? Concentration on the heart is not good. It interferes with the working of the heart, to some extent. The heart has its own way of operating, and we are not supposed to go on bombarding it with our thoughts. Actually, we should not think of any part of the body, properly speaking, because the body has its own way of operating in a harmonious manner. If you bombard any part of the body with your thought, the harmonious working of the organism gets disturbed a little bit, unless you have a specific purpose in doing that. Otherwise, there is nothing wrong; you can go on. And your *guru* is sitting here. You ask him.

24

THE CONNECTION BETWEEN BODY AND MIND: THE ISHTADEVATA

Visitor: What is the connection between body and mind?

SWAMIJI: In a large ocean, in cold countries, the upper part of the ocean becomes solid. It becomes ice. Do you understand what I am saying? The bottom is liquid and the upper part is solid. And, the solid suddenly does not emerge at one particular spot. There is a gradual solidification of the water becoming thicker and thicker, as it goes up, until it becomes very thick and hard on the top; and when you go down it becomes thinner and thinner, until it becomes very thin like water. Now, how do you reach this ice with the water underneath? What is the connection between the two? What is the connection between the ice on the top, and the water at the bottom? Is there a connection, or no connection?

Visitor: No connection.

SWAMIJI: There is no connection. So, I have answered your question, or you have answered your own question.

SWAMIJI: So don't talk much now. That is sufficient. Actually, the answer has to come from the questioner himself. The questioner has the answer within him, deeply hidden. Only, it has to be brought out by an analytic method. What do you say? The answer is inside you, and you are unnecessarily putting a question, not being able to bring out the point. The *guru* is like a midwife. He brings out what is already there, not creating something new. So, I have brought out something, as a midwife. Anybody else wants to ask anything? Liquefied body is mind—that is all—to give you a brief answer. When body liquefies, it becomes mind; when the mind solidifies, it becomes body. There is no "connection," actually; it is one thing only, appearing as two things. Water and ice are one thing only; they are not two things.

You cannot concentrate on something with a desire for something else. Your mind is the same as your desire. As a cloth is made up of threads, and a cloth is not independent of the threads, the mind is made up of desires, and it is not independent of desires. So, how would you concentrate, except through the mind—which means to say, with your desires only? And, where are your desires? What are the things that you require?

If there is a chaos in the way of your assessment of desires, and if you are not very clear as to what it is that you really need in this world, the mind will not be prepared for meditation or concentration.

You will be able to concentrate your mind only on that which you desire. You cannot concentrate on anything which you do not desire. Or, to put it more plainly, you can concentrate your mind only on that for which you have deep affection from the bottom of your heart. You cannot concentrate on anything for which you have no affection. Some people say, "concentrate on the dot on a wall"; "do *trataka*"; "concentrate on the flame of a candle"; "concentrate on a rose flower, or a streak of light." All right; these are wonderful methods of concentration. But, is your heart there, really? Is your heart welling up with joy because it is thinking of a dot on the wall? Or, do you consider it as a kind of imposition inflicted upon you by a hard taskmaster? Is Yoga meditation a kind of unpleasant discipline that is imposed upon you by someone? Or, is it a joyful, spontaneous outpouring of your own feeling, because you want it?

These are certain aspects of the background of thought, which you have to keep in mind. How can you love or be affectionate towards a dot on the wall, as you know very well that it has no meaning? But somebody tells you that it is good to concentrate on it, and so you are doing some forced attempt of concentration on that particular thing, which is the dot.

In the Indian tradition, we conceive of or define the object of meditation as *ishtadevata*. It is a Sanskrit word which means "beloved object," or "beloved God." That which you love most is a god for you. When you love a thing immensely, one hundred percent, it becomes a deity for all practical purposes. It is a god. A god is one, beyond which there is nothing, outside which also there can be nothing. If a mother has one child after expecting it for years together, that child becomes a god for that mother,—she is always thinking of it, hugging it, worshipping it as the most dear delight of the soul. Is anything there in this world which you consider as the dear delight of your soul? That is your *ishtadevata*, your beloved object of meditation.

Each one of you has to choose your beloved object for meditation. That which your mind cannot accept as beloved cannot become an object of attraction; therefore, it cannot become an object of concentration, also. Otherwise, you will go on thinking that you are meditating; for years together you will be humming something and thinking something. After even twenty years of concentration, you will find that you have received nothing, practically, because you have undergone a discipline, like a school-going activity imposed upon you, but your heart was elsewhere.

Our Swami told me that you speak on *yama-niyama*. Actually, *yama-niyama* is the analysis of your heart and your feelings. Where is your heart; where is your feeling? What is it that you are attracted to? Tell me, and I will tell you what kind of person you are. You need not tell others what kind of person you are, but you can tell it to yourself. You tell yourself: What kind of person am I? Will you consider yourself as a very important person, perfect person, all right in every way, beloved of the gods? Or, do you find that you are a puny nothing, a nobody in this world? Is it like that?

A seeker of God is the most suited student of Yoga meditation. One who loves God wholeheartedly can also practice concentration wholeheartedly. But he who loves paltry things in this world, the petty little tinsels which look attractive and beautiful and very worthwhile, but forgets what is really valuable in life,—such a person cannot concentrate spiritually. A teacher, a guide, is absolutely unavoidable.

The ultimate object of love is that which will give you salvation of soul, that which will free you from mortality and death and make you immortal. That you should consider as the object of your meditation. Who can save you in this world, except that which is not of this world? This world is brittle like a glass. It will vanish like a wisp of wind one day or the other. There is something immortal, which is essential in this cosmos. They call it God Almighty, the Absolute, the Supreme Being. On That you have to concentrate. You can concentrate on the tip of the nose, the point between the eyebrows, or heart, or any part of the body. OK, you can go on with that, but finally, the mind has to be led to that Supreme Being, which alone can be called the *ishtadevata,* or the object of beloved affection. Nothing else can attract you. Nobody can love you more than how God loves you. And nobody you can love also, more than God. God loves you, and you love God. This is religion, and this is Yoga. And, if this is clear to your mind, the mind will concentrate. Otherwise, it will go jumping here and there because it has not chosen its real object.

The chosen object is the *ishtadevata*,—the most beloved, the most attractive, the most liberating, and the source of security for you. You will find nothing is so secure as God Himself. Everything else is insecure, and finally unreliable. So, Yoga is a religion in the sense that it is love of God, and it is a discipline in the sense that it is concentration of mind. These two go together. Deep concentration by the power of will should get blended with the feeling for God. Religion and Yoga go together, and they become one in the form of an upsurge of your entire personality in the direction of the great Creator of the universe. This is my little message to you. What else can I tell you? God bless you.

25

GOD AND LIBERATION

SWAMIJI: You are perfectly right in saying that you would like to know yourself. Scientists, philosophers, ecologists, politicians, sociologists, whoever they are, make the fundamental mistake of thinking that they are outside the universe, that they can handle it, and harness it as if it is a bull, or a horse, or an elephant,—not knowing that they are included in that which they seek.

You cannot know the environment, unless you know yourself first. Why should people have such problems, but for the fact that they have misconstrued the whole structure of the environment, which includes themselves, as if the environment is outside? We always think that the environment is sticking to us, like a shawl or a blanket, but, it is not so. The environment is not a blanket with which we are covering ourselves, so that you can throw it away also, if you want. It is rather alike skin; you cannot remove the skin. The environment is your skin itself, so when you handle it, you are handling yourself. Yet, no politician will understand this point because he is selfish, and is concerned with a little temporary gain, and not thinking of the future in a spirit of a statesman.

The environment is sticking to you like a skin. How will you handle it, unless you handle yourself first? What do you say? Do you agree with me? Very slowly, reluctantly, you are agreeing.

Know thyself and be free. You have to find out how it is possible for a person to be free by knowing oneself.

What is the connection between knowing myself and freedom? This question also is a big thing. The relationship between freedom and one's own self also is not clear. The whole thing is a mess. We require a new type of education altogether. It looks like that.

If you are in a hurry, nothing substantial will take place. Nothing happens by mere human effort, finally. There is a cosmic order which takes care of itself. The only thing is that you should not obstruct its movement by your egoism and adamant behavior, and all such things. If you are open to it, it will take you in a boat. But, if you obstruct it by your affirmations, then that is a bolt that you put on the door, so that it will not open. Be not afraid.

Indian Visitor: No, I am not afraid.

SWAMIJI: It will come. One day or other, it must come, and everybody must get it. Nobody is barred from it. It has to come.

Visitor: It has to come, but I have to make that point clear to me.

SWAMIJI: Yes. Now it is clear that you will get it. That is all you want, to know whether you will get it or not, and you are going to get it. It is certain. So, you can smile nicely and be happy. Don't cry and weep. Be happy. It will come.

Visitor: Can you contemplate anything without conceiving it?

SWAMIJI: What are you going to conceive? You can conceive anything you like. What is it that you want to conceive?

Visitor: How the universe was created.

SWAMIJI: Yes, I understand. How will you conceive it? What is your method? What method are you going to adopt? What conception have you got at present?

Visitor: It was created by God for His enjoyment.

SWAMIJI: All right. So what is the matter now? You contemplate like that?

Visitor: No, that is OK, but some desire has to be there.

SWAMIJI: Yes, yes. Correct.

Visitor: But how can a liberated soul indulge in desires?

SWAMIJI: There is no liberated soul who indulges in desires. There is no such person.

Visitor: Then how did this come?

SWAMIJI: There is no such person. There is no liberated soul who has desires.

Visitor: So God is not liberated?

SWAMIJI: God is not a liberated soul. He is not a soul at all. He is something different. He is not a human being, so why do you call Him a liberated soul? You don't know what God is; therefore, some wrong ideas you have. He is not Mr. Bannerjee sitting there. The Creator of the universe is not a liberated soul. They are two different things. The eternal Absolute has no desires, and It is not a human being, and It is not a liberated soul.

Visitor: So, the aim is just to realise that you are part of Him but never become Him?

SWAMIJI: You become united with Him and cannot feel separate afterwards. Just as the soul and body are one, the individual will merge into the Absolute. You will feel unitedness and universal comprehension; omniscience will enter into your consciousness. For that you have to do this meditation, deep meditation every day, for as long as possible. Conduct meditation on desireless Universal Existence.

You can do prayer and *japa*. *Japa* and prayer are the initial stages of spiritual practice. Then meditation will come of its own accord. Chanting the name of God, and prayer are the initial steps; and you should not have unnecessary desires, distractions, worries, emotions, tensions. All these must be absent. If they are there, you cannot meditate. These weaknesses are emotional, and they must be eradicated gradually by effort.

Visitor: What will we feel toward other people at the time of liberation?

SWAMIJI: There are no other people at that time. They do not exist. You will merge into That. You will not see them also, at that time. They will not be visible to your eyes because just as you don't see dream objects in waking, this also will vanish there. The whole world will disappear.

Visitor: For a person who has attained it...

SWAMIJI: Attained what?

Visitor: Attained salvation.

SWAMIJI: Then he will not see the world at that time. The world will not be visible at all, just as you cannot see the dream objects when you are in waking.

Visitor: So, the moment you are liberated...

SWAMIJI: It is finished. You will behold only Universal Existence. You will not see people at that time, just as you do not see dream people. In dream you saw some people. Where are they, just now? You do not bother about them. They don't exist at all. This will happen to this world also, at that time. It will vanish like dream objects. They will merge into the Universal Mind. The question itself will not arise.

26

THE LAST THOUGHT

Mila (Venezuela): I thought that the last thought is the most important thought. I was told now that it is not like that,—it is not important. The last thought is not like as if you think of a deer and you will become a deer,— that it is not like that.

SWAMIJI: If you think a deer, you will become a deer.

Mila: But, I was told that it is not like that, that the last thought is not important. So, how is it?

SWAMIJI: The last thought is the force exerted by all the thoughts that you entertained throughout your early life. It is like the fruit of the tree of your life.

Mila: But, how does the thought of the deer come?

SWAMIJI: The deer comes if you have got attachment. If you have got a little kid in your house and you are always taking care of it, and every day you are thinking of it, that is it. You are doing meditation and prayer; that is all right, but you are looking at the kid, also. A little small rabbit, or something you have, and you go on thinking it, and it will come in the last moment. It will come,—whatever be the meditation you are doing, it will have no effect, if you have attachment to the kid. That kid-thought will never leave you, because your emotion is in the kid, and your emotion is not in the meditation. Your intellect is working in meditation, and emotion in the kid only. So, the kid will come, and that is the danger. Your love for God should be emotionally charged, not just intellectually accepted. For a child, our connection is emotional, so the emotional thing only will come at the last moment. The whole day, what are you thinking, from morning to night? Tell me the answer.

Mila: Well, to see the consciousness in everything,— in the trees, in the stones.

SWAMIJI: All right. Do you think anything else also, in the mind?

Mila: I hope not to think other things, because they say that even on the door of heaven, you can fall down. What is the course that we can take in the last moment?

SWAMIJI: If day and night you are thinking this only, as you mentioned, and you cannot forget it at any time, under any circumstances,—morning, evening, when you go to bed and sleep, when talking, wherever you are, at whatever condition, you have got only this thought—it will come at the time of ending. But in your heart you must feel. Where is your heart? Where have you kept your heart? That will come in the end.

If you have a secret affection for something which you are not telling anybody, that will come with great force at the end, and that only will work. But, if it is not so,—emotionally, also,—and you are thinking only this great wonderful thing, you do not want anything in the world, you have no friends, you have nothing, you are concerned only with the Supreme Being and He is everything for you, and all day and night you are thinking That only—then, in that case, the last thought will be That only. Whatever your emotion says, that will be the last thought. So, this is your question?

Mila: This is just because they were telling me that Swami Chidananda said that the last thought is not important. I was thinking that the Bhagavad Gita says that the last thought is important, so I wanted to ask you.

SWAMIJI: How can the last thought be something different from what you have been thinking your whole life?

It will be the same thought. Why should the last thought be different? The last thought is the cream of all thoughts.

Mila: Some distraction may come.

SWAMIJI: No, it cannot come, because the last thought is the strongest thought. There is no distraction. How can it? Unless your mind is thinking very strongly about something,—you have a property, a legacy, a bank balance; "if I die who will take all this property"—some people think like that, then is the trouble. They may be meditating and praying to God; everything they are doing. But, there is a fear: "When I die, who will take my property?" That thought will come at the end, it is a property thought preponderating.

But, if you say, "Let the property go to hell. I do not bother; I have done my duty. Let anybody take it. I will do charity, finish everything, and stand alone to myself and God. I have got nobody except myself and God. I am standing before Him. Always I am standing before Him, day and night. I am looking at Him, and He is looking at me." If this thought is there, you will have no problem. Think over the matter.

Mila: And, what are the future obstacles? We can achieve indirect knowledge.

SWAMIJI: Every day you are praying and meditating. Is it not? And, what obstacles are coming?

Mila: No, you say that there are three kinds of obstacles: the past, the present, and the future.

SWAMIJI: But, are they coming to you in meditation?

Mila: No, but I was thinking, what are the future ones? How can I make future obstacles? I can understand the past and the present, but I cannot understand the future obstacles. What can I do in the future?

SWAMIJI: The future obstacle is that desire which

you want to fulfil, but you cannot fulfil in this life. Due to some trouble, your desire you cannot fulfil in this life, and that will be the future trouble. But, if you have no desire which cannot be fulfilled, and everything has been fulfilled, you have now a clean slate, then there is no future problem. The future will not trouble you.

Mila: Thank you very much.

27

FEMALE MOUNTAINS

Saravana Raja: I want one doubt to be removed.

SWAMIJI: OK, tell me.

Saravana: Baba, now I am observing each and every body's movement. Suppose many people are here, so they are moving. I am finding some power in them. That means, I think that God is residing in them. So, I am seeing only God,——men as Shivas and women as Shaktis. Is it right?

SWAMIJI: Please repeat once again what you have said.

Saravana: I see men as Lord Siva, and I see women as the goddess Shakti, Parvati. Am I right?

SWAMIJI: And what do you think about trees and mountains?

Saravana: Trees and mountains,——it is pervaded by some power, natural things.

SWAMIJI: Are there also male trees and female trees?

Saravana: I do not explore in these things. I do not know.

SWAMIJI: You do not know? Male mountains and female mountains?

Saravana: No.

SWAMIJI: Then, there are no male human beings also, and there are no women. That is also a wrong notion. If you think that there are males and females among human beings, then you must think that mountains also are like that. There are female mountains, and male mountains; but, if you think they are not like that, then it is not like that in the case of human beings also. It is a misconception.

There are no such things as males and females. But, if you say they are, then they are everywhere. Even in trees you will find male trees and female trees. It may be true, also. I am not joking. That is why cross-pollination takes place, and then fruits are produced in the trees. That is a male-female action only. Even insects have male and female distinction;—like in honey bees, there are males like drones, and the female is the queen. Everywhere you find the same features.

But, if you try to transcend this consciousness, and feel God's power present everywhere, then the positive and negative, both, will melt into God-consciousness. Then there will be no such distinction as you are thinking. In the lower levels, these distinctions are seen, but in the higher level, they all get fused into God-energy, God-consciousness. So, what is your doubt?

Saravana: And so, man and woman are there. When I am seeing their face, what is the right concentrating object?

SWAMIJI: Concentrating on what?

Saravana: The eyes are there...

SWAMIJI: No, no. What are you concentrating?

Saravana: Suppose I want to be speaking with you; everything has a particular point to concentrate. In the face, what is the particular point to concentrate?

SWAMIJI: Why do you want to concentrate on anyone's face? What is the purpose?

Saravana: Suppose in the future I may get married, so Devi will come in my life. So then, what is the right concentrating object in her face? Which spot—eyes or...

SWAMIJI: Whose eyes?

Saravana: Women.

SWAMIJI: Oh, You cannot judge a person by seeing the eyes, nose, ears, etc. It is a total that is there. The whole thing you have to see at one stroke,—from head to foot simultaneously. It is not only the nose that you are seeing, or the forehead. If you see one part by part, they will all look meaningless. Everything is meaningless, if you take it part by part. Everything is wonderful, if you take it as a whole. So, whatever you want to see, you must see as a whole structure. Now I am seeing you. I am not seeing your nose and eyes and moustache and all that. The entire thing I am seeing as one whole person. Then I can understand what you are. Do you understand me?

Saravana: Yes, I understand.

SWAMIJI: So, what else is the problem now? You think like that, as a whole, everywhere.

28

RELIGIOUS CONSCIOUSNESS

Jose: Swamiji, is religion necessary for religious consciousness?

SWAMIJI: Anyone who feels that there is something above oneself is a religious person. Religion is the consciousness of there being something above and beyond oneself. That is all. If you feel that you are complete, and there is nothing beyond or above you, there is no need for religion. This is a simple psychological definition. The consciousness that there is something above, beyond you, more than you, larger than you, transcending you, which you would like to reach, is religion. You may call it religious consciousness, if you like.

Now, you are asking if it is necessary to have religion. The way in which you conduct yourself in your daily life, in the light of this consciousness, in this world, is religion. Firstly, there is a consciousness. Secondly, it has an impact upon your daily life and you conduct yourself in a particular manner accordingly. Your behavior, conduct and action are all determined by this consciousness; so one is the cause and another is the effect. You may say that religious consciousness is the cause; religion is the effect. They go together. One cannot be without the other.

Jose: But is religion necessary for religious experience?

SWAMIJI: Experience is nothing but direct entry into this consciousness of religion. At present, your religious consciousness is only conceptual. It has not actually *become* you. When it becomes you, it is experience. So, it is one step further, beyond even mere consciousness. One is an external manifestation, then there is a conceptual metaphysical foundation, then lastly, actual experience. You may say that there are three stages.

Being religious means having a consciousness of the finitude of oneself and a longing to overstep its limits. And who does not feel finitude? Thus, everybody has a consciousness of what is beyond finitude, which one would like to overcome. Here is religion.

29

BEAUTIFUL THOUGHT

Mila (Venezuela): You said in your Chandogya Upanishad that the pattern of our thought must be beautiful. This means that our spontaneous thoughts are stupid, but the spontaneous thoughts should be beautiful? Is this the true meaning?

SWAMIJI: What is spontaneous thought?

Mila: That which comes without our instruction.

SWAMIJI: Generally, spontaneous thought is not beautiful because it is an emotional thought, or a distracted thought, or a thought born of anxiety. That is the usual thought that people have, so how can it be beautiful?

Mila: How can we make it beautiful?

SWAMIJI: You must think that which is beautiful. Then, your thought also becomes beautiful. You think that which is most beautiful, and your thought immediately becomes beautiful by the impact of the form of that which is considered beautiful. Which is that which is beautiful? Tell me. What is beautiful?

Mila: The unity.

SWAMIJI: Unity of what?

Mila: To see God in all persons and in everything.

SWAMIJI: If you can plant God in everything, you will see only God. You will see nothing else. If you see only God, and nothing else anywhere, that is a beautiful thought. But no other thought can be really beautiful.

Mila: But why does the spontaneous thought become beautiful?

SWAMIJI: In a very advanced stage of meditation, your spontaneous thought also will be God-thought, but normally, a human being cannot think God always. So, effort is necessary. Meditation requires some effort in the beginning. Otherwise, normally, people are not thinking of God in their minds. They are thinking of their own problems, and business, and all that, so that such thought cannot be called beautiful. But, if you are able to spontaneously manifest God-thought only, and no other thought, then you can say that spontaneous thought also is beautiful. Is it possible to think only God, and no other thought will come?

Mila: No.

SWAMIJI: So, the other thought, which is spontaneous, naturally will not be beautiful. It will be a fragmentary and broken thought. Only God-thought is beautiful; no other thought can be called finally beautiful.

A complete structure is necessary for anything to be beautiful. Nothing that is not complete can be beautiful. So, who is complete in this world? Tell me. Nobody. And, therefore, nobody is beautiful. Sometimes the most beautiful thing, which is God, gets reflected in something; then, that also looks beautiful. Do you understand? Though God alone is ultimately beautiful, that in which God is reflected also looks beautiful. A child is beautiful, and a saint is beautiful, because both child and saint have no ego. Wherever there is no ego, that state looks beautiful. Wherever there is ego, it looks ugly. Egolessness is the nature of God; and God gets reflected in a child, and also in a saint. So, both look beautiful; but the middle people are not beautiful, because they are neither saints nor children. Do you understand me?

Mila: Yes.

SWAMIJI: It is very important. So, either you be a child or a saint. Otherwise it is no good. In the middle you are hanging; that is no good as a beautiful thing.

Mila: I am in the middle. I am old and still not beautiful.

SWAMIJI: So, you are a child, or a saint? What are you?

Bhavagrahi: Child.

SWAMIJI: Saint?

Bhavagrahi: Child.

SWAMIJI: If you are a child, then you are beautiful, because in a child there is innocence, absence of egoism, and self-affirmation, so God reflects Himself in that condition. God can be reflected in the things of the world also, provided these things are "minus ego," and are innocent. Then, God will be reflected there.

There are beautiful things in the world, like small babies. Small children are beautiful. Anybody's children are beautiful, but when they grow with moustache and beard and ego, they are no good. A saint also has no ego. He is like a child, so he also is radiant. Finally, it means that God is beautiful. The essence of it is that and anything that reflects God also is beautiful. So, if your thought is spontaneous, and spontaneously you are thinking this kind of thing, then your thought is beautiful.

Mila: We can achieve it only by practising more and more?

SWAMIJI: Yes, by practising total thinking.

Mila: It is the only way to have those spontaneous thoughts?

SWAMIJI: Yes,—by practising. It requires great effort on your part in the beginning to entertain a "complete thought." Only a complete thought can be a beautiful thought.

Mila: What is a complete thought?

SWAMIJI: A complete thought has nothing outside it. It is holistic. And, only God can be so complete. That is Beauty.

30

EASTERN AND WESTERN THINKING

American Visitor: To bring some of the Eastern mind, or intuition, in. And, I would like to hear what you think about what is important for me to remember when I am trying to teach Americans, Westerners, to think creatively.

SWAMIJI: Where are you teaching,—in a college or school?

Visitor: Both. Small children and college,—adults and children.

SWAMIJI: What are you teaching?

Visitor: I am actually teaching creative thinking. I teach the bright children, the gifted children.

SWAMIJI: Creative thinking?

Visitor: Yes.

SWAMIJI: Is it psychology?

Visitor: Some of it is psychology, but mostly creative thinking means how to be creative in your thinking.

SWAMIJI: But actually, it is a part of psychology only. You mean that you want them to drop their rationality?

Visitor: To fuse it with the intuitive.

SWAMIJI: Yes, you are right,—not dropping, but fusing.

Visitor: Yes. Fusing.

SWAMIJI: It is a philosophical subject, almost.

Visitor: Yes.

SWAMIJI: It is the meeting of the East and the West in a comprehension of values. In a few minutes I cannot answer your question. It is a huge, world-shaking subject.

Visitor: I know; I know it is huge!

SWAMIJI: Are you studying anything on this subject? Have you got any book?

Visitor: I just finished writing a dissertation and I did research where I asked...

SWAMIJI: What is your dissertation?

Visitor: It is on the creative thinking processes of investors. Over the years I have studied different authors on creative thinking.

SWAMIJI: Now, what is the defect that you find in Western thinking?

Visitor: The defect? The defect is that they do not appreciate or use the intuitive mind. They do not use imagery or visualisation as thinking processes. They do not listen to the source of the universe or the within. Their body is separated from their mind, and their heart, and their emotions.

SWAMIJI: The body is separated from their mind and heart in every Westerner?

Visitor: No, not every Westerner,—I hope not! But I am saying that in the elementary schools now...

SWAMIJI: The European way of thinking is, as they usually call it, empiricist.

Visitor: Yes.

SWAMIJI: It is based on sensory observation, and on inference based on that perception through the sense organs, believing in nothing that cannot be proved rationally. That is one of the traits of Western thought,—believe nothing which cannot be established by rational investigation. And, it is also socially oriented, to a large extent;

they think in terms of society, and individuals. The value of the individual and the society of individuals is not given up. In the Eastern side, the emphasis is on the universal principles of life. It is not just empiricist. It is also rational. Its emphasis is on the basic principles of all the values of life, which the East thinks is universal in its nature.

Western thinking deduces the universality of a thing by observation of particular instances. If many horses are there, there is a general universal principle called horseness, etc. The Universal does not exist by itself, according to Western thinking. It exists as a corollary followed from the observation of many particulars. In the East, the Universal precedes the particular, whereas in the West, the particular precedes the Universal. Here is the great difference between Western thinking and Eastern thinking. The fact is that the Universal is not derived from observation of particulars; the Universal can exist even without there being particulars.

We are going deep into philosophical realms, and I am not thinking of speaking too much to you on this subject. I can only suggest to you to read certain things where people have attempted to bring harmony between two types of thinking. I was wondering if you have been studying any book of this kind, where a blend has been effected between Eastern and Western thought.

Visitor: No, I have not.

SWAMIJI: You have not seen anywhere any such attempt?

Visitor: Somewhat, I can think of one educator in California. Her name is Barbara Clark. She attempts to weld the rational with the more intuitive, Eastern thinking.

SWAMIJI: Eastern thinking is not irrational.

Visitor: No, no! It is rational, plus intuitive.

SWAMIJI: Yes, it is based on intuitive perception.

Visitor: Yes.

SWAMIJI: Rationality cannot contradict intuitive perception, though its validity is accepted. Have you read any book on Eastern philosophy?

Visitor: What specifically? Educational, no.

SWAMIJI: What we are discussing is not an educational matter. It is something philosophical. Have you come in contact with any treatise on this subject?

Visitor: No, not specifically.

SWAMIJI: In order to know what it is that we are trying to know, we have to know what this universe is made of. You are living in a world, isn't it?

Visitor: Yes.

SWAMIJI: What is the stuff of this world? What is it made of? If you look at it from a larger dimension,—the universe itself,—what is the structure of the universe, which determines the structure of everything that is in the universe,—you and I included? Everything that is in the universe is determined in every way by the structure of the wholeness to which all the particulars belong. So, first of all, you must know what this world is. What is this universe? Here is the beginning of philosophy.

There are umpteen answers to this question. The world is totally external to the individual, according to well-known Western thinking. The world is not touching you; it is external to you, so you are treating it as an object. You are the subject of the perception of an object, which is the world. So, you can handle it without affecting yourself, or your having anything to do with the world outside. The subject has nothing to contribute to the nature of the object. This is the modern scientific approach. The world of science considers the objects of the world as totally independent of the observer. Here, in India, in Eastern thought, the position is quite different. The world is not standing outside, because you are a part of the world, how then will you study the world? Are you studying your own self? You just think over the consequences of this kind of thinking. Are you concluding that the world is so totally outside you that it does not touch you at all? I think it cannot be said that it is like that.

Visitor: It is a big mistake.

SWAMIJI: The world influences you in a tremendous manner, and the influence must be understood,—what kind of influence it is. There are two kinds of influence: mechanical and organic. An organic influence is something like the influence of the whole body on the limbs of the body. The mechanical is like a machine; the parts of the machine influence the structure of the machine. Likewise, you must consider how you are influencing the world. What is the relationship between you and the world? This subject comes to what you call epistemology, in philosophical circles. You are going into deep waters if you go on thinking like this.

You conclude finally that inasmuch as you cannot stand outside the world, *you are the world.* It will come to that. *If you are the world,* how will you handle the world? It must be handled in the manner in which you handle yourself. Now, I should not speak to you more. I should introduce you to some study, and you will see what a tremendous difference it makes in thinking. The study of the world would mean the study of yourself only. "Know thyself and be free," is the Oracle of Delphi.

Visitor: I am going there, after India.

SWAMIJI: I will see you tomorrow again. Hari Om.

Visitor: We ended with "Know thyself." And, the Western mind has an aversion, it seems, to "Know thyself."

SWAMIJI: It is because the Western mind does not know what the Self is. "Call a dog a bad name and then condemn it," is an old saying. If you want to criticise a person, find fault with that person first; then, criticise. A person who does not know what the Self is has no right to speak about it, so the Western mind cannot speak unless it defines what the Self is. They have a wrong notion about the Self Itself. What is the Self, according to Western thought? It is the purely physically bound psychological self. This is what they think; but this is a wrong definition. The Self is not sitting inside the body.

Visitor: The Self to the Western mind is also, oftentimes, just the cognition, the thinking process.

SWAMIJI: That shows the poverty of thinking. It is very unfortunate. This is not correct. The Self is not sitting inside the body. It is not in the cortex; It is not inside the brain. It is a consciousness, a principle of awareness. Now, why are you bringing this question to me? What relevance has it to your teaching of psychology?

Visitor: I am a teacher.

SWAMIJI: You need not bring the subject of Self to the students, because, perhaps, it is not a part of your curriculum.

Visitor: Oh yes, it is!

SWAMIJI: Why do you talk about the Self? Psychology does not require a Self. It is a study of mind and reason and emotion. It is a study of the psychic functions, and why do you worry about the Self? Let It be there, or let It not be there. What does It matter to us?

Visitor: Let It evolve, as It is?

SWAMIJI: Let the Self not be there at all. What does it matter? Why should there be a Self? Your mind and reason, emotions and psychic operations are there, and you are concerned with these. That is the human being, actually. What you call a human being is a conglomeration of psychological functions. And more than that, what do you find in a human being? What is there in a human being other than this body, and the psychological functions? So, here Western thought ends, and it does not want to say anything more than that, because anything more than that is not visible; it is not perceptible, it is not thinkable, and it is not necessary also for one's life.

What is of utility to life? There is a system of thinking called pragmatism, and utilitarianism. That which works well in life is real, and any other thing is irrelevant, and you can live a happy life without there being a Self. What is the good of thinking of the Self? There must be a point in it. How does the Self come into the picture at all, when you study psychology? There is no Self in psychology. There is only a mental operation. So, I am asking why you raised this question of Self, when It is not a part of your curriculum of studies?

Visitor: For the Western mind?

SWAMIJI: Yes.

Visitor: I am saying that It should be. It should be brought in.

SWAMIJI: Why should you? Suppose you do not bring It. In what way are you at a loss?

Visitor: What do you lose?

SWAMIJI: Yes. What do you lose? You can get along well even without It.

Visitor: Oh, you can get on well, supposedly.

SWAMIJI: Yes, yes. So, what is the problem? If you touch It, you will be in hot waters immediately.

Visitor: Yes. But for me as a teacher, doesn't It need to be touched?

SWAMIJI: You see, as a personal aspirant, an inquisitive seeker, or a lover of the Ultimate Reality, you may take It into consideration and try to find out what It is;

but as a teacher of psychology, It is not necessary. If you are inquisitive, curious, and aspire for higher realities than what are available in this world; if you are not satisfied with anything visible in the world; if you feel that there is something more than this world, that all things are finite and perishable, and therefore, something must be there which is not subject to the process of time; if you seek an endless reality; if that aspiration is there for you, then the question of the Self comes in. But, are you pursuing that line, or are you satisfied as a psychology teacher?

Visitor: No. I am not a psychology teacher, but I think in teaching in general that people should come to a level of awareness, and dismantle the aversion to knowing thyself.

SWAMIJI: You must have some training in this Ashram. You have to undergo a course of studies here. This is not a subject for market-place discussion.

Visitor: No, I understand that.

SWAMIJI: This is a serious matter. It cannot be easily understood, but once you know what It is, you will never want anything else in the world.

Visitor: True.

SWAMIJI: You will be simply thrilled to know what It is.

Visitor: True. So to have a sense of the Self, my question is, as a teacher, how to develop it in children, and in others,—in other teachers who teach teachers.

SWAMIJI: That is psychology. Again, you are coming to psychology. You can be a very good student and teacher of psychology without bringing in the Self. Actually, psychologists never talk of the Self. It does not exist, actually. It is a kind of illusion for psychologists. Like David Hume—have you heard of a philosopher called David Hume? And also Freud?

Visitor: Yes, I have.

SWAMIJI: They say that there is no such thing as the Self,—It does not exist.

Visitor: Well, I would not agree with them.

SWAMIJI: And, if you agree with them, what do you lose? If you lose something, then that is a different matter. Many stalwart thinkers of the West hold this view (except a few, of course), that Self is a dubious, conceptual, and hallucinatory existence. Freud and such other people will say that it is an illusion: religion is an illusion, and so God, Self, everybody are bundled up with this illusion, and we can be happy without them. You can be happy without God, also. Why do you want a God? You ask Freud. He will tell you everything about these matters. Do you know Freud's psychology? What does he say about the Self? It does not exist!

Visitor: Yes. He is vacant.

SWAMIJI: You ask Freud whether he is existing. Ask him! I can ask Freud himself, "Are you existing or not? Or, somebody else is existing?"

Luciano: Swamiji, you said that life can be happy in the psychological sense, but experience shows that lives are not all happy.

SWAMIJI: Everybody is happy; who is not happy? Let me see. Who is not happy among these people seated here? They are all well; they have got breakfast and lunch and good sleep. They have got money. What is wrong with you? Tell me. Let anybody say something is wrong. You have a good job, good salary, good health, and you have got medical attendance; you can travel anywhere. You can have whatever you want. What is wrong with life?

Luciano: Nothing.

SWAMIJI: What is wrong with life? Everything is

fine. This is what the gross Western mind says: All is well. But, all is not well!

American Visitor: True.

SWAMIJI: There is something at the back of it. You are dreaming that everything is well, and the Damocles Sword is hanging over your head, which is not anybody's concern; nobody bothers. Do you know of the Damocles Sword?

Visitor: Yes.

SWAMIJI: There is a Damocles Sword called death which can wipe out all values of life in one minute. All your glory, all your study, all your pomp and possession can be negatived in one second by somebody who is called Death. Where is Death sitting? I ask you a question, as a psychologist: Why should anybody die? What is the harm if nobody dies? Let all people be alive.

Visitor: There is a cycle.

SWAMIJI: Do you want people to die?

Visitor: They need to die. It's part of the natural cycle.

SWAMIJI: Now, do you believe in the existence of Nature?

Visitor: Oh, yes.

SWAMIJI: Are you subservient to Nature, or are you independent? You have no free choice? Are you a servant of Nature that you have to obey orders of Nature, and it will kill you, and you can be reborn, also? Are you a slave of Nature's laws, or have you some independence? Tell me. Who would like to be a slave of a law of somebody? Even in political circles, people seek independence. They do not like to be servants of the government. They want independence. Everybody strives for independence. How can you say that Nature is so very hard upon you that it would want to kill you one day?

What kind of Nature have you? And, who created that monstrous Nature? Who is that dangerous person who created such a Nature which swallows up everybody? You have to answer these questions, and you cannot simply bypass them. These are the seeds of the beginning of philosophical thinking—questioning and questioning and questioning until you get the answer to every question.

Visitor: Yes.

SWAMIJI: I cannot talk to you much. I told you that you have to stay here for a long time and undergo a course, as it were; meanwhile, you can only make some studies, and they will solve fifty percent of your problem. I can give you some literature to study.

Visitor: Good. I'll do that.

SWAMIJI: These questions that you are raising and I am talking about are questions of life as a whole. It is not your problem or my problem, it is entire creation's problem. You cannot thrash it out in a minute, you should have time and patience enough, and desire enough to know it.

Visitor: Yes, I understand that.

SWAMIJI: Otherwise, if everything is well, be happy.

Visitor: I cannot stay, but I will leave my heart here with you. Thank you.

31

THE SENSES: TWO KINDS OF SACRIFICE

SWAMIJI: Sharmaji, in the fourth chapter of the Bhagavad Gita, Bhagvan Sri Krishna says that there are varieties of sacrifices. There are some who practise sacrifice
by offering the objects in their senses. There are others
who do sacrifice by offering their senses in the objects.
So, there are two kinds of sacrifice. What does it mean?
They look opposite, like two contradictory things. In one
case, you offer the object in the senses; in the other case,
you offer the senses in the objects. So, what does it
mean?

*Sri Krishna Sharma: Is it not the same thing,
Swamiji?*

SWAMIJI: You offer the senses in the objects, and you
offer the objects in the senses. How can you say it is the
same? They are two different things. But what is the
meaning? Both are considered as sacrifices, though they
are opposites.

*Srotradini'ndriyany anye samyam'agnisu juhvati;
sabdadin visayan anya indriy'agnisu juhvati. Sar-
vani'ndriya-karmani pranakarmani ca'pare; atma-
samyama Yogagnau juhvati jnana-dipite.* This is the
sloka. Some people perform sacrifice in the form of re-
straint of sense organs from contact with objects. That is
the meaning. Some people offer their senses in the fire of
objects; they say, *"Om svaha,"* and they put *ghee* into the
fire. Like that, the senses are offered into the objects.
How do you do that? If you offer senses into the objects,

it becomes indulgence. It cannot be called sacrifice. Everybody offers senses to the objects; there is no need of saying anything here. But yet, it can be a sacrifice.

Sharmaji: Then, these are two opposite things.

SWAMIJI: It requires to be understood. The Gita is not an easy book to read, and you cannot imagine that you have understood it, also. It is a very deep secret, the secret of the operation of the Universe Itself. That is mentioned there. It is not meant for you, or me, or any particular person. It is an address of the Universal Being to the whole creation. It is God speaking to the universe. It is not Arjuna or Krishna; they are representatives of the Universe.

The objects of the senses are enemies if they are considered as different from ourselves. It is only under that condition that people run after the objects of sense. They will never run after the object of sense, unless it is outside,—totally outside. If it is not outside, you will not run after it. You will not run after your own nose, or your own ear, and all that; but you will run after the nose of somebody else, because it is outside you.

The relationship of the object to you is to be understood properly. What is your relationship to an object? Is it outside you, or not outside you? A person walking on the street, whom you see when you go for your evening walk, is totally outside you. You have no concern with him. But, you may go for a walk with your own brother. He is not totally outside you, though for ordinary vision, both are outside only. The brother who is walking with you on the road, and the pilgrim who is walking on the road,—what is the difference between the two persons? They are both outside, and yet your brother is not entirely outside you. Why?

Sharmaji: He is mentally connected with us, and the other person is not mentally connected.

SWAMIJI: Yes. This is the way you have to understand the objects of sense, also. You will run after them, you want to pursue them, because you don't pursue something that is with you, or which is within your capacity, within the ambit of your understanding. You don't go on thinking of your dear brother day and night, but you will think of somebody outside, who has a connection with you, positively or negatively. The objects of the world are neither good, nor bad. They are bad if you treat them as alien, foreign elements; then you want to grab them, or reject them, as the case may be. But if they are set in harmony with your senses, the senses will never go for them.

When two water tanks have water in the same level, the water will not flow, but if one is higher than the other, it will flow. So, if the senses and the objects are on a par, the senses will never go to the objects; but if they are either above you or below you, they will run to things. If they are kept on par, they are your friends, and contemplating them would be to contemplate yourself only, in a way.

This is what Sri Krishna means here. When you offer your senses to the objects, it means to say that a friend is meeting a friend. But, there is a difference in meeting your sister and meeting your wife. Both are women only; what is the difference between the two? Is there some difference, or no difference?

Sharmaji: There is a difference.

SWAMIJI: Why should there be a difference? Both are equally ladies, and there is absolutely no difference between them. Here is the whole point. All your problem is here, in this little analogy. Both are equally women of the same category. But, why is one a wife and another is a sister? Why is there such a distinction?

When you love an object, it becomes your wife;

when it is on a par with you, like your sister, it is a sacrifice, and it is meditation itself. When you think of your sister, you have no agitation in your mind. You think nothing, practically, as if you are seeing a tree or a mountain. But if you see your wife, there is a different way of looking, though both things are identical statistically.

Sharmaji: Yes, Swamiji.

SWAMIJI: You are unnecessarily creating a distinction between two things and get agitated in one, and be calm and quiet in another. The objects are neither yours, nor not yours; they are neither a wife, nor a sister, but you convert them into this or that because of your prejudice. So, in two half verses, the Lord mentions both things. The senses can go in this way, or they can go in another way, also. The world is not a bad object, nor is it meant for your enjoyment. It is just what it is.

In a family, the members of the family are all on a par,—you neither love them, nor hate them specially. But if it is a kind of property, a belonging, then it is different. When you say "my brother," or "my sister," or "my wife," you are uttering practically the same sentence grammatically, while you mean different things. Even the word "my" has two different meanings. What do you say?

Sharmaji: Yes, Swamiji.

SWAMIJI: "My sister" and "my wife"—the "my" has the same meaning grammatically, but the intention is different. Even your mind works in a different way with this "my." So when I see an object, you can say either it is "this" or "that." Just as all women are the same, all objects are the same, but you can convert them into your wife or sister, as you like, by the impulses of your mind.

This is such a complicated verse that nobody cares to understand its meaning truly. In commentaries, they sim-

ply pass it on, gloss it over, as if everything is clear. It
cannot be understood so easily.

Do you consider the object as your sister or your
wife? It depends upon your intention. Objects are not
your properties. Therefore, you cannot consider them as
your wife. A sister is not your property; she is an independent person like you, and the objects of the world also
are equally as important as you. They are not servants;
therefore, you cannot indulge in them.

All indulgence is a mistaken notion of the mind. The
world is not a binding rope created by God to hurl you to
hell, as people think,—it is Satan's creation, evil, and so
on. The world is not a thing. It is just like you. If the
world is a source of bondage, you are also a source of
bondage, because you are a part of the world. You cannot
say that you are perfectly all right, and that the world is
evil. In a most harmonious manner you must look at
things, and then any perception becomes like *samadhi*
only. Every perception is *samadhi* under a condition.
Whatever you see with your eyes, consider it as yourself
only. Then, you will never have any agitation afterwards.

Sharmaji: There is no binding also to that thing.

SWAMIJI: So much meaning is hidden in two half
verses of the Gita: Your self is your friend, and your self
is your enemy, as the case may be, according to the two
viewpoints. The bondage is in the viewpoint, and your
freedom also is in your viewpoint. Unnecessarily we create a mess by our ignorance and stupidity. That is all.

Sharmaji: By taking the things as our possessions.

SWAMIJI: So, I have given you a commentary on this
verse.

Sharmaji: We are fortunate, Swamiji.

SWAMIJI: But, still you must remember this. I have
mentioned a very subtle point. It will slip out of your
mind. It is not easy to catch it. People always say that the

world is a bondage; this is commonly said everywhere, but it is not so. It is a bondage because you are looking at it as an enemy, an outsider. Who asked you to look at it like that? God never created enemies, nor friends.

Sharmaji: Yes, that is true.

SWAMIJI: Has God no other work than creating enemies? You have converted things into alien forces and, then, you are looking at them as friends and enemies. The world is not an alien object. *It is on a par with you*, so it is neither your friend nor enemy. If you look at it thus, the world is a wonderful beauty. *Viratsvarupa* it is! I asked you what you are reading, and this idea came to me.

32

INTELLECTUAL UNDERSTANDING

Norma (Lebanon): We foreigners come here because we have been unable to solve the problem that we have set before ourselves, and we come for your help. Many times when I come here with a question in mind, I have found that by thinking about it enough, I come either to some form of an answer, or I feel from reading your book <u>Problems of Spiritual Life,</u> *that in any event you will give me an answer that "you will only be able to know if you do this," and that I am sort of putting the cart before the horse. In life we apply ourselves to a dramatic problem, and eventually see the problem as a whole, and solve it by having seen it as a whole; but day after day, maybe year after year, I try to change my way of thinking, and it doesn't work. Maybe for ten minutes at a time I can see that "a thing is a thing because I call it a thing," and by calling it "a thing" I posit "I." I can understand this, but the understanding of it does not alter my condition.*

SWAMIJI: You are not supposed merely to understand it. You have to apply that understanding in your practical life.

Norma: I apply that understanding, but it is as if I cannot be aware all the time, for some reason. So, what I am asking is, why?

SWAMIJI: That understanding has to become part of your living itself. That is the essence of living spiritual life. Understanding is not sufficient.

Norma: Yes, I know.

SWAMIJI: The understanding is only an information given to you so that you may apply it in your personal life. This virtually means meditation. You deeply sink into your heart the content of your understanding, and *become it*, practically, and change your personality into the character of that thing which you have understood. The object of your understanding has entered you to such an extent that *you have yourself become that. Knowledge has become being.* Your knowledge, your understanding, has become yourself. Do you understand?

Norma: I understand, but then I go out and I live; I interact, let's say. For some time, I maintain some sense of this, and then everything goes screwy on me. I become "I" and again think "this person wants that from me." Even if I can control this to some degree, and not become scatter-brained at the first moment...

SWAMIJI: You can hold it only to some degree, in the earlier stages. You are just beginning it and, therefore, you may be able to retain such a consciousness for some minutes, or say for an hour, if you are able to sit quietly and meditate; but it is not possible to keep it in mind for all times, throughout the day.

Norma: And, are you able to, then?

SWAMIJI: Well, we are trying to do that. We are existing only for that purpose; otherwise, what is the good of living?

Norma: Yes, but most of us don't do that. And even when you read the religious texts, they say if you want to get there, you are going to be one in a million. They don't get there.

SWAMIJI: Day in and day out, you have to brood over this matter. You have no other work in this world, except this. You are saying that you have a lot of work to do, and your mind goes here and there.

Norma: No, I am saying that though I know, I can

*see that this is counterproductive to me, it seems that it is
sometimes impossible for my mind to change.*

SWAMIJI: That is because you have not been able to
make your understanding a part of your life. You are
living in one way, and your understanding is somewhere
else, in a book, or in the intellect. You are not an intellect,
you are a soul; so, what you call understanding is the appreciation of truth by the intellect. This appreciation has
to enter your soul. This is what I mean by saying that
knowledge is being. It requires great practice for a
protracted period, and whatever you have understood in
this respect is not inadequate; it is sufficient.

You know something, and it is good enough. The
only thing is that you must have a little time to sit alone
by yourself. You may be a busy person; that is all right,
but even then, at least in the earlier stages, you must find
an hour or two, or even less than that, as much as possible, to sit quietly and identify your consciousness with
what you say is your understanding. Later on, if God
wills, you may be able to think it throughout the day, and
your distractions of life will not then upset you.

They are really not distractions. They are only different things which you are not able to harmonise into an
integrated whole. The things of the world are not distractions. They look like that because you are unable to
place them properly in their proper context.

God has not created distractions. He has created a
universe which is complete in itself. And so, you have to
see the whole world as God Himself would see it, as a total whole, in which all distractive elements find a proper
place. And in their own place, they are perfectly all right.
If you take them out of context, they look irregular and
undesirable, and all that. Put everything in its own context and everything is all right. The whole world is perfect, and you are also perfect, because you are a part of

that. This kind of meditation is what I have suggested in my little book <u>Problems of Spiritual Life</u>. Think over that. When you go to Lebanon afterwards, you can write to us, if you have any questions.

God's creation is full of contradictions. Nothing is like something else. One leaf in the tree is not like another leaf in the same tree. One person is not like another person. Everything is different. There is so much contradiction; yet, it is a perfect blend of harmony and beauty of creation. This is symbolised in the contradictions of the family of Lord Shiva, and the perfect harmony also that He maintains. The worst poison of the snake is the nectar on His body. Nothing will harm Him. So, God is all perfection, and in Him every contradiction that you see in life is harmonised beautifully.

In our own body, there are pleasant things and unpleasant things also; yet, they are all harmonised in our personality. You have got lungs, heart, stomach, entrails, blood, bone, flesh, marrow. They are all unpleasant things to see, but they are encased in a bag of skin so that the person looks nice. Suppose the skin is removed; how beautiful will that person look? You would run away from that person as if a ghost is coming. Such a contradiction and horror! An unpleasant admixture of things in our own body is made to look beautiful with a skin covering, and we are looking wonderful. So, even in our own body there is this contradiction harmonised. We are also like a little cosmos, a symbol of God. They say the human being is a mirror of God, symbolising the Almighty. Whatever God has, you also have.

33

THE TENTH OBSTACLE

Swamiji addressed Bhavagrahi: How will you manage to control the natural impulses and live in the world? You have to steer the course in the middle, like fire-walking. People walk on fire, without getting burnt. The world is like that, like a fireplace, and you have to live in it without getting burnt. You must live like a water drop on a lotus. The water drop is always on the lotus leaf, but it won't stick; it is like an oily thing, not getting stuck. Like that, you have to live in this world without sticking.

How is it possible? The mind has to stick to something. You think some object, and it will stick there. If you allow the mind to stick to some better thing, it will not stick to some worse thing. Swami Sivanandaji Maharaj used to say, "attach, detach, attach, detach": detach from this world, and attach to God. If you want to withdraw from one thing, you have to connect yourself with something else. Suppose you want to move away from the West; you have to move towards the East. If you move towards the East, you are automatically away from the West. So, if you move towards the Universal, you are away from the particular, automatically. If you move towards God, then you are away from the world of appearance.

But finally, you will have the greatest of doubts: Even if I see God, what is He going to give me? What has He given to anybody? In addition to Patanjali's nine obstacles, you will have the greatest of doubts as a tenth obstacle: Even if I see Him, what is He going to give? This doubt will be harassing the mind. "Even if I go there, how long will I be sitting with Him?" "He may push me back, and again I will be in the world. Already He has pushed me once, so what is the guarantee that He will not push me a second time? If once He has done it, a second time He can do it also."

This is a very serious matter. "So much suffering and hardship I have undergone to see God; I go there, and He will push me back." Suppose He does that. What will happen? You will run to all the *gurus*. All the meditation is stopped, because the highest doubt has come,—doubt in God Himself, that He will create trouble when you go there. This doubt may occur to the greatest of learned people. It is a heart-rending question.

Then a second problem comes. Someone says that this question is foolishness, because you will not be there to raise any question. If I will not be there, then why should I go there? What is the purpose of doing anything? I will not get anything because I myself will not be there! So why should I suffer, unnecessarily doing things for a purpose which has no meaning?

Who is there if I am not there? God alone is there. Let Him be alone there, but what is my fate? Your fate is that you will not be there. Or, if you are there, then you will be sitting and looking at God for the whole day. Either way you are caught. Now the brain will start agitating, pendulum-like.

The greatest *tapas* is the ability to understand this point. Starving and sitting in cold water and sleeplessness are not *tapas*. The ability to understand this problem is the *tapas*. Some great problem has come to the mind; if you are able to understand what it actually means, and why this problem has arisen, there cannot be a greater *tapas* than that solution.

How has this problem arisen? If I am there or not, both ways I am in trouble. If I am abolished completely, it looks very horrible; and if I am there, what shall I do there after going? If you can answer this question to yourself, you have done the greatest *sadhana,* and nothing further is necessary. Let anybody answer this question: What will happen to you? The heart will jump in fear. This is a question as to what God-realisation means. The question is final. Let each person answer this question for oneself.

34

FOUR KINDS OF CONFLICT

SWAMIJI: There are four kinds of conflict; every conflict is included in one these four. First of all is the conflict within one's own self, which is sometimes known as
non-alignment of the inner components of personality:
the reason, the feeling, and the will do not agree with
each other. It is called inner non-alignment, causing inner
distress. It is a psychological malady, due to which everybody remains in a state of anxiety, restlessness, and fear
from unknown sources.

This internal conflict which keeps one inwardly sick
creates social conflict, which is the second one. You cannot get on with your own self (that is internal conflict)
and so you cannot get along with others also. You don't
like anybody, as if there is some trouble with everybody.
This is social conflict.

Now the third thing is that you are not reconcilable
with the law of Nature operating, with the universe of
five elements (earth, water, fire, air, and space-time gravitation). They operate on some laws, and you are not in
harmony with them. So, you get a kick from your own
self, from society, and now the universe also has started
giving a kick. Lastly, you are not reconcilable with the
Creator, God Himself. Whatever law operates in the
realm of God is not reconcilable with your present condition. So, there is psychological conflict, social conflict,
cosmological conflict, and finally conflict with the Absolute,—everything in the world is included within these

four problems. Even if there are millions of conflicts, they can all be boiled down to these four.

The Bhagavad Gita, for instance, tries to solve all these four conflicts. If you read the Gita from beginning to end, chapter-wise and verse-wise,—all the eighteen chapters,—you will not know which one is touching which subject. In many places, several things are touched upon. Anyway, if you classify and analyse the verses and arrange them in a logical way, you will find that the Gita has a solution for all these four conflicts. And, if it is studied properly, with earnestness, deep concentration and dispassion, it will point out to you the way ahead.

The nature of the end that we wish to achieve will determine the means that we employ. To whatever extent our end is clear to our mind, to that extent the means we employ also is successful. People have different ideas of the purpose, which will decide the nature of the practice and the amount of success. When you know which place you want to reach, you also know the road to reach that place.

According to the Bhagavad Gita, there are four kinds of people who seek help. There is one kind which seeks material help; there is another kind which seeks knowledge. There is a third kind which comes because of suffering in society, and a fourth kind which seeks only God. These are the four kinds of seeking, according to the Bhagavad Gita. So, seek only God. That includes all other seeking.

35

ACTIVITY AFTER ENLIGHTENMENT

Visitor: There are some teachers who seem to be enlightened but still are involved in the world.

SWAMIJI: Either they are not really involved and you have a wrong notion about them, or they are not enlightened. One of the two it is. Either you are making a wrong judgement about them and they may be really enlightened, or they are not enlightened. There are only two aspects of it.

Visitor: Can an enlightened person do something bad?

SWAMIJI: Our outlook of life has to be properly oriented. What do you mean by good, and what do you mean by bad? That has to be clear to the mind first, before you make any judgement. Your ideas of good and bad may be conditioned by certain factors which are delimited. You may not have a cosmic view of things. So, whatever judgement you make may not be complete. It may be partial. That is one aspect of the matter.

Visitor: Can a person lose his enlightenment? Can they fall?

SWAMIJI: A person who is really enlightened cannot fall. It is like saying a person who has woken up will sleep again. If you have already woken up from sleep, will you sleep again? It is not possible, because you have already woken up. If you again go to sleep, it means that you have not fully woken up. You are still half sleeping. You have to define what you mean by "enlightenment."

It is like waking up from sleep. You are asking whether a man who has woken up can sleep again. Why will he sleep? He has already woken up. Otherwise, he has not fully woken up; he is half dozing.

Visitor: What is morality?

SWAMIJI: You have to become a disciple of a *guru* and learn. Even a clever man cannot understand it. We have got political definitions, social definitions. Anything that is good for your country is moral—is it correct? It is one definition, but it is not the whole truth.

Anything that is good for your family is good, moral. But, still it is not the whole truth. Anything that is good for your little family may not be good for the whole nation. So, your morality is delimited here. Anything that is good for your little country may not be good for the whole world; there, also, your morality is delimiting. So, what do you mean by "morality"? You have to judge it from the context.

It is like medicine. What do you mean by "medicine"? You cannot name the medicine for any particular illness, unless you know what kind of illness it is. If you say that you want medicine, they will ask what kind of illness. Then only, a medicine will be prescribed. So, your idea of morality depends upon the circumstances of your existence physically, intellectually, socially, psychologically, and politically. So, there is no off-hand answer to a question like that. Cut-and-dried answers we cannot give to such questions. Everything is conditional and relative.

Suppose somebody says, "Is it good to cut off the hand of a person?" You say that it is very bad, but suppose you are a surgeon and you are amputating a person's hand. Is it good? So, is cutting off the hand good or bad? There again, the question is relative. So, all questions bring a relative answer; under conditions, circumstances, and exigencies you will know what is proper.

Finally, that only can be called good which will directly or indirectly help you in reaching God. That only can be called good. It may be not directly useful, but indirectly, at least. You have to judge yourself: is it going to help you in any way, indirectly, at least, in reaching the Absolute? Then it is perfectly right—nothing wrong with it.

It is said that a person who is starving and about to die can even steal food, though you cannot say that stealing is good. Suppose there is a mentally demented person who is brandishing a sword in his hand, and you silently go behind him and steal that sword from his hand. Have you done a good thing, or a wrong thing? So, stealing is not always bad. You cannot answer any question in an absolute fashion. They are relative and conditional.

Drinking brandy is very bad, but suppose a person has fallen from a tree and become unconscious. You can pour a spoon of brandy into his mouth, and he will wake up. Is drinking brandy good or bad? Here, also, it is conditional. Every question has to be put carefully, and the answer also has to be given accordingly.

Visitor: Swamiji, would you say that anything was immoral if it had a harmful effect on other people?

SWAMIJI: It has nothing to do with "other" people. It is people in general, because you are also "other people" to certain others. For people who are other than you, you are an "other people." So, what do you mean by "other people?" There are no "other people" in the world. Everyone is equal to others. To me, you are an "other," and to you, I am an "other." When you say "other people," who are the other people? Everybody is "other people" only. What do you say?

You have to use the word carefully. You mean everybody. By "other people" you include yourself, also. You are also other people. So anything good for everybody is good. Don't say "other people." Anything that is good for everybody is fine, and you have to judge for yourself what is good for everybody. Be careful.

The best thing is not to judge quickly. There is a wise saying, "Judge not, lest ye be judged." You will be judged in the same manner as you judge others. The world is made in that way. Whatever you think of other people, that others will think about you, and whatever you do to others will be done to you. So, "do unto others as you would be done by." This is the ethics of the highest type. If you want to know what morality is, you can say it in this one sentence: "Do unto others as you would be done by." That is all.

Visitor: Rituals?

SWAMIJI: Images, idols, pictures, portraits, whatever it is, are as good as anything else. As every part is organically connected to the whole, you can contact the whole through any part. The worship of God through ritual is equivalent to trying to contact Him by means of visible manifestations. This is one stage of religion, or spirituality. But if your mind is vast enough to comprehend the total whole in one grasp, there is no need of touching parts. You can touch the total at one stroke. Otherwise, it is better to go slowly, stage by stage. So here is the relevance of ritual for enlightenment.

Visitor: What about after enlightenment?

SWAMIJI: After enlightenment means after reaching God. This is what you mean?

Visitor: Right. After realising the Self.

SWAMIJI: No, no. Go slowly. Are you realising God or the Self? What are you going to realise?

Visitor: God,—the Self with a big "S."

SWAMIJI: Now, you see, after realising God, what happens?

Visitor: What is the relationship of practices after realising God?

SWAMIJI: When you realise God, what happens to you, actually? What will be your status in the condition of the realisation of God? What will happen to you, actually? Do you have an idea about it?

Visitor: It is not that you reach anything.

SWAMIJI: When you reach God, what will happen to you?

Visitor: Then there is no other. Everything is emptiness, or fullness.

SWAMIJI: There is no other.

Visitor: Right.

SWAMIJI: And, you will see only yourself. If you are seeing only yourself, no question will arise afterwards. Who will put the question? To whom? You are putting a question because you are seeing another. And you have already said that there is no "another." So, who will put the question? The question ceases. You will be doing there the same thing which God is doing. And, what is God doing just now? That you will be doing, whatever it be. Inasmuch as you have still maintained a little psychological distance between yourself and God, you are raising this question. If you have actually merged in God, you will not raise a question like that. Already you have asserted that there is no other. What will happen to you, and what will you do after realising God? You will do exactly the same thing as God is doing. Tell me what God is doing.

Visitor: Everything.

SWAMIJI: Then you will be doing the same thing.

Visitor: Another analogy can be: what happens to the river when it merges in the ocean?

SWAMIJI: The river cannot understand it, unless it actually enters the ocean. You are talking about a condition which you have not yet reached. That is why these questions are rising. Unless you have reached that state, it is like a sleeping man asking, "What will I do when I wake up?" When you wake up, you know what to do. Why are you putting a question? It is because you have not woken up that you are putting a question. You have woken up, and you know what is your duty; it is clear to your mind. When you reach the Absolute Being, you will behave in the same way as the Absolute Being behaves. It is up to you to decide what It does. You will be doing the same thing, because you are inseparable from That.

As the Swami said, "What does the river do when it enters the ocean?" It will do what the ocean is doing. It will not behave like a river at that time. It will behave like the ocean only. And, there will be no river in the ocean. The Ganga, the Yamuna, the Mississippi, the Volga, the Amazon—there will be no such thing in the ocean. You will see only ocean. You will not find the Amazon, the Mississippi, etc., in the ocean; yet, they are there. Likewise, you will all be there, yet you will not see anything there. It will all be ocean. This is what will happen to you, and you will do what the ocean is doing.

It is a great joy, isn't it? It purifies the mind, satisfies the soul. You feel healthy and vigorous, even by hearing it. What do you say? That is why *satsanga* is necessary. It makes you healthy, even the thought of it.

Visitor: In my experience before I was with my teacher now, I was involved in doing certain rituals and that kind of thing with another teacher. After I met my teacher and experienced enlightenment from him, all de-

sire to do any of those kind of things just completely van-
ished. It was like there was no need anymore.

SWAMIJI: There is no need anymore, when you have
reached the Universal Absolute. There is no need, because there is nobody to do anything at that time.

Visitor: Right.

SWAMIJI: So, the question does not arise. You need
not do anything, because, who is there to do anything?
Doing is a manipulation of the individual in terms of external relations, and external relations cease there. So, the
question of doing does not arise. Everything vanishes
into the Total Universality. Unless there is an external,
there will be no doing, also.

Visitor: That is why it made me wonder why anyone
after enlightenment would do any kind of rituals.

SWAMIJI: Anyone with enlightenment will do anything,—what are you asking?

Visitor: Why is it that after enlightenment someone
would do rituals, etc?

SWAMIJI: It all depends upon what you mean by enlightenment. If enlightenment means unity with the Absolute, there will be no question of doing anything
afterwards. The question itself is redundant. But, if your
idea of enlightenment is something else, then you have to
define, first of all, what you mean by enlightenment. If in
enlightenment you maintain individuality as Mr. so-and-
so, then, in spite of enlightenment, you will be propelled
to do actions by the very law of your biological existence. You will feel hungry, you will feel thirsty, you will
like to sleep, you will like to travel, you will like to
speak. These are all rituals only. But, you will do that
only as long as you are existing in the body, and are conscious of the body.

But, if enlightenment means merging in the Universal Being, the question is not there. There is no question.

You do not exist there at all. So, there is no doing; what will you do at that time? It is as "being" only, not "doing." God is *Pure Being*, not "doing." In Sanskrit we call this state *sat-chit-ananda*,—existence-consciousness-bliss. That is the nature of God—pure existence, pure consciousness, and pure bliss. This is God in essence.

Visitor: After one realises unity with the Absolute, can there be any thing that is of not living in accord with that profound realisation, according to the depth of one's surrender to It?

SWAMIJI: Once you have become united with It, you do not exist anywhere else as this person. Your questions have no meaning then. You do not exist at all. You become one with the sea of universal force, so you will not put a question like that afterwards. The question arises on account of the persistence of individuality even after enlightenment. But, enlightenment means merging in the Universal. The personality ceases to be there; then, you need not have to raise this question at all. The person himself is not there. Then, what question arises? So, you do not maintain a duality after attainment of That. You should not think that still you are outside It.

Only if you are outside It, the question arises. In the path or the process of realising It, there may be difficulties of this kind. But once you have actually touched It, there is no problem. On the way, there are problems, and many varieties of problems. You will have hundreds of difficulties. Many of them, you cannot even imagine; such problems will arise.

You have to read the lives of saints who passed through all these stages, about the problems they had to face. Like Buddha, for instance—you must have studied or read about the life of Buddha. I am giving one example among many others. He tried many ways of enlightenment. First he went to a *guru* who taught him physical exercises,—*asanas, pranayamas,* and all that. He went on doing it and nothing happened. No enlightenment came. Then, he started fasting: "Let me not eat. I will sit here until my bone melts, and I will not get up from this place." There was no eating, and his body started withering, as if it was collapsing and finishing. He could not crawl, also. Even that strength he did not have. He felt at that time that it was all a waste, a worthless pursuit,— nothing comes: "This is the last day for me." At that time, some lady on the way brought him some porridge, some gruel, and gave it to him to eat. He had some friends who saw him eating this, and they thought this man has fallen. "Oh, you have eaten! You are no good. We will leave you and go away."

He said, "All right, you can go away." Actually, they did not understand, nor did Buddha understand at that time, whether fasting is good, or eating is good. Anyway, he took it and a little strength came, but he was dejected very much. "What is the matter? Nothing comes,—no enlightenment. I am in the same condition as I was." He went on sitting.

Suddenly, he saw in his presence his own wife, whom he had left. The wife was with a little child on the lap: "My Lord, you have left me and come. Are you so cruel?"

He said, "How this lady has come here?" He was in the forest, far off under a tree, and the palace of this lady was somewhere else. "Oh, it is an illusion!" he started telling himself, "My desires are manifesting themselves in the form of this individual. Get away from here!" he said.

It was cruel, you could see, because she was sitting there. She was weeping, "Oh, my Lord, you have left me."

He said, "No, no, no. Get away! You are an illusion.

You are trying to tempt me. Get away!" Anyway, that vision vanished afterwards. Again he sat.

Edwin Arnold has written a poem called "Light of Asia." I do not know if you have read that book. "Light of Asia" is a poetic biography of Buddha written by a learned scholar. He describes in one chapter what psychological tortures Buddha had to undergo. Angels descended from heaven with temptations of thousands of kinds—with dance and music and nectar. They said, "Everything is here. Come on. You have attained enlightenment, Master! Now, stop your meditation. Here is the river of nectar; there is the pool of honey; here are the maidens for your servants; here are the palaces; you are the king of these gods. Come on!"

"Get away from here!" Buddha said, "You are trying to tempt me with all these dances and all that. No! I do not want it." After he persisted in rejecting them, these visions vanished.

Then, another more ferocious vision started: "What do you think you are? We will pound you to dust just now. We will belabour you! Get up from this place! You are an idiot!" Demons started coming and talking to him.

He said, "What is the matter? First some other vision, now another thing is coming. Do not talk to me! You can pound me to dust or belabour me. I do not want to talk to you," he said. He kept quiet and went on with the meditation. Then, that vision vanished.

Then, there was vast wind, tornado, cyclone, with mud and a hailstorm—everything on his head. It was not actually a physical hailstorm. A psychological world manifested itself before the dross of the mind was thrown out. When you sweep the floor, all the dust goes up and blinds your eyes; yet, it is a cleaning process. Even then, he was thinking to himself, "Nothing has happened to me. I am not having any enlightenment or anything." On that day, when he was in this very difficult situation and in a state of despondency, in the middle of the night, light opened; he had enlightenment.

I am just mentioning to you the difficulties that spiritual seekers have to pass through. It is not easy going, a bread-and-jam path. It is a very hard job, difficult to control the mind. The mind cannot be controlled; it cannot be concentrated on anything continuously. It will jump here and there, in twenty places. When you are wanting to think something, another thing will come. This is the difficulty in Yoga practice. Even God you cannot think then. When you think of God, the idea of the market place, or travel, or a railway train, or something, will come and obstruct you.

Months and years of practice, and tenacious, adamantine persistence in concentrating the mind on one thing is necessary—and a perfect faith that after getting it, "I shall get everything." Therefore, tell the mind: "Oh foolish mind! Why do you go here and there? When you get that, everything will come to you, so what is the good of running here and there for little tinsels?" You tell the mind.

The mind feels that it is losing everything when it goes to God. All the friends, relations, money, wealth, and good things vanish. It may feel like that; it is not concentrating. You tell it, "No, it is not like that. This is a shadow that you are seeing. The realities are somewhere else. If the shadows are attracting you so much, what about the realities? And, not only that, these shadows also are included there in that thing which is your goal in meditation, so you are going to lose nothing. You are going to get everything."

Tell the mind. That is one way of controlling the mind. Like a little child, you tell the mind, "Don't cry, don't cry!" Otherwise, it won't listen. Even children don't listen. They are very naughty. So, these are some of the interesting things on the spiritual path. It is very hazardous and takes much time; yet, it is worth pursuing, and it is the only thing worth pursuing, finally. What do you say?

Visitor: You said earlier that after enlightenment, external relations do not exist? Is that right? Could you explain more about that?

SWAMIJI: What explanation? I have told you. It is very clear. I think the sentence is very clear. What difficulty have you got in understanding it?

Visitor: I am wondering about how people live together after enlightenment.

36

ON PATANJALI'S YOGA

Visitor: About Patanjali?

SWAMIJI: There is a system of Yoga called the Yoga of Patanjali. I do not know if you have heard of it. Have you heard of such a thing?

Visitor: I have heard a little bit about Patanjali, yes.

SWAMIJI: He describes eight stages of Yoga. They are called in Sanskrit *yama, niyama, asana, pranayama, pratyahara, dharana, dhyana,* and *samadhi. Samadhi* is the last stage, and *yama* is the first. You are asking me what is the first. That is what you are asking?

Visitor: Yes.

SWAMIJI: *Yama* consists of five principles—the initial steps that you may take. Never hurt or injure any living being in any manner whatsoever, by your thought or by your word or by your deed. You may call it *ahimsa.* Neither by thought, nor by word, nor by deed should you hurt another living being, not merely human beings, but any living beings.

Secondly, never deceive anybody by untruth of any kind. Never appropriate any belonging or property which does not rightfully belong to you. Then comes another thing: do not keep with you anything which is really not essential for your existence; that is, do not be luxurious. Do not have five motor cars, ten wrist watches, and ten-story buildings. You do not require all this for your existence. Else, it is a kind of exploitation. You are exploiting people by living such a kind of over-luxurious life. Do not grab what belongs to others.

Then, there is self-restraint, the control of the sense organs. The eyes want to indulge, the tongue wants to indulge, the ears want to indulge. Every organ of sense wants to indulge. These sense organs should be restrained as much as possible by daily effort on your part. These things that I have mentioned are considered as the first steps in Yoga. We do not talk of meditation and all that in the beginning. A little bit of self-restraint is necessary, along these lines mentioned. They are called *yamas,* the processes of self-sublimation.

You asked me how to begin. This is how you have to begin. I am not telling you much more than that. Then, other things start,—more difficult things.

First of all, be a good person. Before you become a godly person, you must be a good person,—a really good person. And that is your first step.

Visitor: You said, "Don't hurt anybody by thought." Could you explain this?

SWAMIJI: You mentally curse somebody: "Let this person die; this idiot should not exist. He is the very devil incarnate." Like that if you think, you are hurting by thought. And, it can work also. Though it is only a thought, it will have an impact upon that person whom you are cursing in this manner. You are not supposed to do that,—at least, as a Yoga student.

Visitor: Is it not possible just to not believe the thought that goes through your head,—just to laugh at it,—to not believe the thought? If you think a bad thought about someone else, a thought enters your head,—is it just that the thought is there, or can you just not believe it?

SWAMIJI: No, you should not entertain such a thought. The question of leaving comes once it has entered. Then only the question of leaving arises. Let it not enter at all.

Visitor: It means that one cannot control one's mind, and a thought might pass that occurs in it.

SWAMIJI: I understand. If the thought passes like that, you must tell yourself, "These thoughts should not arise in my mind. I shall not think like that in the future." The next day you think: "I made a mistake in thinking like this; it should not be like that. I am sorry. I shall not think it in the future." And you tell your mind not to think like that; then, it will not think. Past is past; let it go, but in the future, at least, you will not do it. You have made a mistake; OK, all right, you repent for it. But at least take a resolve that in the future you will not do it.

Visitor: So, even if you have a bad thought about somebody, and even if you do not believe in what you are thinking, it still could create karma.

SWAMIJI: If you think something, it creates *karma*. Any thought creates *karma*. Unless your thought is organised in a universal manner, unless your thought is in harmony with the Universal Existence, thought will produce *karma*. *Karma* is nothing but the reaction produced by action. Thought also is an action, so every thought may produce a reaction; but reaction, or *karma*, will not be produced if your thought is in harmony with the universal structure of things; but if you think like an ordinary individual, then a reaction will be produced.

Visitor: Swamiji, I want to ask you about what you said about the beginning of the path. From our experience, this behaviour that you described is a natural result of the realisation of the Absolute, but without the realisation, it is impossible to think this way.

SWAMIJI: Even now, when you are not realised, you will be able to appreciate that this is good behaviour. Don't you believe it? Do you want to become a good man only after reaching God, and before that, you will be bad? Is it possible? You have to try to be good even now itself. You must put forth some effort. You may not be perfect, but at least some achievement is as good as a great success. Even one step that you take in the direction of God is an achievement, though it is only one step.

In the spiritual path, there is no loss of effort. Every single effort that you put forth in that direction, even if it is minimal, will be a credit balance in your spiritual bank account. Even one penny, if you put it in the bank, it is a credit for you, though it is only a penny. And many pennies will make pounds. So, go slowly, little by little. Many drops make the ocean; effort is necessary.

Visitor: In your own experience, to realise God, is it necessary to follow all the stages that Patanjali is speaking about?

SWAMIJI: What are you following, then? You must be following something. What are the things that you are following?

Visitor: Well, when I met my teacher, I just stopped doing all the practices that I was doing, like doing Yoga and meditation, and I just felt that I didn't need them anymore.

SWAMIJI: What do you need, then?

Visitor: Nothing.

SWAMIJI: Then, you do not need a *guru*, also, if that is the case. What do you say? Be careful in your thoughts when you make decisions. You should not come to hurried conclusions. You cannot say that you need nothing. You certainly need many things.

Visitor: Right, of course, I needed my guru. That is for sure.

SWAMIJI: Not only that,—you have got many other needs in the world. There are varieties of requirements for the very existence of the body. How can you say that you have no needs? You have to protect yourself by various measures. They are the needs of the person. You want clothing, food to eat, a house in which to stay; are they not needs?

Visitor: Yes.

SWAMIJI: So, why do you say that you have no needs?

Visitor: No, I was referring to the practices. I was just wondering if...

SWAMIJI: When you have got such gross physical needs also, why are you so very uncharitable to the higher needs?

Visitor: I am sorry,—I didn't understand...

SWAMIJI: Finally, what are you telling me?

Visitor: I was just asking you if in your own experience to realise God you went through all these stages that Patanjali was talking about.

SWAMIJI: You need not follow Patanjali necessarily. These technological terminologies are not necessary, but these principles you have to follow. Patanjali says, "be a good person." Now, when you do not follow Patanjali, does it mean that you can be a bad person?

Visitor: No.

SWAMIJI: "I am not following Patanjali, so I will be bad." It does not mean that. The principles are applicable to everybody—Patanjali or anybody else. The stages are applicable to all people. Who would not like to be a good person? Who would not like to have self-control? Who would not like to be unselfish? These are principles for everybody, so you cannot be without them. They are the preliminary stages.

Visitor: Sure. I was referring more to the practice of Yoga, pranayama, pratyahara...

SWAMIJI: You see, for you personally, Yoga physical exercises and *pranayama* may not be necessary. But for somebody else, it may be of some utility. So, how can you universalise any principle? You may be in one stage where they are not necessary. I agree. But for some others who are in another stage, it may be an essential. So, let it be.

Visitor: Thank you.

SWAMIJI: I am glad to see all of you are very good aspiring souls. This is what I find, because your questions are all very intelligent and practical. You have not put any nonsensical questions. That means you are on the right path. Very good. I am glad to see you.

37

SATSANGA

Janie: It seems, from the way I understood it, that you were speaking about, ideally,—that it was an ideal situation to be able to be happy, and be on your own.

SWAMIJI: I don't remember what I said. Can you repeat it?

Janie: I don't remember your words exactly, but it was something to do with being on your own.

SWAMIJI: You mean to be alone, to be alone to yourself. Yes. What I said was, the more you feel happy when you are alone to yourself, the nearer you may be considered to be to your Self. The nearer you are to your Self, the more you will feel the need to be alone to yourself, because the Self has no friends. It has no contact with anything external. It is Universal Existence. It is present inside you, and so the more you move toward the universality that is inside you, the more you feel the need, and the more you feel happy to be alone. This is what I said. And what is your question now?

Janie: Well my question is, in the experience that we are having with our teacher is the growth of a sangha...

SWAMIJI: *Sangha? Sangha* means a group.

Janie: A group, but of people who are sharing the same experience of the Self, and who are standing alone with the Self, but out of that there is a celebration and a joy in being together. And it is not in the way of being social friends, it is being together in the Self.

SWAMIJI: This is one stage of consciousness. There are degrees of the ascent of consciousness. You don't jump into something at once. Gradually, you move from the lesser, or the more external, to the higher, and the more internal. From the external, you move to the internal; from the internal, you move to the Universal. These are the three stages of spiritual ascent.

In the beginning, the consciousness is involved in externals. Now, when I am speaking to you, or when you are speaking to me, it is moving in an externalised atmosphere, but it is also aware that it is so moving. So there are two types of movement. Consciousness moving in an externalised atmosphere, not knowing that it is actually moving in that manner, is binding activity of the ordinary people in the world. They are externally impelled towards satisfaction of sense organs, by means of contact with objects outside. That is one way of the movement of consciousness.

The other way is the way in which it moves just now, for instance. You are not involved in me, and I am not involved in you. Yet, the consciousness moves in an externalised fashion in the sense that I am aware that you are sitting outside me, and you are aware that I am sitting here outside you. This is the second stage. The first stage is movement without knowing that there is a movement. It is the life of desire, passion, anger, conflict, etc., the ordinary life of the world. The first one is social life with involvement and bondage; the second one is involvement in society without attachment and without bondage. That latter is what is called *satsanga,* spiritual group, common meditation, etc., as you are mentioning, but this is not the highest stage. This is a better stage than the involved stage. The consciousness of Universality is the final aim, and you are aware of that.

When you are conscious of the Universal, what do

you see around you? Can you imagine that condition? You will feel in the third stage,—I am mentioning to you the different stages,—in the third stage you will feel that all the people around you, all the things around you like hills and dales, and forests, and mountains, and rivers, and what not, are the limbs of your Universal Body. Do you see them, as you are seeing your own fingers and hands? You see objects,—you see, this is an object. When I can see it, it is an object, but, yet it is not an object, it is part of my organism itself.

So, consciousness of an object as totally different is the first stage. Consciousness of an object as a part and parcel of a congregation spiritually is the second. Consciousness of an object as organically connected with one's own cosmic existence is the third. In the higher stage, the limbs also will not be there, because the consciousness of the limb arises on account of space and time being between the two. If space and time are not there, you will not see the hand, also. You are projecting a limb, and being conscious of it, on account of space-time delusion, and that which you call God or Universal is beyond space and time. We have been mentioning something about it in the morning. It is timeless being, as I said to one of your friends. "What happens afterwards?" he asked, and I said, "There is no 'after' or 'afterwards'." There is no "after" because the question of "after" arises because you introduce time there. There, you will find no *satsanga*. God has no *satsanga*,—just *Being as such*.

So what you are mentioning is one important stage. It is a higher stage than ordinary involvement, but there is still a higher stage. The scriptures tell us that there are seven stages of ascent. I am not referring to Patanjali's Yoga System. It is some other thing called seven stages of knowledge. In the highest seventh stage, you will not know what will happen to you, because mortals, people thinking in terms of body and social diversity, cannot imagine at this moment what it would be like when the mortal becomes immortal, or that which is in space-time enters into the spaceless and the timeless Eternal. We can only imagine something in a figurative, symbolic way; actually, we cannot know what it is. We cannot know what is ahead of us. We can know by memory what has been behind us, or what is the past. We can know only one step in front of us; a hundred steps ahead we cannot know. The mind is limited in its capacity in knowledge.

What I mean to say, finally, is that this particular stage that you are mentioning, *satsanga,* is a happy thing, because it is higher than the stage of involvement in ordinary society, but still there are higher stages than this, where you will be alone in a different sense. By aloneness I do not mean that physically you are alone; it is a consciousness-aloneness. It is Universality feeling aloneness by Itself. It is the vast sea of cosmos feeling that It alone is. That kind of aloneness is what is referred to, and not a physical aloneness of someone sitting inside a room. That is not what I mean. Do you understand the point?

Janie: In my experience, it is the more the people who are involved in the sangha stand alone, the more I stand alone...

SWAMIJI: In Buddhist philosophy, there are three things called *Buddha, dharma* and *sangha. Sangha* is the first, *dharma* is the next, *Buddha* is the highest. In the beginning, it is *sangha,*—a congregation of devotees, brothers, sisters, etc. It is a necessary one. It is an institution, and it is called institutional life. Higher than that is pure *dharma,*—only law is there before you, not in terms of persons and things as when you are in congregation or *sangha,* but pure law. The universe is nothing but law operating, ultimately. It is abstract law, though it looks like a solid object before us. The universe is not made of hard substances. That is only a perception of the sense organs. It will melt into a pure abstract law, when you go higher up,—operative, interconnected law. Higher than that is *Buddha*, which is Pure Being.

So, in every religious parlance, these stages are recognised, only people call them by different names.

38

TEST OF OUR PROGRESS ON THE SPIRITUAL PATH

SWAMIJI: When a child cries, sometimes you will be able to know what it is wanting; at other times, you may not even know why it is crying. Often children cry, without even telling you why they are crying. They go on wailing. If you ask them what the matter is, they will not speak. Rarely they tell also, "I want this."

So, either way, you must take notice of this phenomenon. Thoroughly you have to put a question to your own self. Is it true that you have got everything that you want? Or, do you have a feeling that it is not the whole issue like that? "Everything that I want, I have not obtained; there are certain things which I have not got." See whether such a voice arises from inside.

These are the ways by which you can test yourself. How many times do you get angry in a day? You can ask a question to yourself: "For the last one month, how many times did I get angry?" If you never got angry, it is well and good, fine. If you did get angry, what was it for? You can put a question to your own self: "Am I justified?"

There are two kinds of anger. The mother's anger with the little naughty child, just to protect it from going too far; the physician's anger with a patient who is disobedient; the teacher's anger with a schoolboy who is not studying properly,—these are all educational angers, but not really anger. That is fine, because here the emotions are not stimulated. If a lawyer does not argue properly, the judge may get angry, but he is not angry from the emotions. It is an intellectual resentment.

The pernicious anger is that which arises from the feelings of the heart,—not like the judge, the teacher, or the mother. You really mean harm to somebody. That is emotional anger, and you must be guarding yourself against it: "Have I got anger like that? If so, I must see that it does not arise in the future."

Yesterday, somebody asked me what is the first step in Yoga, and I mentioned four or five principles. Are you violating any one of them in your daily life? They are important basic principles because they concern your attitude towards other people, and the extent of emotional self-restraint that you have achieved. With these little things, you may have some idea of the progress that you are making.

There is another thing. Do you feel happy in the midst of people, or do you feel happy when you are absolutely alone, unknown to anybody? Suppose for three days continuously, you have not seen anyone's face, and nobody has seen you, also. You are somewhere far off, in a sequestered place, in an isolated, far-off region. Do you feel that you are happier in that condition than you would have been in the midst of other people, or do you feel, "No, this is a misery; I cannot be alone like this. I must have some social atmosphere around me."

The more you feel happy when you are alone, the more can you be said to have progressed spiritually. The more you feel misery when you are alone, the less is the progress you have made. Actually, as the great mystics sometimes tell us, this superb attempt of yours is a "flight of the alone to the Alone."

We are alone in this universe, ultimately. We do not realise this fact because of illusions. Our mind is caught up in a cobweb of the network of errors, due to which we feel that we have many friends who are sustaining us. The fact is different.

In this world, which is relatively constituted, no part can be said to be a friend of another part. All are intertwined, like the warp and woof of a fabric. In that sense of the interdependence of the parts of the Universal Whole, no one is a friend of another, and no one is an enemy of another. It is cosmic democracy you may say. Neither do you have an occasion to like anything, nor do you have an occasion to dislike anything. Like threads in a cloth, things are intertwined warp and woof. They are so closely mixed that they can be said to be brothers, sisters, or friends; yet, you cannot call any thread as a friend of the other thread. It is a cooperative activity going on among the threads, and cooperative activity is a transcendental operation, rather than an emotional friendship.

So, anyway, it means, finally, you are alone, and you do not belong to anybody, and nobody belongs to you. In this consciousness, you are actually nearing that Supreme Aloneness which is the Absolute. God has no friends, and He has no relatives, and He cannot be considered as less happy. Can you say because God has no friends, no family, therefore, He is a miserable person, and we are better because we have all appurtenances? The other way round is the truth.

The nearer you are to aloneness of the ultimate type, the greater is the progress that you have made in the spiritual field. But if you are enmeshed in society, politics, communalism, and all that, and you cannot be happy unless you are in the middle of a market place, or a cinema house, or a ballroom, or a club,—without these you cannot have peace,—then, it is clearly a tragic condition of the mind. When you are happy with yourself, and you do not require anything from anyone,—"My condition of consciousness is such that I can obtain anything I want just here, because of the cosmic operations",—then, you do not have to tell people to bring you anything. "All these things shall be added unto you."

The universe is not outside you, as the cloth is not outside the threads. If the thread has to go and speak to the cloth, it need not have to travel by an airplane. It is just there. So, if you want anything from the cosmic operations, you need not have to go here and there. All is touching your nose. Just assert, and it is there.

So, these are a few words about the nature of the test that you can apply to your own selves concerning your progress in the spiritual path. This is my short message to you. So, I've told you something even without your asking [*group laughter*].

39

AFTER SELF-REALISATION

Amy: When desires arise, or anger arises in the mind, then what I am wondering about is since the Self is beyond the mind, and has no relationship to the mind...

SWAMIJI: It has a relationship. If It has no relationship, then how will you contact the Self through the mind? It has a connection, in the same way as the light of the sun has a connection with the light of the sun reflected on a mirror.

I will give you an example. You keep a mirror here, inside this room, and imagine that there is a ray of sun falling on the mirror. This mirror receives the light from the sun, and projects it on a wall. Now, that light on the wall cannot be regarded as actual sunlight, because actual sunlight, if it had been there, can be seen even if the mirror is withdrawn. You cannot see this unless the mirror is there; nevertheless, it is sunlight only. So, the mind is a reflected consciousness, though it is not the same as Self-consciousness.

In the same way as through the reflected light you can contact the original light, through the mind you can reach the Supreme Self. It is not that there is no connection, though they are not identical in the same sense as in the analogy mentioned. Now, what is your question, finally?

Amy: So, my question is that many thoughts will come and go in the mind, just by the nature of the mind itself. Rather than measuring or watching each object that arises and passes away in the mind, try to be rooted somewhere else, and to not act, or take too much importance. Say, if anger arises in the mind and passes away, there is no action taken on it...

SWAMIJI: Anger, etc., arise in the mind because your consciousness is not settled in itself. It is moving outside; otherwise, there is no occasion for anger. The mind and the Self are not two things. You cannot separate them. You are now talking to me through the mind only.

Amy: Yes.

SWAMIJI: If the mind were not there, you would not be talking; and yet, the consciousness that is behind your talking is coming from the Self. You are conscious that you are speaking to me, and here a double activity is taking place. The mind is operating, and the Self also is operating. Both are acting directly, spontaneously. That is why you are speaking, and also you are conscious that you are speaking. Speaking is the act of the mind; the consciousness of the act of speaking is of the Self. So, you are having a dual function just now taking place. And when the mind is thinking of anger, desire, etc., actually, it has diverted the consciousness elsewhere, instead of centreing it in the Self Itself.

The whole problem of spiritual life is that the consciousness should not divert itself outside the Self. Self should not become non-Self. You should not become another thing, or other than what you are. You have to be what you are. When the consciousness thinks of something other than itself, *A* has become *B*. You have become another. How can you become another? You are what you are. The thought that there is something outside you is actually the affirmation of consciousness wrongly that there is something outside itself. It is affirmation of particularity, rather than universality. I hope you catch my point. So, these are important things. It is a very subtle psychological point.

Amy: Yes.

Amir: I know the fact of the Absolute, and I know that I am not my mind, no matter how I feel, and what thoughts go through my mind. I know that always for a fact. And from that perspective, it does not make any difference if confusion or anger arise in the mind.

SWAMIJI: Why does it arise?

Amir: Because this is the mechanical action of the mind.

SWAMIJI: No, it is not mechanical. If it is mechanical, you will not be consciousness that you are angry. It would then be like a bulldozer moving on the road without knowing that it is moving. But you are not a bulldozer; you are conscious that you are angry. That shows that it is not a mechanical action: it is a deliberate action. That is the whole danger behind it. If it is mechanical, you would not be even aware that you are angry. It would be going on like a motor car without a driver, but this is a motor car with a driver. That is why there is a difference.

Amir: So, you mean that I am actually creating the anger?

SWAMIJI: You are creating the anger for a purpose. That is the whole point. Without any purpose, you will not get angry. Unnecessarily, who will get angry, unless one is crazy? There is a deliberate attempt behind it. You want to achieve something, purposefully; therefore, the anger arises. And, you are conscious of it, also. You are not unconscious. If you are unconscious, that is a different matter; you are pardoned. Unconscious actions do not produce results. It is a conscious action that produces a reaction. That is the whole point behind it, and so you must be cautious.

The entire life of a person is a drama played by consciousness, in many ways. And wherever consciousness is there, there you are, and you are involved in it. If consciousness is not there, you are not involved. If unconsciously something has happened, you are not responsible for it; but if you are conscious of it, you are responsible.

Janie: Swamiji, from my understanding, that awareness or consciousness of the anger in my mind does not come from my mind; it comes from my Self which is beyond the mind. And, it is from my Self that I can have the discrimination over those thoughts, and choose to see them for what they are, and not act out of them—not react to them.

SWAMIJI: Not react?

Janie: Yes.

SWAMIJI: Yes, yes. Certainly. You should not react.

Janie: But I am saying that is the freedom—that is where the freedom lies.

SWAMIJI: Freedom?

Janie: Freedom from the mind, in knowing that which is beyond the mind.

SWAMIJI: You see, I do not know exactly what you are speaking. If you are beyond the mind, you cannot get angry. It is the mind that gets angry. The Self cannot get angry. It is Universal Being. You are somehow not fixed in the Self. You have identified yourself with this medium, like a mirror, as I mentioned, which is the mind, and that agitates. When it agitates, you feel that you are doing something, thinking something, anger or otherwise. The consciousness does not agitate. It does not vibrate, act, or do anything, but the mind does all these things. When the sun is seen shaking on the water, the sun is not shaking, actually. It is the water that shakes, yet you may see it, and unintelligent perception may conclude that the sun is shaking. It looks as if the sun is moving.

So, likewise, you may feel that you are thinking something, while actually you are not doing that. It is a double action, as I mentioned already, of mind and consciousness. The awareness of it is from the Self; the activity is from the mind. They are blended together, and it looks as if you are doing it.

Amir: Swamiji, in your experience, is there a difference or change in the content of the mind?

SWAMIJI: Content?

Amir: Yes. What arises in the mind after realisation,—is there a change in the content of the mind after Self-realisation?

SWAMIJI: You see, yesterday we had been discussing this matter. You have to, first of all, be sure as to what you mean by "Self-realisation." We have already threadbare discussed this yesterday. By "Self-realisation" you mean identity of yourself with the Universal Self?

Amir: Yes.

SWAMIJI: Then the question of "after" does not arise, because there is no time there. The word "after" you have used is a temporal expression. There is no "after" and "before," because there is no time. It is timeless eternity, so there is no question of "after." It is eternity, and eternity cannot be understood in terms of time. There is no "after" for God, or for a Self-realised person. There is no such thing as "after," because you are thereby bringing the time factor into it, which will not be there at that time.

Amir: But still, the event of Self-realisation does occur in time.

SWAMIJI: When the event of Self-realisation has taken place, the character of events ceases. It does not any more exist as an event then, because an event also is a temporal concept. Through time you move towards that which is not in time. But, once you enter that which is not in time, you cannot judge it any more in terms of time. The time factor has gone. It is like waking from dream. The laws of dream will not operate in the waking condition. So, there is no before and after. "After Self-realisation what happens?" Such questions should not arise, because there is no "after." Time itself has gone. You will be universal, all-pervading. The Self is prior to time.

Kelly: You said either somebody is awake, and they cannot go back to sleep, or they are not awake. Then you said, otherwise they are dozing. I wondered if you could say a little bit more about that.

SWAMIJI: What is the matter? You have already explained it correctly.

Kelly: I did not understand quite how you could either be awake or asleep or...

SWAMIJI: Just now you are awake, isn't it?

Kelly: Yes.

SWAMIJI: Now, are you asleep, also?

Kelly: No.

SWAMIJI: So, here is the whole point. You cannot be asleep and awake at the same time. If you are asleep, you are not awake; if you are awake, you are not asleep. Now, what is the question?

Kelly: But, you also said it is possible to be dozing.

SWAMIJI: If you are not fully awake, and if the impressions of sleep are still persisting, you may be dozing. But if you are fully awake, and the need for sleep has gone, you will not doze.

Kelly: Impressions of...

SWAMIJI: Impressions of sleep. Sometimes you have

not slept well, and you get up and feel like sleeping once again. Though you are speaking and doing some work and having your breakfast, etc., you have not slept well, so you feel like this. But if your sleep is complete, and you have woken up thoroughly, you will not doze. So, the fully awake person will not fall asleep. Otherwise, the impression of the old sleep will continue, and you feel like dozing. But in Self-realisation, all is everywhere awake.

Amir: Is it not possible to have moments of complete awakening, and then times of dozing?

SWAMIJI: You cannot use the word "complete."

Amir: Being completely awake.

SWAMIJI: You are not completely awake,—rather semi-awake. The word "complete" dissociates itself from every other factor. You cannot bring another factor, and then call it "complete." If you are a complete person, you will desire nothing; because your personality is complete in every way, you have no desires. Complete awakening is totally different from having any other factor getting introduced into it.

Amir: I understand.

Michael: Swamiji, I would be very interested to hear your story of what happened to you, and what you went through.

SWAMIJI: Nothing has happened to me. I have gone through nothing. I am very fine and happy. What can I tell you?

Michael: I mean, how you discovered That.

SWAMIJI: I have not discovered anything. It has come to me somehow,—God only knows. Maybe in the previous birth I must have done some good deed, and the impressions of it have blossomed forth in an aspiration which has spontaneously acted in this birth. In my case, I was religious right from my age of six. Even at that age, I wanted God, and that cannot be attributed to any personal effort. What effort can be there? I have a memory even now of what I thought at six. That makes me feel, with a sense of wonderment, how things work.

I was born in a highly religious family. My father and grandfather were saintly persons, masters of the Vedas, and religious experts. Their blessing also must have been there. If you believe in the transmission of genes, their genes must be in me, also. Real sages they were,—my father and grandfather. That also may be one factor. And also, it might have been some good deed that I did in the previous birth, all have acted together and made me what I am. This is my short autobiography.

Janie: ...main thing is being guided by one's intention to be free. Think about one's intention to be free.

SWAMIJI: One goes on thinking one's intention to be free. This is what you mean?

Janie: And every other thought, you know, I think...

SWAMIJI: Every other thought is different. I'm talking especially of thoughts that are connected with your final freedom.

Janie: Yes. Right.

SWAMIJI: How do you generate that thought?

Janie: Really, just by staying with the intention to be free, that's all.

SWAMIJI: The intention is something that you maintain in yourself as an awareness. You are constantly aware that you have an intention to be free.

Janie: Yes.

SWAMIJI: It is very important that you must maintain the awareness always, and you should not miss it. But it is possible sometimes that the mind can get diverted into another thought. Sometimes it is unavoidable. When you are traveling, when you are purchasing a ticket, when you walk in the market, you will have the necessity to think in a manner that is not exactly as you are describing. What do you say?

Janie: Yes, it happens, but home is always the intention to be free.

SWAMIJI: Though the other thoughts are not in any way inconsistent with this main thought, they may look like distractions, when you are not able to discover the harmony between the secular existence and your life of aspiration. Most people, the majority, ninety- nine percent, do not see the vital connection between the humdrum life of the world and the life of spiritual aspiration. They think they are two different things. Actually, they are not two things. They are two aspects of the working of the human circumstance. And if you always feel that they are two different things, you get disgusted with the ordinary life of the world. You get fed up with it. You want to renounce, as people generally say. That is because you want to give up something which you do not consider as in any way relevant to your spiritual aspiration. This is the psychological impasse through which people have to pass. And, everyone has to pass, big or small, whoever he is.

You can never be able to reconcile, usually, the two things that are before you, this world of activity and conflict and war and what not, and God Almighty. We do not know how to bring them together, in spite of the fact that we may accept that God has created this world. What kind of world has God created? You will feel that everything in this world is not fine and peaceful. You would have liked the world to be better. That would be a complaint against God, to some extent: He has not created a proper world. When you expect the world to be a little better than what you see with your eyes, you are intending thereby that God has not thought well before creating this world. This is not a proper attitude on our part. God has thought well. He has not created unseemly, unaesthetic things in the world; yet, they seem to be there before our eyes.

The problem before a spiritual seeker is a reconciliation of these two things, the integration of the visible and the invisible, the outer and the inner, the empirical and the transcendental, the secular and the spiritual, the world and God. If you can blend them together, harmoniously, as you are able to blend your soul with your body, you can be said to be living an integrated life. This is the problem before spiritual seekers, and this rift that one perceives in consciousness is due to the impulsion of the sense organs which work in one way, and the consciousness which moves in another way. They have to be brought together. Here is a great task before spiritual seekers.

Janie: Before I met my master, I always felt that I could only be in touch with God if I was away in a quiet place, meditating. And after I met my master, I knew that that was not true, that, as you know, God was everywhere.

SWAMIJI: Yes, you are not making those complaints which you made earlier. That is good. In your *satsanga*, the Master gives discourses, is it?

Janie: Yes.

40

CREATION OF THE WORLD

Visitor: Swamiji, sometimes I wonder how all this came into being—you know, the whole human condition.

SWAMIJI: The human condition did not come. The world came.

Visitor: Yes. Sometimes I wonder how it all came into existence. And, it seems unanswerable.

SWAMIJI: Some say it came into existence by the thought of God. Some say it never came into existence. It is there, as it was, and nobody created it. It is there. Existence is not created by anybody. Who will create existence? To create existence, somebody else has to exist, prior to this existence, and existence is a general principle, so nobody can create existence. Existence is a word which does not require any further explanation. It has been there, and it is there. It is what it is. Nobody created it. That is one view—some kind of scientific view, we may say—the view of modern scientists, to some extent.

But the religious view is that the Absolute Supreme Being, God, willed, "Let there be heaven and earth," and immediately, space manifested itself. Then, vibrations started moving inside space, and it became air. Friction started after that, which is heat, fire. Then, condensation took place, which is water. Then solidity appeared, which is earth. Here is the beginning of creation, according to descriptions in religious scriptures.

And, inasmuch as God willed this creation, His consciousness is present in every little part of creation,—this

space, this air, this fire, this water, this earth,—which are
the five physical elements that you see before you. And,
then, emerges a group of little, little individualities,
which is the beginning of what you call the evolutionary
process. There is, in the beginning, inanimate matter,
which is described in the form of these five elements I
mentioned just now. Then, there is animation starting—
like fungi, amphibians, fish and so on. Then, you know
the whole story of evolution; some small creatures, insects, and animals,—but animals come later. In the beginning there is only fungus-type plant kingdom, and all
that. Even in the scriptures you will find that God created
not man first; He created only this plantation,—trees,
etc., because trees are the first creation. Higher than plantation kingdom is the animal kingdom; higher than that is
the human kingdom. So, we have come like that, by gradual evolutionary process, in the act of creation.

And among human beings also, all are not of a uniform type. They say that there are about eight million
types of living species in this universe. You cannot know
who they are, where they are, and all that. You cannot
count them; and, the human species is one. But, as you
know, even among the human species, all people are not
of the same category. Some people are like animals, some
people are cannibals, some people are intensely selfish,
some people will do tit-for-tat. Some people are very
good in nature. They will do only good. Some people are
saints; some people are geniuses; some are God-men. So,
even among human beings, you see how many varieties!
This is just to answer your question, how things came
about,—in one way.

Visitor: Thank you.

*Visitor: What are the stages from a good man to a
God-man?*

SWAMIJI: A good man is one who considers other

people as equally important as he considers himself. Do you understand the point? When I consider you as a person as important as my own self, I will treat you in the manner in which I treat myself. This is the characteristic of goodness. Do you understand me? When you treat others as you treat yourself, it is considered as goodness. But a saint is a further step towards God-consciousness. It is something above goodness. The saint is also a good man, because he is moving in the direction of God-consciousness. Thus, there is a gradual ascent from the lower to the higher;—the higher includes the lower and transcends the lower.

Higher than all is the God-man. He lives like God Himself. Practically, there is no distinction between his consciousness and God-consciousness.

41

KARMA

Carol: Does thought create karma?

SWAMIJI: Any thought which is connected with an object other than yourself, with a motive behind it, or an intention behind it, will produce a reaction. I am looking at the wall. I am thinking of the wall. It won't produce any reaction, because I'm not looking at it with any motive or intention. It is just there, visible.

There are two ways of seeing things. One is the general perception of things, like when you walk, you see a tree, or a building; you are not concerned with it. Another is a thought which is connected with objects with a purpose, intention, or motive, with a like or dislike—to get something from it, or to avoid it. Such thoughts will produce a reaction. That reaction is called *karma*. It does not mean that every thought will produce a reaction. General perceptions do not produce *karma*. Only emotional perceptions will produce it.

If we are seeing a thing with a feeling behind it, it will have a reaction; but I have no feeling about the wall. I am just seeing it without any feeling about it. It is impersonal perception. Now we are all sitting here, and I am seeing so many people. I have no feeling of any kind in regard to you. I am seeing you, as I see anything else. But if I see you with a purpose, intention, motive, like or dislike, then it will produce a reaction.

Carol: And then there will be a gap between,—it will create a gap.

SWAMIJI: It will create a bondage. That kind of *karma* is what causes rebirth.

Carol: A bondage.

SWAMIJI: That kind of *karma* it is that causes rebirth.

Carol: I see.

SWAMIJI: Every *karma* is not binding. Only thoughts charged with desire of any kind, positively, or negatively, create a psychological cocoon around yourself, and that cocoon materialises itself into a solid formation, which is called the body, in rebirth. So, your body is nothing but a concentrated form of thought, which has arisen on account of your past thoughts, of many births, several births. But if you don't have any kind of desire, for or against anything,—you are thinking only in an impersonal manner; neither you want anything, nor you don't want anything; you have no opinion about anything; you are just what you are,—then these thoughts, which are impersonal in their nature, will not produce any reaction, and they will not produce *karma.*

Carol: So, the psychological cocoon you talk about, another word might be preoccupation? You are just in your own thoughts around that object, concerning that object?

SWAMIJI: Any thought with a feeling behind it.

Carol: Thank you.

Amir: Is it not possible to have a thought with a feeling behind it, and then to recognise that this is bondage, and to disengage before any reaction happens?

SWAMIJI: If you can do that, well and good. Suppose you look at a thing with some feeling for it, or against it, and you are disturbed by that, and you realise that it is causing a disturbance, and you avoid it immediately. Then you are free from the reaction.

Several people: Right.

SWAMIJI: But what happens, generally, is that the emotions are so strong that they take possession of the person. It doesn't happen always, but sometimes. This is what they call "love at first sight" or "hatred at first sight." And you cannot disentangle yourself from that. Because something has happened to you, you pounce on it, for wanting it or hating it,—one of the two. At that time you cannot use the discretion in your mind that "I am caught in this and I must absolve myself from that." Very rarely the intellect works at that time. When passions are strong, the intellect ceases. If the intellect is strong enough, and the desire is mild, then what you say is all right. You can apply that method.

Amir: The Buddha said that this is why mindfulness is necessary, all the time.

SWAMIJI: Mindfulness. Constant thought of the thought itself,—"what is happening?" Every day you have to maintain an observation of what is happening to your mind,—a spiritual diary, as they call it,—a check-up of the personality. From morning to evening, what have you been thinking? You just sit for a while and think: "What have I been thinking from morning till now? Is it a useful thing, or an absurd thing?"

Sometimes, the thoughts will be meaningless thoughts; they will not produce any good or bad results. It is something like what is called woolgathering, a lethargic, half-dozing condition. You will think nothing; you are neutral. That is a waste of time. You have not achieved anything by that kind of thinking. Neutrality, also, is not good. Love also is not good; hatred also is not good. They are called *sattva, rajas, tamas*—the three qualities of Nature. When you are free from all these three aspects of thinking, neither should you be simply neutrally in an unconscious state, not knowing what you are thinking; nor should you love, nor should you hate.

That is called an impersonal way of consciousness. You must maintain consciousness; it is not that you should be sleeping, but careful. What are you conscious of? It is incumbent on the part of everyone to keep a direct watch on one's own thoughts, and see to what extent it is in harmony with the universal set-up of things.

You are a citizen of the universe, not from America, and all that. These ideas must go away. You belong to the whole cosmos. Don't say, "I am American, I am an Indian, I am a man, I am a woman, I am this." All these ideas must go, gradually; otherwise, you are bound by these thoughts. You belong to the whole universe. It is not only theory, it is a fact. You are in the universe just now. Why should you say, "I am on the earth, in the room; I am in the city." These are all paltry, silly thoughts. Spiritual seekers should be a little above it.

You are regulated by the law of your government. In a similar manner, you are regulated by the law of the universe, and how can you be completely ignorant of its operations? Ignorance of the law is no excuse, is an old saying, and it applies also to the universe. You cannot be simply oblivious of the laws of the universe operating in terms of you, and then simply go scot-free. It is not possible.

It is necessary to know the law of the area where you are located. You cannot say, "I don't know the law." Then, you cannot exist there, and if you don't know the law of the universe, you cannot exist in the universe, also. That is the cause of suffering and rebirth. There is no use pleading ignorance. You must be cautious.

One of our Swamis went to the United States. He did not know the law of parking of cars in the States. He put it in the wrong place, and a policeman came. The Swami said, "You see, we have come from a long distance, and we do not know."

"You can talk like this in the court." the policeman said. "Do not tell me anything."

Like that, the universe will tell you. If you say, "I never knew," it will say, "Tell it in the court." [*laughter*]

Anyway, the law of the universe is more stringent than the law of man. You may be pardoned by the law of man, but you cannot be pardoned by the law of the universe. It is just, to the very core, and you cannot escape it.

Amir: Our teacher teaches that we always know. We always know...

SWAMIJI: Right, right.

Amir: And we claim ignorance to escape responsibility.

SWAMIJI: Just now you are connected to the centre of the cosmos,—even now. To know it is a great strength, and also a great fright. It is both things at the same time. The law of the universe will not permit any kind of self-ishness. Here is the essential point.

42

QUERIES OF SEEKERS

Satoko (Japan): How can I do meditation on Om?

SWAMIJI: *Om* is not a word; it is a vibration. It is a name for universal vibration. The whole cosmos is vibrating like this, and it started the vibration at the time of creation. You are trying to concentrate on that in your mind. You feel the sense of a universal vibration everywhere, like an electric energy emanating from the top of the universe till your heart. It vibrates everywhere. Feel deeply that the universe is vibrating through you.

You are not one person sitting; you are only a little drop in the ocean of universal force, and because you cannot think it properly, one creates a symbol in the mind. *Om, Om, Om.* If you chant like this, you must feel a thrill in the body, a vibration inside every cell of the body. All the *pranas* will do like this, shaking, as if some electric shock is given, and you feel as if you are connected with the universal energy. To create that feeling, you recite *Om* like that. You should chant it properly, not quickly, with deep thought and feeling from the middle of the heart, directly.

You start with a deep sonorous sound, and slowly it tapers off, like a ripple in water. When you throw a stone in water, it makes circles which will become wider and wider. Like that, you start the vibration here. Then you feel as if it is expanding little by little, by circles, until it reaches the top of the universe.

Eva: Reaching enlightenment through the mind, and

*in my own experience, what I experienced when I met my
Guru was that I realised something that was other than
the mind, where my own life, and all of existence was
coming from.*

SWAMIJI: You see, when you say "I" and "my," to
what are you making a reference? That is the mind. You
have already accepted that there is a mind when you say
"I," "my" and all that. It is not the Universal Consciousness that is speaking here. It will not say "I," "my," etc.
You have already concluded that you have reached It
through your mind, because you are remembering It, and
you are still having a mind. The mind has not gone away.

There is no problem with the mind. It is not a bad
thing, though people always go on saying that the mind
must be controlled, the mind must be transcended, and all
that. The actual subtlety behind it is rarely understood by
people.

The mind is neither a good thing, nor a bad thing. I
told you, it is something like a mirror that is reflecting
the sun, and you can have some idea of the sun through
the mirror, though the sun is not in the mirror. The reflection in the mirror is not the sun, and yet, through the reflection you can have some idea as to what the sun is.
And, if the reflection is to be considered as you, it can
contemplate the original and reach the original.

So, as the reflection can reach the original, the mind
also can reach the Absolute. There is no objection. The
mind is not a bad thing like that; it is a medium of gradual ascent. Only, you should not misuse it for personal
purposes. It is like money. Money is good or bad? You
cannot say anything about it. It is an impersonal thing. It
is up to you to see how it is utilised.

*Visitor: I was wondering if there are any differences
for men and women in reaching the Absolute.*

SWAMIJI: No. There is no difference. What reaches

the Absolute is not a man or a woman. What reaches the Absolute is an enlightened soul. The soul is neither a man, nor a woman. It is like a flame of light; therefore, there is no difference. God is neither a man, nor a woman. He is absolute radiance, and only the radiance in you will go to that Universal Radiance. The radiance is not man or woman.

Visitor: Thank you.

Vilaidan: In Hinduism, we say that we have to destroy the ego. But, how can there be initiative without the ego?

SWAMIJI: The initiative should arise from the Universal Being, which includes all the egos. So, it is a greater power of initiative than the individual egoistic motivation. You know, God can do more things than man can do. God is not an ego, It is universal existence. So, it implies that the lesser the ego, the greater is the entry of universality into you, and, more is the capacity for innovation, motivation, or initiative. And, the more is the ego or individual affirmation, the less is the power of the person. An egoistic person is a weak person; the lesser the ego, the greater is the strength, because of the entry of universality into the person. Ego is not a virtue. It is an obstacle to any kind of proper initiative in the real sense.

Luciano: In this case, when a man decides to follow a spiritual path, is it the ego that decides, or is it the grace of God?

SWAMIJI: The spiritual path is the technique which the ego employs in diminishing itself and allowing more and more of universality into it, by gradual degrees. You cannot say whether the spiritual path is trodden by the ego or by the Universal Being. It is a dual action taking place at the same time. When health improves, disease goes. Now, which comes first,—the disease goes first, or health comes first? They are simultaneous occurrences taking place in the person. Night goes and day comes. Which is the first thing—night goes first, or day comes first? You cannot say which is first, and which is afterwards. It is a simultaneous occurrence. So, likewise, is the entry of the Universal into you, and the diminishing of the ego. They are not first and afterwards; it is a simultaneous action, a total evolution.

Luciano: Then, in that case, the ego is in tune with God-will.

SWAMIJI: Certainly. When it comes in tune with God-will, it ceases to be an ego. It is God Himself operating through the so-called individuality.

An American Visitor: In the USA there is a large interest in channels,—people who go into a trance, or close their eyes, and come out with words that others call wisdom. They talk about all kinds of things. The voice changes, the mannerisms change.

SWAMIJI: They come in contact with some force through which they speak. There is nothing wrong with it. Mostly, the forces are disembodied souls.

Visitor: Why would a soul of a higher being condescend to come through a channel?

SWAMIJI: Instead of them coming down to your level, maybe you are ascending to their level. It does not necessarily mean that they will come down to your level. You adjust your consciousness to a higher status, and then you come in contact with them.

Visitor: Is it the higher soul that would be talking?

SWAMIJI: Yes, higher than your present level. You can come in contact not only with higher souls, but with God Himself if your mind is purified enough. God can speak through you, which is finally your aim. Why do you want to come in contact with ordinary souls? It is better to directly contact the Ultimate.

An American Visitor: Is there any benefit to knowing our past lives?

SWAMIJI: There is no benefit. It is an unnecessary curiosity. You have taken thousands of births; would you like to know all the things of all the thousands of births? It will be a hierarchy of all unpleasant things, which will make you miserable in one second. God has been kind enough to brush aside all those memories and confine your consciousness to the present birth.

If you knew all the miseries of your previous existence, you couldn't even live in this world for a few seconds. You might have been a bandit. How horrible to remember all these things! God is very merciful to remove this memory, to keep us sane. You have passed through every kind of species in existence. You were crawling reptiles, cockroaches, lizards, good people, bad people. It is a frightening drama which you would not like to remember.

You do not remember many of the things that you experienced even in this very life. Maybe fifty percent has been forgotten, and you would not like to remember it, also. So, memory is a good thing, but it is also a bad thing, in many cases.

Visitor: Is reincarnation a progressive evolution?

SWAMIJI: It is generally considered as a progressive evolution: from mineral, to plant, to animal, to human, to super-human. You have yet to go ahead. You are now a limited human being, but you are expected to become an advanced divinity, not merely an ordinary super-human. From man to God-man is the ascent yet ahead of you, for which you have to struggle through the practice of meditation, Yoga, or religion. You have to become a God-man—perhaps God Himself, ultimately.

Visitor: Some believe that we shouldn't have to

struggle, we should just go with the flow, go as our life takes us.

SWAMIJI: That is one way of thinking, but you should not hinder the normal process by any kind of selfish action. If you are totally unselfish in your behavior, action and thought, I think the natural process will take you ahead; but if you hinder it by selfishness of any kind, then it may be difficult go with it.

Roger: Any intelligent person can see that the life in India is being choked by the excessive growth of population. India is a very religious country...

SWAMIJI: You see, I am not handling India.

Roger: Swamiji, please just let me finish, and then tell me your opinion. Why don't the holy men of India preach to the masses of the people that they should limit their family sizes, and thereby bring happiness back to the country?

SWAMIJI: The saints do nothing else but that. They are doing only that work. They don't say it bluntly as you suggest, but they are doing it in a highly cultured fashion, and you will be surprised that they are doing no other work than this. They are doing only that for all-round human welfare.

Roger: And the people are not listening?

SWAMIJI: They are listening. It is like a sick man being told not to eat food, and as soon as you go away, he starts eating. They are doing it slowly. They understand, but instincts are very strong. Social, biological instincts sometimes go rampant, though good advice is received.

So, it doesn't mean that the saints are not doing anything. They are doing it very well. To make the whole ocean sweet, it requires a large quantity of sugar. If we put ten quintals of sugar in the ocean, we have done a good deed, but the salt is so much that it's not sufficient to make it sweet. So, it is not that the saints are not doing it; it is slow work that is going on, and finally you have to trust in God. One day it will be successful. It must be. When God is great, all shall be well.

An American Visitor: There are a lot of problems in the world that we have never had before.

SWAMIJI: It will be like this forever. It won't change. The world will be like this only, and that is part of the process of evolution. There is a coming of something here, and a going somewhere else. You are seeing only this particular earth, but you do not know what is happening in the whole cosmos. If you widen your vision to the entire creation, you will never put a question like that afterwards.

They say the evolutionary process is like the movement of a wheel. The spoke that is above will come down, and that spoke which is down will go up after some time, so nothing is in a permanent position. There is a cycle; everything is moving. Today the world is in one condition, tomorrow it will be in another condition. Nothing is permanent, static or in one position only. Everything is a flux, finally aiming at Self-realisation of the universe. The universe is aiming at Self-realisation, which includes the Self-realisation of everybody and everything in the universe. A total merging of the universe in the Absolute is the purpose of evolution.

Visitor: Many people in the West fear that, because of man's selfishness, perhaps we will wipe civilisation off the earth, without evolving. We will destroy ourselves, instead of becoming better.

SWAMIJI: The world cannot destroy itself. Cells in the body are destroying themselves every minute, in order that you may become better. The destruction also is a process of becoming newer and fresher. Otherwise, you would have always been a baby, and would never have become an adult.

Every seven years, they say, the whole biological process of a person changes. You become a new man every seven years. Cells were destroyed; if they weren't, you would have been a stunted individual, and not the person that you are today. Your biological evolution is an indication of what is happening in the whole cosmos. Cells dying, and changing, is part of the natural anabolic and catabolic process in things. It takes place simultaneously. You cannot always be in the same condition; otherwise, there would be no movement and growth, no betterment. Death is meant for a better life; it is a part of evolution.

The world is moving forward and it has to move onward. Though there appears sometimes to be a retrogression, ultimately it is a progression.

43

HINDU GODS AND THE ONE GOD

American Visitor: Who are the Hindu gods?

SWAMIJI: I do not know if you know the names of these Indian gods. You are not acquainted? Have you heard of Vishnu?

Visitor: Yes.

SWAMIJI: The three great gods of Hinduism are Brahma, Vishnu and Siva. Brahma is the creative aspect, Vishnu is the protecting, sustaining aspect; and Siva is the transforming, dissolving aspect. Brahma creates, Vishnu sustains, and Siva dissolves. These are the three aspects of the Supreme Being.

Vishnu has several incarnations. Rama and Krishna are the most prominent of his incarnations, and they are worshipped as veritable Narayana. Narayana is also another name for Vishnu. The supreme creative principle, the absolute creative will, you may say, is called Narayana, or Vishnu.

So, we have various concepts of God, for the purpose of religious worship. You have got Badrinath, in the Himalayas. It is a very famous place of pilgrimage; in summer, millions flock there. Worship starts from the month of May, and goes on until October. It is on a mountain top. It is also a temple devoted to Vishnu, Narayana; and there is another, for Siva, at Kedarnath. It is also a mountain peak. That is Lord Siva's temple. These are the most prominent of the shrines in the

Himalayas,—Badrinath and Kedarnath, of Narayana (Vishnu) and Siva.

Visitor: Lord Buddha and Lord Christ were also incarnations of Vishnu?

SWAMIJI: Lord Buddha is considered as one incarnation of Vishnu, but you can consider Christ, or anybody else also as an incarnation of the Supreme Being in a wide philosophical sense, but not in a strictly Hindu religious sense. A Hindu will not consider Christ as Vishnu's *avatara*, though in a broader sense, you can consider any great divine manifestation as the incarnation of the Absolute. From the purely religious point of view of a Hindu, they will not consider Mohammed and Christ as incarnations. But, in a highly transcendental sense, everyone is an incarnation of the One Being.

Visitor: There is one Hindu goddess. I do not know much about her, but she has eight arms, right?

SWAMIJI: I did not want to complicate your mind with all these things, so I closed with Brahma, Vishnu, and Siva.

Visitor: I do not know much about it, and I see all these post cards, and they are very beautiful.

SWAMIJI: Brahma, Vishnu and Siva represent the Universal Consciousness at the back of the processes of creation, preservation, and destruction. Consciousness, when it manifests itself as creation, preservation and destruction, is conceived also to have a force, because manifestation is nothing but a demonstration of power, or force. These forces of Brahma, Vishnu, and Siva are called *shaktis*, which means power. The *shakti* of Brahma is called Sarasvati, the goddess of learning; the *shakti* of Vishnu is Lakshmi, the goddess of prosperity. The *shakti* of Siva is Durga (and various other names also she has.) Durga is sometimes identified with the Power of the One Absolute.

These *shaktis* that I mentioned are also independently worshipped as goddesses, apart from conceiving them as part and parcel of Brahma, Vishnu, and Siva. In the earliest forms of religion, they were all considered as one only. Later on, when it became very difficult to conceive this totality of divinity in worship and meditation, there was personification of these universal forces.

Actually, you cannot consider any god as a person, like a human being, but we cannot think anything except in terms of personality, due to the habit of the mind; so, though Brahma, Vishnu, and Siva, or Durga, Lakshmi and Sarasvati, cannot be regarded has having a body like ours, we can think them in no other way. We consider Brahma as an old father of the universe; sometimes he is even considered to have a beard, as the supreme father. And, Vishnu is a grand, majestic, beautiful person. Siva is an austere, inwardly drawn, ascetic. They are with their consorts Durga, Lakshmi, and Sarasvati,—Durga having so many hands, as you say, Lakshmi also is having so many hands, and Sarasvati has four. Everyone has four hands. They can have more, also.

But they all have an inward mystical meaning. They form an outward symbology of an inward spiritual connotation. All the powers of the psyche are concentrated in a single act of thought, or awareness, in these divinities. In our cases, the facets of the psyche are separated,—understanding is one aspect; feeling is another; willing is a third, and remembering is a fourth. In Western psychology, three aspects only are considered: understanding, willing, and feeling; they emphasise three aspects of selfhood, but there is a fourth aspect which is subconscious, or subconscience, we may say, which is the medium of memory. All these act independently in us. It does not mean that understanding is the same as feeling, or feeling is the same as willing, etc. Each one is independent. We cannot think in a total fashion. If you can merge all these faculties into a single act of perception, it will be intuition, but we cannot do that. We are always separated in our psyche. We understand one thing, feel another thing, will still another thing, and subconsciously we can be a fourth thing; but the gods represent a total intuitional power of a blend of all these four faculties. So, the four hands, we may say, actually symbolise the four aspects of the psyche, through which a single consciousness is operating as intuition in their case, and as ordinary perception in our case.

All these religious figures are symbols of a higher abstract principle, which ordinary people cannot comprehend, and so we require figures, pictures, idols, images, sculptures, paintings, all sorts of things; otherwise, we cannot think of God, because the mind has come down so low in its psychological operations and power of thinking that we want everything to be just like us. God, also, should be like us only. So, God, we think, is a huge man; this is what we think. If you read any scripture, you will find God described as a huge Body occupying the entire space, and having eyes and nose, like us.

If you say that God is not like that, then what else is God? It may end in denying God altogether, if you cannot think God in some form. So, it is better to have some inadequate conception of God, than have no conception at all. We need something, at least, to hang on.

Dr. Goel: Finally, we must have a true conception.

SWAMIJI: It is not possible for ordinary mortals to have a true conception. People cannot have true conceptions even of themselves. How will they have a true conception of somebody else?

Dr. Goel: So, we must have first a true conception of ourselves.

SWAMIJI: Yes. Unless you know yourself correctly, how will you know another thing correctly? You are the medium of knowing anything else, so whatever you are is reflected in the process of your perception and knowledge of things. Whatever you think you are, that you will think anything else also is. This is the difficulty with us.

Actually, you are also not a physical body. You are not the son of so-and-so; you are not six-foot high, with so much weight; you are not flesh and bone, and all that. You will find it difficult to know what exactly you are. Much time is necessary to go deep into this matter, and realise that you are totally different from what you appear to be. But yet, you will not forget that you are Mr. so-and-so, and you have come from such and such a country, you have got this height, this weight, etc. You cannot forget these features.

You will never imagine for a moment that you are a concentrated formation in space and time of a universal bit of consciousness. If you can maintain this awareness always, you will not be this person that you are. You will become different every day, and what you will be, God knows; but, who can think like that? It is not possible. The mind will pull you down—"Don't go too high," it will tell you.

You are only a little eddy in the sea of universal consciousness. That is what you really are, but who can think like that? For a moment you may think it, but afterwards it slips down, and you are once again the same man that you were.

So, all this requires hard meditation to raise the consciousness to that level of universal perception, and feel oneself as commensurate with the total setup of the universe, and not existing independently as Mr. so-and-so. You are part and parcel organically entwined with the whole universal fabric. If you can maintain this consciousness always, you are perpetually in a state of meditation.

American Visitor: On gods some details, please?

SWAMIJI: Durga sits on a lion, Sarasvati sits on a swan, and Lakshmi sits on a lotus, representing three functions of these three forces. It is difficult to explain all these things, in a few minutes. The lion represents the ferocity of human desire. Desires are not ordinary simpletons; desire is ferocious when you oppose it. Because we do not oppose many of our desires, they do not look terrible. The subdual of the ferocity of desire by a divine power is symbolised in this divine force of Durga riding over the lion.

Lakshmi sitting on a lotus implies beauty, prosperity, magnificence, aesthetic rejoicing, all pleasantness.

Visitor: Is usually water in the background?

SWAMIJI: Yes. Water, but not necessarily. And Sarasvati on a swan represents intelligence, purity. Sarasvati is dressed in pure white; Lakshmi is dressed in gorgeous drapery; Durga is a little more picturesque, with varieties, you can see many hands and phases. One represents the purity of knowledge, transparency of understanding, which is symbolised in white color. Another is all-conceivable prosperity in this world, which is slightly tinged with human desire. (Unless we have some desire, we cannot understand what prosperity is.) Durga is the force that controls the cruelty of human passion. These are the aspects of it, briefly.

Visitor: Thank you.

Andrea: Swamiji, you mentioned the four arms of the deity, and you said that there was willing...

SWAMIJI: Understanding, willing, feeling.

Andrea: And you said remembering, and then you said...

SWAMIJI: Subconscience.

Andrea: Is it like the subconscious?

SWAMIJI: It is the same thing.

Andrea: It's not to do with the conscience?

SWAMIJI: The conscience also is in the subconscious. It is one of the functions of the subconscious.

Andrea: I see.

SWAMIJI: Memory also is a part of it. It has got many functions. Memory is one. Conscience is another as the voice of God, you could say. Something tells you this is proper; that is the work of conscience, and it is the work of the subconscious, also.

Dr. Goel: What is the difference between conscious and subconscious?

SWAMIJI: You are now working in the conscious level. In dream you are in subconscious level. The conscious level is withdrawn into the subconscious, which is dream. In sleep you are in unconscious.

Dr. Goel: And in deep sleep?

SWAMIJI: Unconscious.

Eva: Swamiji, along those same lines I have another question. You mentioned on the same day that those four faculties, they are together in one.

SWAMIJI: If all the faculties work in unison, it becomes intuition.

Eva: So, intuition is bigger than conscience?

SWAMIJI: It is bigger than all the four. It is a total blending of all the four.

Andrea: I was thinking about how people really wouldn't want to stay in the body if there's no point, really. You know, I understood why some people wanted to leave the body once they realised...

SWAMIJI: It is not a desire to leave the body, actually. It is a desire to leave the consciousness of individuality,—body or no body,—that is a different matter. If you have a body, but you are not conscious that there is a body, it is not going to trouble you. The body is not the source of trouble; your consciousness that there is a body is the source of trouble. A wealthy person is a person who is conscious that he has a lot of wealth. Suppose he has a lot of wealth, but he is not conscious that he has wealth, you cannot call him a rich man. What do you say?

Visitors: Right.

SWAMIJI: So consciousness is wealth. This is a very interesting thing to hear! [*laughter*]

Dr. Goel: Consciousness is everything.

SWAMIJI: Yes. Suppose you have got a lot of money, and you are not conscious that you have got it. Can you call it a worthwhile thing? It is useless. So, consciousness is money, also. Very interesting! Everything is consciousness. Minus that, there is no meaning in anything. So, bondage is consciousness of finitude. It is not the existence of anything, but the consciousness of the existence of something; so, the bondage is consciousness only, of some type,—limited consciousness.

The question then is not of leaving the body, or holding the body. Let the body be there. There are bodies; so many people have got bodies here. Are you worried about them? [*laughter*] Why are you worried only about *your* body? What is the importance? If you are not at all concerned with the bodies of other people, why are you concerned with *your* body, as if it is more important than others'? That is called attachment of consciousness to a particular localised individuality.

Dr. Goel: That is the worst thing.

SWAMIJI: The whole point is that. It is not the existence of something, but the consciousness of it. In liberation, the world is not destroyed, only you will not be connecting it with your finitude. Your consciousness will pervade everything; therefore, there will be no particular attachment to any individual object. Liberation is the recognition of consciousness being present in all things, and not only in some things. If it is only in some things or one thing, that is bondage. If it is everywhere, it alone is, and is free. Now you are, and somebody else, also, is there, whereas there, only one is there.

Dr. Goel: In liberation?

SWAMIJI: In liberation, only One Being is there.

Dr. Goel: And that is Universal Consciousness.

SWAMIJI: Yes. Bondage is not in the existence of things, it is in the consciousness of the existence of things. It is a peculiar operation of consciousness. Now, the Universal Consciousness is locked up within one body only, which is what you call yourself. Therefore, it is frightened because of its limitations, because of its isolation from others—and because of its dependence on many external factors, etc., and also because of the fear of losing this individuality, one day or the other.

But suppose it is present in everything, which actually is the case. Then, there is no such fear. Fear arises from a dual existence. Fear arises from another outside you. The outside-consciousness must go; then, the fear also goes.

Andrea: I actually feel peaceful somewhat, when you say that.

SWAMIJI: Yes. When we hear it we feel a little peace. We are genuinely acquiring peace.

Dr. Goel: So we must detach it?

SWAMIJI: We need not detach it. We must attach it to all things. Then automatically, detachment takes place from one thing. Always there is a fear of detachment, so I suggested that such fear need not be there. You like attachments? Then attach yourself to all things, and then it is equal to detachment from one thing. So, you like to be attached; it is your happiness. If you are detached, great fear comes. Nobody wants detachment, so we never use such words. Don't say "renounce" and all that. Have attachment, but to everything. Let us see what happens. [*laughter*]

The mind is such a trickster. Neither will it want attachment to everything, nor detachment from anything. You want something? All right, take all things. You should not ask for something only. Everything you take; otherwise, don't ask. What are you asking for? Everything I will give you. Everything, also, you cannot take, because you have no place to keep it. The whole earth you take! [*laughter*]

Nobody can be so mischievous as the mind. It doesn't know what it wants, and yet, continuously goes on wanting, without knowing what it wants. Here is the trouble. Why don't you get attached to everything? What is wrong?

Visitor: Ego.

SWAMIJI: Ask the ego to get attached to everything, to every person in the world, every building, every tree in the forest and every river, every mountain, every sun, moon, and star. Get attached to all of them, and let us see what happens to you. It is possible you will not get attached. Here is the whole thing. Most unreasonable. Even in attachment you are unreasonable! [*laughter*]

There is a story: Acharya Sankara was inside the room. The door was bolted, and the disciple knocked from outside. "Who is there?" the *guru* asked. "I." "Let it be either nothing, or everything," the *guru* said.

There are three kinds of "I's": the I that is nothing, the I that is something, and the I that is everything. This "something" is a dangerous thing. Let it be nothing, or be everything. Then you are free. You cannot make this

"I" nothing, nor can you make it everything, so you are hanging in the middle. [*laughter*]

Dr. Goel: That is the problem of life.

SWAMIJI: Even when you are given everything, you don't want it. What kind of person! Have everything, and get attached to everything. Then you will have Virat-consciousness. Attachment of consciousness to everything is another name for Universal Consciousness.

44

ON WORK AND MEDITATION

German Visitor: What is the relation between the active and meditative living? How to find the balance?

SWAMIJI: It is a very simple matter. When a person feels that meditation is the most important thing, and higher than any other thing, it will mean that one wants to do only meditation, and does not want to do anything else. This is the idea behind the feeling that meditation is the highest. But, is it possible for a person to be doing only meditation and doing no work?

German Visitor: No.

SWAMIJI: Why is it not possible? Let that person answer the question. When you say that meditation is the highest and the most important thing, why cannot you do only that, and you want to do some other work? What is the reason? It is an individual matter; each person should answer this question.

Why are you working so much, when you say that only meditation is necessary? There is some reason for your work. What is that reason? The reason is that you cannot exist in this world, in this body, without doing some work; and if the body does not exist, the meditation also does not exist. The whole thing goes. You are asking me the connection between work and meditation. Inasmuch as without existing, you cannot meditate, and without some work you cannot exist, the connection is simple. It is essential for maintaining yourself as a seeker of truth, for the purpose of meditation.

Actually, every work done with a feeling of devotion is also a kind of meditation. When you work, you are not doing it for a selfish purpose. You are doing it as a necessary medium for keeping you fit and secure for the purpose of higher worship and meditation.

Work also becomes a preparation for meditation. Therefore, it is a part of meditation itself. So, work becomes worship, and contemplation and action are interconnected, like body and soul. You cannot keep your body somewhere and your soul somewhere else. They are together. So, the body is connected with work; the soul is connected with meditation. But, they are not two things. You know, your body and soul are together; so, likewise, work and meditation also go together. They are one integral whole. That is the relation.

45

ON WORLD CRISIS

German Visitor: How do you see the increasing world situation, about maybe a possible coming world crisis, or about the increasing population?

SWAMIJI: What do I see? I see nothing. I have no opinion in this matter. It is the work of God. He has created this world, and so He is creating and also destroying, both, for different purposes. It is the work of Nature, just as you are growing from a little child to a man, and become old, and afterwards, die also. Now, you are asking, why should a person be born, and grow, and become strong, and be happy, work hard, become old, and then die. Why does this happen? Tell me. It is the work of Nature; it is the way in which the universe operates. It is the process of evolution and involution, and we cannot have any say in this matter. The history of the world is a history of Nature, a history of the universe. As you are considering yourself as something outside the world, you are unable to understand what is happening in the world and why.

If you are a part of the world, it is difficult to imagine this situation. You have to feel that you are one with the world. At that time, you will feel that you are thinking like the whole Nature thinking, the whole universe thinking; then, you will not put questions, because it is happening within yourself.

A thing that is happening within yourself does not raise questions. You are raising a question because you think that something is happening outside you, but the world is not outside you. You are also part of the world. Do you understand me? So, you cannot stand outside it.

The whole cosmos is evolving from one stage to another stage, until it reaches the Supreme Absolute. Population, or dying, or war, or whatever it is,—they are all part of the processes of evolution. The meaning of it you cannot understand, unless you identify yourself with the whole cosmic structure, and feel like a cosmic man, rather than Mr. so-and-so, like an individual outside the world. No man can understand the mystery because he thinks that he is outside the world. It is a wrong notion. Your meditation should feel one with the whole creation, and then you will never put a question afterwards.

German Visitor: Thank you, Swamiji.

46

THE SELF IN THE DEEP SLEEP STATE

Dawn: Swamiji, how can I know the Self through my meditation?

SWAMIJI: You are in the state of meditation for the purpose of knowing the Self. Now, what is this Self? You may say that you are sitting there and talking to me; this is the Self, but it is not the Self. The physical body cannot be considered as your real Self, because even when you are fast asleep and not conscious of the body, still you are existing. So, if you can exist even without the consciousness of a body, it follows from that experience that you can exist without the body. That means you are not the body.

This analysis may enable you not to get attached too much to these bodily comforts, physical associations, social engagements, etc. Social, political, material, physical engagements are all connected with this body; if you are really not the physical body, but something more than that, all this drama of life loses its significance. You belong to another world altogether, above and transcendent to the physical world.

What is the condition in which you existed in the state of sleep? You may say that you knew nothing. Maybe, but how did you know that you knew nothing in the state of deep sleep? It is a contradiction in statement. To say that you knew that you did not know does not make much sense. "I know that I did not know anything in the state of deep sleep," is a sentence which has no sense, but yet we make this statement always. This implies that you had a consciousness, but it was covered by some peculiar veil.

You may ask me what this veil is made of, and why it is harassing and covering you like that. This veil is constituted of desires. Every human being has desires. Fulfilled desires produce impressions, and they act like a cloud on consciousness. Unfulfilled desires are still worse. If you know something of psychology, you will know that the mind has various strata—the conscious, subconscious and unconscious level, etc. The unconscious level also is a kind of mental level only. These are all forms taken by unfulfilled desires. This is the reason why you are not really conscious of your existence in the state of deep sleep, and you are only inferring afterwards that you slept, though you did know what it was all about.

With this analysis, you concentrate on the consciousness of your being, minus association with the body. You deeply concentrate, with the concept that you are consciousness; you are not the body, and nothing connected with the body also—just pure consciousness, intelligence, resplendent light.

Consciousness cannot be limited to any particular place, because if consciousness is to be limited, you must be aware that it is limited. In order that consciousness may be aware that it is limited, it should exceed the limit. Otherwise, you can't know that it is limited. Now, this second inference shows that your consciousness is unlimited. It is an astounding conclusion that you are arriving at, that perhaps your essential Self is all-pervading. You are not an ordinary human being.

Of course, this is a brief introduction that I am giving to you on a large subject; for the days you are here, keep in mind that you are consciousness pervading all things, universal in its nature, not this mortal body. You are the immortal self, immortal consciousness. Go on asserting this again and again. Then, you will find, because of the fact of your consciousness being universal, everything will be connected with you, and nothing is excluded from you. Then, all your desires will subside, and some better things will take place; what they are, you will know yourself.

Dawn: But Swamiji, I am having trouble with concentration. My mind is always wandering.

SWAMIJI: At that time you must chant a formula—any formula you like. In India, people chant a formula called a *mantra.* If you don't have a *mantra,* you can chant anything; in regard to whatever you want, you make a formula. In Christian theology, Jesus' name is taken. Loudly they chant it, so that the mind may concentrate. In India, they take the name of Rama, Krishna or any other god, or they chant *Om* several times. Some *mantra* or formula or name of God is resorted to, and chanted loudly in the beginning, until the mind comes back to a point of concentration; when it is concentrated, you may not chant the *mantra* loudly; slowly mutter the name. The best way of controlling the mind is reciting a formula—*Om,* or any other *mantra* you like. Some audible sound must be there.

Otherwise, if that practice is not possible, you gaze on some picture, statue, form, etc., which is projected outside, which you like best, and which you consider as the suitable object for concentration. Keep a picture, and go on looking at it, and close the eyes. When the mind wanders, again open the eyes and go on looking at it. When you look at the object, the mind will not wander here and there, because where the eyes are, there the mind also is. After some time, when you are successful in concentrating on the thing in front, close the eyes and mentally, conceptually, feel the presence of that object. Again when the mind wanders, open the eyes and look at it. This is another method.

Chanting a *mantra* is one method, and concentrating with open eyes on a portrait or picture or some symbol is another method. If that is also not possible, at least study a scripture, read a holy book. Go on reading it again and again, until the mind gets absorbed into that thought. If nothing is possible, chant *Om* for fifteen or twenty minutes at one time. It must be done every day, and after one or two months you will find the mind coming down.

47

KNOWLEDGE AND MATERIAL POWER

SWAMIJI: Even if I explain it, it will not enter the mind, because a fundamental problem will prevent you from understanding it. It will prevent you from even appreciating what I am saying.

How will you remove the fundamental problem? It is the basic defect in thinking, which applies to every human being, barring very rare exceptions. It is that fundamental defect in thinking which has given rise to certain doctrines of psychology called behaviorism, pragmatism, utilitarianism, materialism, etc. You cannot say that they are foolish doctrines, but they are really untenable, for the reason that they are imagining that the mind of a person is subsidiary to the physical body, is an emanation of the body, or a function of the body. This is a fundamental defect in thinking.

If the mind is subsidiary to the body, whatever the mind does is not of any worth,—it has no value. Education comes under mental activity; therefore, it will have no value. A person would like to be a wealthy businessman, rather than a highly educated man. The desire is not for education. You will not like to be a educated genius so much as you would like to be wealthy businessman wielding power. Here is the essence of empirical thinking.

Behaviorist psychology says that the mind is an exudation of the body. As fire is emanating from a match stick, to give an example, the mind is exuding from the body, so that the body is the source, the cause, and the mind is the effect. The effect cannot have so much importance as the cause. So, anything that satisfies the affirmation of the physical body, the ego included,—what you call egoism, self-respect, are all names for the affirmation of the body,—attracts. Physical affirmation includes acquiring wealth and also name and fame. All these are connected .with the physical body only, and supersede any mental or intellectual activity under the wrong notion that the mind is an exudation of the body.

Very learned, highly capable, scientific thinkers of the West were not foolish people, highly intellectual and sharp thinkers, but they have come to the conclusion that the mind is subsidiary to the body at least impliedly. The body is the primary thing; the mind is number two.

This is the fundamental defect in human thinking, as such, from which I cannot say any person is exempt. No human being can be free from this wrong way of thinking; therefore, an academy of education is not succeeding in its aims. Education is not attractive; and therefore, an educated person does not receive so much respect as a millionaire magnate. The magnate has greater force than an educated person. This again is a fundamental defect in thinking, which cannot be rectified unless a divine orientation takes place, a tremendous *shirshasana* of consciousness.

Can anybody believe that mere thinking in the mind is superior to physical existence? Nobody will believe that. Physical existence is more important than merely thinking. What is the good of thinking? This is the reason why meditation also has no effect in the case of many. That meditation which one does becomes useless, because you consider the mind as secondary, and the body as primary. So, in meditation, it is the body that is thinking, rather than anything else!

This is a very serious matter. In meditation, the body starts thinking, rather than something else. Think over this issue. It is the body that is vibrating and thinking, and then you are imagining that you are meditating on God, which is not true. The truth is otherwise; the mind is the cause; the body is the effect. The body has come from the mind; it is not true that the mind has come from the body. This kind of philosophy is wrong, but the body is so strong that it can defy the mind and say, "You keep quiet. I am strong; that is all."

All political activity, all warfare in the world, anything that you see in the world taking place is an activity of the body conditioning the mind. The body is affirming itself. The world does not want a mental genius so much as a physical potentate,—call him a king or a minister. Who is greater, a minister, or a learned man? Tell me who is greater. You cannot answer this question. The answer is a tremendous earthquake. The President of the country is great, or the highly qualified genius is great? Who is great? Now the answer will come.

This answer will decide the fate of your academy of education, also. The answer will decide the fate of all educational institutions, and anything that you call learning. So, your heart will not answer this question. It will say, "It is better that I don't say anything." You should not say anything, because it is very dangerous to offer an answer. You are landing on prohibited zones. The earthly calls can defy even a divine aspiration. The world vies with God.

This is why nobody wants to come for the academy. And, nobody is interested in it. So, I have given the final judgment of the Supreme Court as to why knowledge will not succeed, due to the idiocy of man, which is at the root of all things.

So, I have given you the first academy lecture. I

spoke from the heart. I am not talking as a mere thinker.
My heart is vibrating; it is revolting against this idiocy of
worship of power, social appraisal, money, and physical
strength. The soul is revolting against the very thought of
material superiority. The soul says, "Do you think I have
no strength?"

Do you think the Commander-in-Chief is stronger
than the soul? Don't you think like that? Tell me, honestly. The Commander-in-Chief is stronger than the soul
of man. Is it so, or it is not so? The heart cannot answer
this question. It is revolting inside: "What is the matter?
You are raising a tremendous turmoil before me." It is
afraid to say anything. So, let it go. I won't say anything
further.

The strength of the body nobody can imagine. It has
such strength that it can defy the soul, and push it underneath; and it has already done it, also. That is why the
world is going on like this. The world is going on in the
manner it is going, because the soul has been trampled
under the foot of bodily weight.

It is not easy to know God, however much you may
chant and jump, because the body will say, "I am superior to God. What are you talking?" And even the idea of
God is only an emanation from the body only. That is the
worst part of it,—even the idea of God is an empirical,
non-substantial notion says the German philosopher, Im-
manuel Kant. People like Kant have decried the idea that
thought is reality. He differs from Hegel; Hegel and Kant
are opposites on whether thought is reality, or it is different from reality. If you think something, actually it is
there, or you are only imagining something? According
to Kant, if you think something, it does not mean that it
exists. But Hegel says, if you think, it is there. Why are
they talking in two different ways? That is up to you to
know,—the empirical and metaphysical ways organising

the mind. Kant says that even your idea of God does not prove the existence of God. Mere thinking does not bring any object into existence. This means that thought is not reality. In empirical thinking, the object is outside thought. In metaphysical thinking, which is true meditation, thought is identical with the object. Here is the difference between Kant and Hegel, epistemology and metaphysics.

Then, this question also goes to affect the meditation process. If thinking is not reality, meditation has no effect, unless you bring about a Hegelian transformation, which is contrary to Kant's opinion. What Kant says is correct empirically. The thought in your mind is actually a function of the body only. It is a physical vibration that thinks in the form of thought, and imagines that what it thinks is there already; your idea of God is not God Himself. So goes the great Kant.

Unless the idea becomes God, the meditation will not yield its result. So you must find some way where the idea and God do not stand apart. They are to be identical. *Thought is being; consciousness is existence.* If this is asserted, then meditation will succeed well. If consciousness is not existence, then existence will run away from you, and you will have only consciousness minus existence, which is another way of asserting non-existence.

People will cooperate immediately in going to a club dance, or a moving picture, or a large *bhandara,* great feast. You will see whether people cooperate here or not. What do you say? The most magnificent feast is going to be given to you. Will you come, or will you say, "I am very busy." There is a wonderful dance in the club tonight. Will you come? Or, will you say that you are very busy? At that time, you will not be busy. If I ask for cooperation in the academy, you plead being busy. You cannot find time to go there, teach or attend the classes.

This physical body has such powers, and it can manifest its strength in so many ways that you will not even know what is happening. You will be in a dreamland under the impression that you are a big, matured person.

Sri Krishna Sharmaji: But can one think something which is not existing?

SWAMIJI: It appears as if it is existing. That is another trick of the mind affirming that it is existing, but it is the body that it is existing. It is the body that is saying, "I am existing," and making you feel that something else is existing; otherwise, materialism would not have succeeded so much in this world. Materialism is the ruling law of today, and do you think that everybody in the world is a fool? But, it looks like that. I asked just now whether a highly qualified, learned man is great, or a Commander-in-Chief is great. Who is great? The President of the country is great, or a master genius is great? That is, whether the mind is great or the body is great?

When a President comes, what do you do? And, when a learned man comes, what do you do? See your difference in behaviour. This is the trick of the body. The body says, "I am great," under any circumstance. Though you theoretically accept that the mind is there, but it is *"me"* that is operating, says the body. It is the body that is operating as the mind also. So even the learned man is afraid of the Commander-in-Chief. Then, what happened to that learning? Why is the mind afraid of the body? The whole essence is here. The fear of the Commander-in-Chief, or the President, is the fear the mind has for the body. The mind is afraid of the body; and such a mind is meditating on God. What happens?

Sharmaji: Swamiji, if a learned person is afraid of something, it means he is not still learned.

SWAMIJI: This is the mind that we have. It is that kind of mind only that we are endowed with. The real metaphysical mind is not present, and is not operating. Only the sensory mind is working. The empirical, sensory mind is working; the metaphysical mind is not operating. These two subjects, the metaphysical mind and the empirical mind, have been studied in great detail by two great thinkers of the West, Hegel and Kant. Everybody should understand why they are talking in two different ways. Both are equally great; you cannot say who is inferior. Equally great people are teaching two different things. How is it possible? It is necessary to know it, and this knowledge we are trying to instill into your mind in the academy,—and people say they are too busy!

Even when a man is about to die, he is afraid of what will happen to his financial deposits. "I have kept deposits and gold chains in so many places. What will happen to these?" "My dear boy, I am going. Where are my deposits?" His *prana* is going away. What God will he think at that time?

You require mighty grace of God in order to get over these problems. Or, you may say, the mighty grace of a spiritual master, a *guru*; otherwise, the devil of this body will not allow you to think correctly.

Birgit: But in meditation, don't the two work together? Doesn't meditation work through sensory perceptions, and watching the breath?

SWAMIJI: The mind is not supposed to work through the sense organs, and in terms of the physical body in meditation; but, unfortunately, the mind is slavish to physical existence, and is conditioned by the operations of the physical body, and is afraid of losing itself. Fear of death is the greatest fear. It is not the death of the mind that you are afraid of. You are afraid of the death of the body. Nobody likes to die. Actually, in death, the mind does not die; it continues. But the body will vanish. The fear of death is nothing but the fear of the loss of one's physical existence. That shows the wrong connection of the mind with the body. The mind is independent of the body, actually. It is not a slave of the body. But in ordinary thinking, we imagine that the mind is an emanation of the body, and so the love of body is much more intense than the love of the mind. Meditation or true knowledge is non-empirical identity of thought and being.

48

THE RELATIONSHIP BETWEEN
BRAIN AND MIND

Spanish Visitor: Swamiji, what is the mind, and how do thoughts originate? How do these thoughts originate in our mind?

SWAMIJI: When your personality starts, when you come into being, the mind also comes into being, because you are the mind itself. The one who is speaking to me just now is the mind speaking, and it originates the moment the Mr. so-and-so that you are originates. When did you originate? How did you come into being?

Mind is the consciousness of individuality, and the moment individuality arises, the consciousness of individuality also operates, simultaneously. In early babyhood, it is in a very minute incipient form. When the individuality becomes more and more mature, the consciousness of individuality, which is called the mind, also becomes more and more clear. When you were a little baby, your consciousness of your individuality was very vague. Now it is very clear, as in broad daylight.

So, briefly, the answer to your question is that the mind is the consciousness of individuality, and it is present in every created thing. Even an atom has a kind of mind. It will not allow its individuality to be disrupted by any kind of external interference; it maintains a self-identity. The nucleus of the atom, around which electrons revolve, constitutes the atom's individuality, and that distinguishes one atom from another atom, as one person is different from another person, as one thing is different from another thing.

Everything in the world, right from inanimate matter up to the human level, maintains a self-identity, and it will not become another thing. You are what you are, and you cannot be something else. That self-identity consciousness, which maintains itself and cannot become other than what it is, that is the mind, and it operates universally everywhere in the cosmos. It is not only inside you. When it operates as an individualised affirmation in one particular centre, it becomes an "I" in the case of some person; and when it operates in another person, it is the "I" in another. When it is in an insect, it is the "I" in the insect. When it is in a tree, it maintains an individuality of its own, also; it has its own mind also, in a biological state. It is not so very conscious, but it is biologically alive, in protoplasm and other things.

Essentially, the whole mind is cosmic. It is operating everywhere. There is only one mind, finally. It is called the Cosmic Mind, like an ocean, a sea. And it appears like drops, or waves, or ripples operating individually in different persons, things, individualities, etc.

Whenever there is a consciousness of individuality, of any person or any thing, the mind at once starts operating, because mind and consciousness of individuality mean one and the same thing. If anyone is conscious that one exists as an individual, that consciousness is called the mind. So, the origin of individuality is the same as the origin of the mind.

How the individuality arose is a cosmic question. It is a question of cosmology and creation, and there we go beyond psychology. Your question is partly a psychological question, but when you go deep, it becomes a cosmological question of creation itself; it is very deep, farther than how the mind works. Then, you have to know how the individuality has started at all. There, we go beyond ordinary human concepts of experience. This is my answer to your question.

Spanish Visitor: Thank you, Swamiji.

SWAMIJI: They say the mind is inside the brain. From where did the brain come? Their idea also is that the mind is different from the brain.

Spanish Visitor: Yes. They say so.

SWAMIJI: Is the mind touching the brain, or is it separate from the brain? What is the relationship between the mind and the brain? What is the brain made of? What is the mind made of? You see, you have already accepted that they are two things.

Spanish Visitor: Yes.

SWAMIJI: So, you may say that the brain is made of material stuff. Is the mind also made of material stuff? Or, is it made of something else? Let the scientists answer this question. If it is made of a different stuff, what is that substance out of which it is made? If it is made of the same stuff as the brain, it becomes as material as the brain; then, it cannot be conscious, because matter is not conscious of itself. So, how is it that you are conscious, if the mind also is made up of matter only? Is matter aware of itself? Matter requires another thing for it to be known. Matter cannot know matter; the non-matter only knows the existence of matter, so we must say that the mind is made of non-matter. If it is non-matter, what is that non-matter? What is it made of?

They are making a muddle. Their idea is not correct. They are not two different things. If the mind and brain were two different things, you would be feeling that you are two persons, like a split personality. But do you feel that you are two persons? You are one whole, integrated, solid being. How did this consciousness arise, if there are two things operating in your personality? Are you two fractions put together? Do you feel that you are a dual individual? Or, do you feel that you are a total whole? What do you say?

Spanish Visitor: I feel like a total.

SWAMIJI: Then, how did these two things come there? You cannot be made of two things, and then feel that you are one. It is impossible, so there is a mistake in the concept of the mind being inside the brain. It is not so. It is a different thing altogether. The mind is not inside the brain.

Actually, the brain is a solidified form of the mind itself; as water looks like ice, the mind looks like the brain, and the body. That is why you are feeling that you are one integrated whole; otherwise, you would have been feeling that you are a split personality,—some matter, and some non-matter. You would never be happy for one second, if you are a split personality. The identity consciousness, and the total consciousness that you feel in you, is possible only if there is no distinction vitally between mind and matter. It is one thing appearing as two things. You are from Spain. There was a great philosopher in your country called Spinoza. Have you heard of Spinoza?

Spanish Visitor: Yes.

SWAMIJI: Do you know what he writes? You have not read him. You are a philosopher?

Spanish Visitor: I am not a philosopher, actually.

SWAMIJI: You are teaching philosophy? Spinoza says that mind and matter are like two wings of a bird. The bird is the most important thing; if the bird is not there, the wings will not be there. So, I told you that the mind is vitally inseparable from the brain or matter; but actually, as Spinoza, Plato or Aristotle, or Indian thinkers, mystics, etc., would say, it is one Universal Substance that appears as thought and matter. This is what Spinoza will tell you. And, you are actually Universal Substance, and not either this or that. Due to some peculiar phenomenon that has arisen in the act of creation itself, you have separated yourself from the Cosmic Substance, and are looking like an individual, isolated from the Cosmic Substance.

The Ultimate Reality is Substance, according to Spinoza. You may call It God, if you like. He calls It the Universal Substance, and It is conscious of Itself. That Self-consciousness of Universal Substance is called God, and you are inseparable from It, ultimately. But in the act of creation, due to the interference of space and time, this separation consciousness has arisen, unfortunately, and each part of the Universal Substance began to assert itself as something totally different from It.

A part of that mind gets separated from the total whole; It asserts itself as I am so-and-so, even down to the insects and the atoms. And, then that consciousness of isolatedness from the Cosmic Substance solidifies itself into sense organs, and instruments of action,—called the body, the brain, the heart, the lungs, and so many things. So, actually, I am slowly, unconsciously, jumping into a cosmological subject, which I wanted to avoid.

You are then a cosmic being, basically, and if you know this, you shall be free. You shall have no problems. This is another way of saying that your consciousness is a part of God-consciousness.

Spanish Visitor: And to be aware of that is through meditation?

SWAMIJI: It is through meditation, and great self-restraint—control of the sense organs, and meditation correctly practiced under the guidance of a competent person.

Spanish Visitor: There is a lot of confusion about meditation.

SWAMIJI: Yes, I know. It has to be carefully conducted, and it is not an easy thing. In the beginning, it looks easy; afterwards, it becomes a little difficult. It requires a competent teacher in the case of every person.

49

THE HIGHER REALITY AND THE ETERNAL IMPULSES

Dr. Goel: The mundane things also go in the Higher Self?

SWAMIJI: By accepting that the Higher Self includes all these mundane things, so that you need not have to ask for mundane things separately, it includes whatever you want, even your train fare is included in that, so, why are you worrying about these little things, when it is already there? The idea of avoiding something is painful, but I am not telling you to avoid anything. Just realise that what is here, is also there, in a better way.

Dr. Goel: What is here, is also there.

SWAMIJI: So, why should you go here, when it is already there? And it is in a larger dimension that you will get it there; it is only a fraction you will get here. That is the original; this is a reflection. So, why do you want a reflection, when the original is ready there?

Dr. Goel: So, that is why I always want to go in the Higher Self.

SWAMIJI: If you want it, it will come. There is no qualification necessary, except wanting it. That is the only qualification. If it is not wanted, it will not come. It comes when it is wanted,—but wanted wholly, not a little.

If I like you only for some time what kind of statement is it? Is there any sense or meaning in it? Like that, you tell God, also: "For some time I like you, because I want some help from you; otherwise, I can manage myself." What kind of person are you?

Dr. Goel: Too much selfishness is there.

SWAMIJI: "When I want something from you, I like you. When I have nothing to do with you, well, you mind your business." This kind of thing you tell to God, also.

Dr. Goel: Yes. Selfishness is there.

SWAMIJI: Yes, we sell a lot of fish. How much fish will you sell?

Dr. Goel: I want all my thoughts always to be in the Infinite, in tune with the Almighty.

SWAMIJI: When you can find everything there, why should you have problems? The problem is that you cannot believe that everything can be found there. "The heart has a reason which reason does not know," is an old saying. So, whatever you may say, the heart will say, "Do not be too optimistic. Be cautious." Like that, it will tell from inside. "After all, you are going to some unknown place. Be cautious." So, there is a hesitancy in going there.

If you say everything is there, yes, I understand; but, still the heart has a reason which reason does not know. It will whisper something: "Don't be too optimistic; don't be foolish; go slow." All this, it will tell. So, what to do? Whose voice are you going to listen to?

And the world will tell you, "I have taken care of you for so many years, and now what is your idea of kicking me out, and going like that? Are you ungrateful? What kind of person are you? So many people have protected you and taken care of you, and made you what you are, and you will simply throw them out, and go somewhere? Is this a gentlemanly attitude?" This it will tell from within.

A hundred questions will come from inside. One by one, they will come. They do not come always together; sometimes, finally, one questions comes: "It is a hopeless thing, a hopeless affair; nothing has come, and nothing may come, also." This trouble also may arise from inside.

There are some intelligent lawyers in the court. Before any question is raised by the other party, they can visualise what questions will arise. All the questions they themselves will raise, as can be put by the opposite party, so that the other one has nothing to say, and they will furnish the answer also subsequently. If he is a very able lawyer, he can already assume what questions can arise, contravening his position, and answer them then and there. The other party will then have the mouth shut.

Sankaracharya's commentaries are highly polemical. "If you say like that, this is the answer to you. But you may counteract and say this is wrong; for that, I rebut like this."

It has to be clear what questions will arise. They are only two or three questions the mind has generally, and these manifest as hundreds, as light becomes manifold by passing through a prism. Questions are only two or three, basically. All of humanity has only two or three questions, but it appears to be manifold because of this prism of the ego which converts the issues into a manifold form, and then tantalises, and troubles you.

Place one image, and then keep two glasses on both sides. Then you will see millions of images reflected on both sides. Only one is there, but it looks like millions; likewise, only one desire is there, finally. But it looks like a hundredfold, because it passes through the ego, which is the peculiar medium that deflects a centrality of aspiration, and makes it appear as manifold.

Dr. Goel: You have said that nothing exists outside;

everything is in you. How can we convince ourselves that nothing exists?

SWAMIJI: Who are the "ourselves"? Where are they? You have again defeated your own self by saying, "Nothing exists outside, but I am existing." You have already asserted that you are existing outside, and then you say, at the same time, that nothing exists outside. Thus, your statement is self-contradictory. If nothing is outside, you also do not exist; then, why are you wanting to convince yourself? That means that you are still existing as an outside object.

You are, somehow, by the back door, coming to the same point. By the front side, you say it is not there; by the back side, I am here. So, what is the purpose? It is back-door entry. You close the door from the front, and behind you open it. This is what you are doing.

Dr. Goel: That is what happens in life.

SWAMIJI: No, that is no good. Back-door entry is no good. Dr. Jekyll and Mr. Hyde are the two friends you have. Sometimes this man speaks, and sometimes that man speaks. You don't know what to make out.

Dr. Goel: Yes, that is correct. That is the problem of life.

SWAMIJI: Two voices will be telling you two different things, like one man with two wives. They will quarrel, and then say different things, and the man has to hide, afterwards. He has to run away from there. So, likewise, these two friends are telling you two things. Sometimes this looks all right, and sometimes that looks all right, according to your mood and requirement and the voice heard from within.

Dr. Goel: But what is the solution? That is the problem.

SWAMIJI: Already you have given the solution. That which you want is everywhere; therefore, you are also there. Hence, you should not raise a question. If you raise a question, you are asserting your externality still, and then your assertion that externality does not exist gets defeated. The question defeats itself.

Andrea: Swamiji, what are those two basic questions?

SWAMIJI: I did not want to tell all these things, but you are a very clever person. You understood what I said. You want to know everything before you leave this place.

Andrea: Yes.

SWAMIJI: Do you want to know everything?

Andrea: Yes.

SWAMIJI: Very good. They say everything should not be told at once. There are certain things which are not supposed to be told suddenly. They touch the very core of the personality of an individual, and such things are discussed only between a *guru* and a disciple; otherwise it will go over the heads of people, or will be misconstrued.

The basic desire is to exist, but that existence is conditioned by various other associations. The primary desire is to exist only: "If everything goes, may I exist." Survival is the basic desire. If survival itself is threatened, then other desires go, automatically. When a person is in water, and goes inside, will he ask for some profession, and a higher salary? Will he want a bungalow? Will he talk all that? He is inside the water. Then what happened to that desire for a bungalow, and salary, and all that? Why has it gone away at that time, when it was there previously?

That means the other desires are redundant, and auxiliary to the basic question of survival. You want to exist, and this basic instinct of existence, survival, has certain tentacles, ramifications, expressions: to possess things as much as possible. You need possessions, what you call wealth, generally. By the desire for wealth, you try to convince yourself that you are secure in this world.

People feel secure when their possessions are large. Whether they are justified in thinking like that or not is a different matter. There is always a hunger for larger and larger possessions because of the feeling attached to it that it will be a great security for the person. If the possessions are not there, security goes. But, simultaneously, there is another feeling that this body will not survive eternally.

There are two desires simultaneously working: a desire not to die, and a feeling that death will take place certainly. Who wants to die? Nobody. And who will believe that tomorrow death will come? Nobody. Nobody will believe that death will be tomorrow. Everybody will say that it cannot be tomorrow, it will be a little later on. We push it as much as possible. Simultaneously, together with this peculiar hope that death will not occur, there is a feeling that death will certainly come. Thus, there is a contradictory clash of feelings about one point.

Because of the feeling that death will not occur, we go on purchasing land, and putting investments in the bank, and then building bungalows, and having estates, and conquering kingdoms. Why do you do that, if the certainty is that tomorrow is the last day? The foolish feeling is there that tomorrow will not be the last day,— "I'll survive." Who told you that you will survive? This is a jugglery of the mind.

If this foolish conviction was not there, nobody would do anything in this world. People are very busy doing all kinds of things, because they never think that tomorrow is the last day,—it may be after fifty years. Simultaneously, there is a fear that death may come.

There is also a necessity felt by the ego to perpetuate itself. Self-preservation and self-reproduction,—these are the two basic instincts. We want to preserve ourselves, somehow, by the accumulation of wealth, riches, and all that, as I mentioned to you. But the other feeling that one day death will come creates a fear in the ego, and so the ego wants to see that it continues; and it wants to continue in a very foolish way, through progeny.

That is why there is so much pressure of this particular urge. The desire to continue for all time is actually the pressure of eternity in you. The eternal masquerades in a wrong way in the form of a desire for progeny. That is why the sexual urge is very strong. And there is also a desire to see that you are secure; for that, another foolish desire is added to it by accumulating wealth, property, this, that, etc. So, two foolishnesses are there which catch hold of a person perennially.

The world is living an idiotic life, under the impression that the everything is fine. This is why I do not want to talk about these matters. It has got further implications, so I told you briefly something in answer to your question. It is a very deep subject.

Andrea: Thank you very much.

American Visitor: This love that just keeps spilling out and overflowing, how it can be limited in any way, and how any kind of conditions can be put on it.

SWAMIJI: If you want to put conditions, you can put, but if you don't want to put conditions, it need not be conditioned. It depends upon your will. If you want to love only certain things, and not all things, it is conditioned love, but if you can love everything equally, that is unconditioned. It is up to you to decide.

American Visitor: I go with unconditional love.

SWAMIJI: Think over it properly. Can you love God and the devil equally?

American Visitor: There is no devil.

SWAMIJI: The very idea that you are existing is contrary to the Ultimate Reality. Who told you that you are existing separately? That itself is the beginning of the problem. You may not call it the devil, but it is something contrary to God's existence. You are not thinking that only one thing exists. You are also thinking that you are also existing. And you are making a statement about something; that creates duality. When you speak, you are not speaking about yourself, you are speaking about something else. That "something" and yourself create a duality.

We have to be cautious in the conducting of our thoughts. At different times we feel different things. At different stages of evolution, we have different types of experience. Sometimes we feel everything can be done by us, we don't require anybody's help. At other times we feel that nothing can be done by us,—everything is spontaneously taking place. Both these feelings will arise in your mind at different times.

There are people who sometimes feel that everything is hopeless: You can't do anything in this world. That dejected despondency can also arise in certain conditions of mind. It is not that everybody will feel like that. There are conditions, circumstances, which may create such feelings. Those who have lost everything, all relations have died, their own life is at stake,—what do they feel at that time? You ask that person. They will not even believe that there is such a thing called justice in the world. Though they may not be right in thinking so, the tragedy in which they are placed will make them feel like that. They curse God Himself. "Such a God exists that everything has gone from me, and I myself am not secure."

Does God exist? Draupadi, in the Mahabharata puts such a question. I don't know if you know Draupadi's story. It is an interesting epic of India. She cursed God

Himself. "I don't know whether such a God exists Who has landed us in this tragedy," she cried. That is the condition where the mind breaks, and cannot tolerate the experiences through which it is passing. There are experiences which are intolerable, and many people pass through it as if through pangs of death.

Everybody is not born with a silver spoon in the mouth. There are different experiences which anyone can expect. Great kings have been pounded to dust, empires have become one with the earth. Potentates who ruled the earth, and thought that they were masters of all things, have gone into thin air. Why do things happen like that? Is it not a tragedy?

People cannot swallow all these things. They don't know what is happening. Then war takes place, and nobody knows what will happen as a consequence. Who goes? Who comes? Nobody knows. Now, who is doing all this?

Only a person who is involved in it will know what feeling will arise at that time. You must be in the thick of a tragic war, and then you will see what you feel at that time. When you are far away from it, your thought is a different thing.

Suppose a person is a prisoner of war and is thrown in a concentration camp. What will he feel at that time? Will he believe in God at that time? He may or may not. It shows the conditions through which the mind has to pass, and every condition it cannot swallow. Certain things it can, certain things it cannot; it breaks.

It is a great thing for a person to expect everything in the world; even the worst you have to expect, so that when it comes you are not surprised. You should not say, "Oh, this I never expected." There is nothing which you cannot expect, even the worst, hell itself,—let it come. Even that, you are expecting. Because you are expecting it already, you can face it. But if it comes as a surprise, then you don't know how to handle it.

As we are not omniscient, as our personality is not connected to every event in the whole cosmos, we cannot know what will happen at what time. The reason is, we are outside the operating medium.

We many a time feel that certain things should happen; also, simultaneously, we feel that certain things should not happen. We have got dual feelings there, also. Why should we say that certain things should not happen? We have created a duality in creation itself, because those things which we do not want to happen are considered unpalatable, and even destructive to our egoistic personality, our individuality, our so-called dear body and mind. There are things which are contrary to its welfare, and they are called bad things, and those which are contributory to its pleasure, we call good things. Our idea of good and bad is connected with our personality's reception of it,—how we receive it.

All people cannot happily pass through the various tests which perhaps God will inflict upon us one day or the other, as a punishment to the ego, which is asserting itself. Our ego is the demon. It is the Lucifer, if at all there is any such thing as that. The affirmation of individuality is the Lucifer, and God has thrown him upside down, with head below and legs up; that is how we are seeing things. We see the outside as inside, the inside as outside. This is what has happened to every one of us.

The world is not outside us; yet, we are seeing it as outside. This is the punishment that is meted out to us by God: "You will see everything topsy turvy, you fellows, because you have asserted yourself as independent of Me. Go! I will place a flaming sword at the gate of heaven, so that you cannot enter it." This is the story of the ego, an opposite of God.

50

WHAT IS YOGA?

Visitor: Swamiji, what is your definition of Yoga?

SWAMIJI: Yoga, finally, means meditation; it is an exercise of the mind. It is also an exercise of the body, but it is basically an exercise of the mind. It is more a system of thinking, than a method of physically doing something. Yoga is not doing something, but thinking something, which incidentally means being something in yourself, because what you are is mainly what you think. Your being and your thought cannot be separated. Whatever you are, that starts operating through the mind as a thinking process. Your mind and you are inseparable things; you yourself are the mind.

What happens to your body is not so important as what happens to your mind. Your happiness and unhappiness depend more on the condition of your mind than on the condition of your body. Even if your body is robust and very healthy, you can become unhappy in one second by a different kind of thinking entering into your mind. So physical health alone does not mean happiness. To make you unhappy, one disturbing thought is sufficient. It will shake up all the balance of things.

Your basic root being the thought process, more importance has to be given to the art of thinking than just to physical exercise. I don't say physical exercise is unnecessary. It is necessary, but that is not the whole of it. You are more than the body, as you know very well. Your feelings and emotions, your understandings and your thoughts are the vital issues in your life much more than your physical appearance.

I am coming to the point that Yoga is the art of channeling the mind in a particular given direction. The difficulty is that you must know what that direction is. The mind has to be established and made to operate in a given direction. What is that direction? Here is the main question. Yoga starts with the answer to this question: What am I to think?

It is not easy to understand what life is. It is not merely what you are; it is also what relationships obtain between you and other people. That also is a part of your life. Your life is not only inside the body; it is connected with outside people also, which have an impact upon you. That also is you only. Any kind of thing which can have an impact upon you is you, so social relation is yourself only. So, you are not merely an individual mental and physical personality, you are also a social personality. Society can make you or unmake you sometimes, apart from what happens to the body and mind. It is not merely that. There is something more about you.

A wind that blows strongly, a torrent of flood from the skies, tremendous heat or cold, also can affect you. That is another kind of relationship you have got with physical nature, so just imagine how complicated your personality is. You are not just one person like that. It is a wrong notion.

Firstly, I told you that you are a body doing exercises. Then, I am telling you that you are also a mind, emotion, understanding, etc. Then, I said that also is not complete—you have a social relation and entire humanity can affect you. Now I am telling you that furthermore, the whole nature can affect you. Even the sun shining in the sky has something to tell you; it can do or undo anything—such is the power of the sun. Finally, last but not

least, God has something to tell you. He is the Creator of
the universe.

So in an adjustment of your personality in this vari-
egated direction (physical, mental, emotional, social, cosmological, natural and divine), all these are brought
together into a systematic arrangement of organic completeness, so that you feel that you are a huge cosmic individual.

This idea that you are a person has to go away. You
are something larger than what you think you are. If you
appreciate that, it is a great advance that you have made
in correcting your life. It is the first step in Yoga and if it
continues, your happiness will be untold. You will feel
everybody protects you. Society, God, your mind, and nature will all be your friends. You will be living in a world
of friends. This is the way you can be happy.

51

METHODIST MINISTERS

Mike: What is the relationship between contemplation and action?

SWAMIJI: There is the subtle feeling of difference between the two. If you say that they are not different, that they are identical, then there is no question of any kind. Do you think that they are two different things? Is meditation one occupation, and action another occupation? If that is the case, there is no harmony between the two, and there is definitely a contradiction; but if the two are only two names for one and the same thing, then the question does not arise in doing both things, because they are not two things.

The right hand and the left hand do two different things; I can write with my right hand, and lift an object with the left hand. They are two different actions, isn't it? But, they are your actions, and therefore, they are not two different actions. Though apparently lifting an object and writing with the hand are not identical actions,—they are totally contrary, you may say,—yet, it is you who are doing it. Therefore, there is no difference between two different types of activity,—call it meditation, call it social service, or anything you like.

All this hinges, finally, upon the relationship between yourself and the social atmosphere outside. Are you a totally independent individual seeking the salvation of yourself, which, of course, is a most worthwhile thing; or, are you also connected with society, and not totally independent of society, in which case, you have a duty towards society?

Here is a question of the relationship between the individual and society. In what way are you connected to society? You may say you have no duty towards society: "I am myself; in what way am I connected with the world? I can do whatever I like." Each one is independent. You can just now go that way, and he can go this way, so what connection is there between you? Yet, there seems to be a connection with even the trees and mountains. You cannot say that the trees, the mountains, the sun, the moon, and the stars are disconnected from you.

You breathe the air of the atmosphere; are you connected to the air, or are you independent? You live in sunlight, without which you will perish; are you connected with the sun and the moon? You drink the water which God has given to you; are you connected to the water, or independent of water? You require heat; are you connected with heat, or totally independent? You want space to live; are you independent of space, or connected to space?

So, are you independent at all, in any sense? Or, are you cosmically involved in a network of relations with the whole of creation, in which case, call it meditation, call it work, do anything, and it is within the framework of the whole of creation. What do you say?

Mike: I understand you to be saying that contemplation and action are two aspects of a deeper reality, the same thing, and we certainly have found that to be true in our own life, and in our desire to develop our own spiritual life, and to help others do so.

SWAMIJI: Inasmuch as you are entwined with the cosmical setup, there is no such thing as "your own." That word has no meaning. "My own" does not apply to the facts operating in the world. You are connected organically with the entire creational setup, so there is no such thing as "my own." This "my own" will mean the universal whole. All of creation is with you. God has created you, and God has created the world, and not kept you apart from the world. As you are not outside the world, there is no contradiction of any kind in your life, if we think of it deeply. Seeking God, and seeking the peace of society, do not seem to be two things because, if at all you are doing anything, you are doing it within the campus of God's creation.

So, there is no such thing as "my own"—"my salvation." When you seek salvation, you must understand the implications of it. The whole thing comes up with you, with which you are connected. An organism cannot be split into two parts, and the universe is an organism as is your body, as is society, as is a family relation, as is anything. The whole of reality is an organism which cannot be split into parts.

So, when you do one thing, you have done other things, also, at the same time. Do you remember the old word of a poet, "When you touch a flower in the garden, you have disturbed the stars in heaven"? So, there is no difference between contemplation and action. There is no difference between you and me, also, finally.

Here is a great vista before us of what true spiritual life is. It is Godly life, which cannot be separated from earthly life, social life, or any kind of life. All life is one, so whenever you do anything, it looks as if the whole world is doing it through you. You are living a total life, and not a personal life. Personal satisfaction, personal salvation, all these words do not carry much meaning in the setup of the total organism of the cosmos. If God is a whole, His creation, also, is a whole, and you are equally a whole. So, fractions, fragmentations, do not exist here. This is, you may say, a cosmic, holistic thinking. So, what is your question? I have said something, and I think I have answered your question, from my point of view.

Alan: I think that we are of the mind that in the Christian tradition, we are discovering anew, maybe, or for the first time, the unity of all of creation, in the sense that we are truly connected, not only with our fellow humans, but with all of creation; and I think for myself, I am coming to understand that out of our tradition, this is what has been best in our tradition, but at times has been lost.

SWAMIJI: What is lost?

Alan: The unity of creation. The awareness...

SWAMIJI: You have lost the consciousness of unity.

Alan: Yes. The awareness that we are truly connected with one another.

SWAMIJI: Yes. We have, therefore, to revive our consciousness of the fact of unity of existence, overcoming the unfortunate limitation consciousness, finitude consciousness, selfish consciousness, physical consciousness, and all that. This, I think, is how we can really worship God. To think like God would be the greatest worship, and perhaps to act, also, as God would act. What do you say?

Mike: The great teacher in our tradition was Jesus, who said, "Love your neighbour as yourself."

SWAMIJI: Why love? You are inseparable from the neighbour. This is much more than love, actually. Your self is implanted in the self of the neighbour. The Self of God is present everywhere, so it is not merely love. It is much more than that. You have to be more friendly with a person than you would like in a social manner,—love another person in a condescending manner. You are not condescending in your love. It is the soul communing itself with another soul, so it is much more than a social teaching. It is a spiritual gospel. It is a divine teaching.

Alan: We also have an expression in our tradition, from one of the disciples of Jesus, who encourages people to put on the mind of Christ,—to find unity with the Christ within.

SWAMIJI: If we can think as Christ thought, then there would be no problem, afterwards. We have to know what he thought, and you think like that. Let us see. Then, no problem will come to you.

Mike: Thank you.

SWAMIJI: Thank you very much. God bless you. We had a very wonderful *satsanga*. *Satsanga* means a holy gathering. We have actually thought of God just now, and I think He should be pleased with us.

52

WHO IS YOUR NEIGHBOUR?

Visitor: We feel it is a privilege to be visiting your country and meeting you and your friends. We like being here.

SWAMIJI: It is a privilege to please God, in whatever manner it is possible.

Bruce (New Zealand): I suppose there are many ways.

SWAMIJI: Yes, so many ways. There are millions of ways. As God has millions of facets of expression, there are millions of ways of serving Him also which, I believe, is going to satisfy God. It is not easy to satisfy Him. He is a difficult Person, but once you know the art of satisfying Him, then you are scot-free. There is no problem, afterwards.

Bruce: That is hard, not easy. For people to come here, as these people are, as well as us, does it do good for humanity that all of us should come here?

SWAMIJI: It is better for you to ask the people seated here. You ask them, "Is it good for you to sit here, instead of going to the market place and doing some service to the shopkeepers?"

Bruce: But is it good for humanity that we should come here?

SWAMIJI: The shopkeepers are also a part of humanity, so if you can make people happy in any way, it is equal to doing service to humanity. Humanity does not necessarily mean an ocean of people. Even if you serve two people, it is serving humanity, and if you can enlarge the dimension of it, quite all right. Each one's heart will know what is good, and the heart decides the destiny of the person. One person cannot instruct another person on what is good.

Each one says "it is good." The tiger thinks it is good to eat a cow. And, a dacoit thinks it is good to rob; a politician thinks it is good to make profit by the exploitation of the masses. Every person has got his own idea of goodness. The whole point is, "What is goodness?" Then, it answers every question.

It is good to do good things. It may be service of humanity; it may not be service of humanity, it may be anything. Doing the proper thing is the good thing, but what is the good thing? This decides and answers all your questions. Let anybody say what is good, and what is not good. The whole philosophy, the entire religion of mankind is summed up in this question: What is good? Everybody pursues what is good, but what is good? What are they pursuing? Let each one's heart open up and answer this question: What do you mean by "good"? And you will pursue it.

It can be service of God, service of man, service of animals, service of trees and plants, or service of anything. All these come under the question of what is good. Let anybody seated here tell me what is good. Then, you will have no problems if the answer to this question has come. Everybody has shut the mouth. The mouth cannot open because if you say something, you are likely to get caught up by some difficulty afterwards. So, it is better not to say anything, and do what you think is good. Whether it is good or not, if you think it is good, do it.

Indian Visitor: Sir, whatever the scriptures say, that is good.

SWAMIJI: Whatever your heart says, that is good, the scriptures apart. Let the scriptures say anything; what does it matter? You cannot do something against your conscience. Though the scriptures may say that, your conscience may say, "No, no. This is not for me."

If the scripture says the hand must be cut off because you have stolen a pencil; this is also one law. Do you agree with it? Or, do you bury a person neck-deep, and stone him afterwards, for some mistake he has committed? Is it all right, because it is mentioned somewhere? What do you say?

Indian Visitor: To me, it seems, those are man-made scriptures.

SWAMIJI: That is another way of saying that we should not bother about scriptures. We shall not think of them. Let the scriptures be there. What do *we* say? What do *you* say? What does your *heart* say?

Every government in the world has a defense ministry to protect itself from onslaught. There is no necessity for a defense ministry unless there is somebody to attack. But, that particular area, from which attack is expected, also has a defense ministry. There is no country which maintains an offense ministry. If nobody is going to offend, why do you want a defense ministry? This has some connection with the answer to your question.

Is it good to have a defense ministry because you are distrusting a neighbour? Unless you distrust your neighbour, a defense ministry is not necessary. This goes against the law, "Love thy neighbour as thyself." Where is the love for your neighbour if you are maintaining defense forces? Everybody is doing that. There is not one area of the world which is free from this difficulty. Is it good to distrust your neighbour, and always be afraid of the neighbour? If you say it is not proper, there is no one in the world who does a proper thing. Everyone is fraught with fear, not of animals, snakes, scorpions, and tigers. It is man fearing man.

You were talking of service of humanity. You are serving the very same humanity of whom you are afraid, and you have to manufacture guns, and all that, to protect yourself against people. You have to protect yourself from human beings only, not from tigers, because they do not come and attack you. It is your brother who is going to attack you, and so you want to keep police, and army.

You have fear of the very same person whom you are going to serve. There is a contradiction in the very psyche, in the thought itself. The mind says, "Be careful about this person," But, at the same time, the mind says, "Serve that person." Now, what kind of thought is this? Who is your neighbour?

Bruce: The Christian scriptures says every man is your neighbour.

SWAMIJI: "Neighbour" is a word in the English language, which grammatically means "that which is adjacent to you." That which is very near you is your neighbour. Now, the nearest thing, I think, is the very earth on which you are sitting. This earth, this floor on which you are squatting, is touching you. The earth itself is the dearest and nearest neighbour. And, this earth happens to be one of the planets, among many others revolving around the sun, who worship the sun as their soul.

Inasmuch as the nearest and dearest neighbour, which is the very earth on which we are sitting, is considering the sun as the dearest and nearest neighbour, the sun then would become our neighbour. The sun in the sky is a very good person! Without him, we would not breathe. And the sun belongs to the entire galaxies. The galaxies will have something to say about the very organisation of the solar system; and the galaxies are controlled by the vaster space-time complex. So, who is your neighbour,—the entire space and time, all creation, living and non-living, visible and non-visible, that which you can understand, and that which you cannot understand.

The very centre of the cosmos becomes the nearest neighbour of yours. It may look that the centre is far away, millions and millions of light years away, but the centre is everywhere, with circumference nowhere as we are told. You are just sitting on the centre of the cosmos. That is your dearest neighbour. Then, where are we actually sitting? What is our duty in this context? These are questions, to which an answer has to come; not from me, but from the heart of each and every person.

Sometimes, when a person is about to pass away, he is breathing his last breath, he may know what is his duty much better than when he was quite all right. When the last breath is being breathed, one will know what the duty is at that time. What will you think at that time, when you are about to leave this world? You will know who your neighbour is at that time, who will come to your aid immediately.

He is your neighbour who will come to your help when you are breathing your last breath; tell me who that friend is. All other friends will desert you, but some friend is there, who will come to help you even at that moment. A friend in need is a friend indeed; but your need is this: your breath is passing away. Who will help you at that time? But, there is somebody, whom we forget completely, due to the egoism of human nature. Then, you will know what your duty is, who your neighbour is.

The good thing is that which will enable you to love that dearest neighbour of yours, who will come to your aid when you are in need. A sidelight I have thrown on this answer to what is good. It is good to love your neighbour, and you find out who your neighbour is.

53

WAR

Israeli Visitor: What about war?

SWAMIJI: If you are a resident of Iraq, you will feel that the United States is doing some aggression, and it is very bad. Suppose you are a resident of America; you may feel that Mr. Bush is right, provided you are in sympathy with him.

It is a question of consequence, finally. An act can be judged from the possible consequence of doing it, or not doing it. If you do not do anything, what is the consequence? If you do, what is the consequence? Use your discretion, as a statesman. Statesmen are those who can visualise the future by inference drawn from present conditions. They do not take any action suddenly without proper thought. If you take some steps, what will be the consequence, finally? And, if you do not do anything, what will be the consequence? You weigh these two consequences, and see which is proper.

Israeli Visitor: Can you feel the result when you weigh the worth in one of these sides,—"is it still worthwhile"?

SWAMIJI: As you say, war is never good. Nobody will say that war is good, but then, why do people start war, if it is not good? Everybody, even a person who starts war, knows that it is not good. Why does he embark upon it? He feels that if he does not engage in war, maybe it will be worse still. From bad, it may becomes worse. He may be right or wrong; that is a different matter. If you don't wage war, it will be worse; so wage war, and it is bad. So, it is a choice between bad and worse; the worse is not good, so bad is better. This is how they choose.

We cannot discuss this just now, as we are not sitting in the field and seeing anything, and also cannot directly connect ourselves to it. Our judgments will be only theoretical. You are asking me a theoretical question, without knowing the actual implications of the issues at hand.

Israeli Visitor: I have been living in a country that has many wars, and this war, for instance, for my country—I come from Israel—if it was not America fighting, I know it would be my country fighting this war, some other time. But I try not to look only from this point of view, because I know that this is very conditional, because I am Israeli.

SWAMIJI: You see, you are Israeli, yes. You will certainly wish that Israel should be protected, and somebody should not attack, isn't it?

Israeli Visitor: Yes, it is true.

SWAMIJI: What will you do to protect yourself?

Israeli Visitor: The question is, is protecting myself is more important than having other people in safety?

SWAMIJI: Other people's safety also is necessary. That is, of course, you do not want to go and kill somebody, but your country also should be protected. How will you protect your country, then? What is the method?

Israeli Visitor: Some people say to protect, you have to attack; some people say...

SWAMIJI: Generally, all countries have forces which are called defense forces, but nobody has offense forces. Do you know what offense is?

Israeli Visitor: To attack.

SWAMIJI: There are defense ministers, and all that.

You do not call them offense ministers. Why should you defend, unless somebody offends? Now, who is there to offend? Nobody offends, because everybody is defending only. What do you say? Everybody has a defense ministry; no offense ministry. But somebody should be offending; only then, you want to defend. But nobody says they are offending,—they are only defending. Now, what is the point? Who is the offender?

Israeli Visitor: True.

SWAMIJI: But, one does not say like that. The man whom you say is offending will say he is not doing like that, but that he is only defending himself against possible trouble. He wants to defend himself against future trouble, though it looks like offending. This is what he will say, though you may say that he has made a mistake and that he is offending.

You place yourself in the position of the leader of the country, and then think through that mind. What will you do at that time? That is the answer to your question. Suppose I am the head of this particular country; what will I do at that time? How will my mind work? Now, you are judging somebody else. That is no good. You judge yourself first, as the person involved in it,—at that time, what would you do? Then, you will see that your heart will tell what is good for you.

Life is a mutual anabolic and catabolic activity, as is the case with one's own body. Creation and destruction are going on simultaneously without a time-gap in every organism for the purpose of a higher form of survival. This is so in humanity as well as Nature as a whole.

54

WHO IS A GURU?

Rita: What is the role of a guru?

SWAMIJI: Whoever guides you is a *guru*. Whomever you consider as superior to you, from whom you can receive blessing and guidance, is a *guru*. As things are not clear to your mind, naturally you have to approach somebody who can guide you. If everything is clear to you, then you need not approach anybody. The *guru* is necessary as long as things are not completely clear.

Rita: What is the relationship between the guru and the disciple?

SWAMIJI: A *guru* is one who initiates a person into the technique of God-realisation and guides that student continuously as long as it is necessary for the purpose of carrying on this technique of meditation for God-realisation. The relationship is as between a teacher and a student. There is no other relationship.

Actually, a *guru* does not mean a person who just teaches something. He is not merely connected with learning. His connection is with spirit, the spirit of God, finally. Learning is a secondary thing. You may learn or not learn; that is a different matter, but the spirit has to be established in itself. Towards that purpose, if anybody can guide you until such time as such guidance is not necessary, that person is the *guru*.

A *guru* cannot be changed. Once you accept a person as your guide, it is permanent. You cannot change the guide from time to time.

Rita: If a person chooses a guru, is there a past association between them?

SWAMIJI: Every contact has a past association, not only a *guru*, but everything. The past association determines the present context, for every kind of contact.

Rita: What happens when the guru drops the body? Is there a sort of individuality, or does he just dissolve in the Universe?

SWAMIJI: He may retain individuality, if he takes rebirth. If he does not take rebirth, then there is no individuality, and there will be no relationship afterwards. It is like the relationship with God at that time, because they have merged with God. But if they have maintained an individuality still, then, of course, the relationship continues.

You can't have a relationship with the Absolute. That is not possible, unless you yourself become the Absolute. If the *guru* merges into the Absolute, then there is no relationship. You can't maintain anything. It is another way of saying that the relationship is with God Himself. But if you maintain an individuality, then the relationship will continue. Even in the next birth, it will continue. Unless there is some individuality, some personality, a relationship is not possible. You can't have a relationship with the Absolute. Only below that level a relationship is possible.

Rita: If a person is still on the personal plane...

SWAMIJI: Then the relationship will continue even in the next birth. Whether the person is alive or dead, that is a different matter. The relationship will continue. If a relationship was maintained in this life, it will be carried over into the next life; but if the relationship breaks for any reason, then it won't be carried forward. If it continues in this life, it will continue in the next life, also. If it has ceased in this life for any reason, then, of course, it won't be carried over into the next life.

Rita: Swamiji, it is not clear. If the aspirant is still on the personal plane and the guru has merged, what happens?

SWAMIJI: Then you can't have any contact with that person. He is not a person at all. No contact is possible. You must then contact the Absolute; that is all. Or else find another *guru*, or take God Himself as the *guru*, because contacting him is another way of contacting God. So why do you say "*guru*" and all that? It is God only. A person who has merged into God is God only, so he is no more a *guru*. He is not a person and, therefore, he is not a *guru* also. He is a Universal Being, so you cannot maintain any personal relationship with him. Otherwise, at lesser levels a relationship is possible.

Rita: How can you know if your guru has merged or not?

SWAMIJI: You cannot know it; it is not possible. You must assume that he has not merged, and then maintain the psychological relationship. God will bring a blessing in some way for that. Many devotees consider God as a person, and it works in some mysterious way. Though God is really not a person, you can consider Him as a person and He will react as a person, according to your feelings.

Sean: The guru cannot really change into God, so he must have been God all along?

SWAMIJI: Why only he? Everybody is like that. You are also God alone potentially.

Sean: So, the relationship with the guru all along is really a relationship with God, and it doesn't change when the guru leaves the body?

SWAMIJI: You cannot have a relationship with God, because He is impersonal, unless you consider Him as a person. There is no such thing as impersonal relationship, because impersonality means non-externality. If it is non-external, there is no relation.

Sean: So then the guru is within?

SWAMIJI: Why do you say "within"? He is everywhere.

An American Visitor: Swamiji, in the USA there is a movement that says that the guru is within; therefore, you don't need to find a guru.

SWAMIJI: These are all very hasty remarks of people who don't understand the gravity of the situation. If the *guru* is inside, then the world also is inside, so why do you travel from place to place? You cannot have only one thing inside, and other things outside. It may be that the *guru* is inside in one sense, but he is outside, also.

Why do people go to colleges and universities when the university is inside the heart? Can you close all the colleges and universities in the world because they are inside the heart? They are inside in some sense, but not literally. There are difficulties in understanding the ultimate problems of life which require guidance.

You go to a scientist in order to learn science, and a philosopher to learn philosophy. Every art and science requires some guidance from somebody who is expert in it; otherwise, you could purchase a book and become a driver, engineer, astronaut, merely by reading a book. That is not adequate. In the beginning, you require guidance from a competent person. Later on, you may become competent yourself, in advanced stages. In the earlier stages, personal guidance is necessary. Otherwise, you may go astray.

American Visitor: Swamiji, one problem is that many people in the West are raised to be independent and free thinking. They don't want to subject themselves to any such discipline.

SWAMIJI: They must understand what they mean by "free thinking." Does it mean thinking anything one likes? Or, is there some system and discipline in thinking? If not, then what is the use of thinking? They need not think, also. It will be only an erratic movement of the mind. Freedom and license are two different things. We may have freedom, but not license.

The way in which we behave with another person is also a kind of discipline. If we behave in any way that we like, then society will crumble one day. Even social existence would be impossible without a code of conduct. If we want to behave in any way we like, then others also will behave in any way they like. This is called rebellion, not society.

We cannot be free unless we share a little of our freedom for the sake of freedom of others also. To the extent that we allow freedom for others, our freedom is limited, so here comes discipline. We cannot have all the freedom for ourselves and nothing for others. People have to think a little rationally, and not make abrupt statements.

55

THE NECESSITY FOR A GURU

Visitor: In my own experience, for me, that has been very true,—I was interested about people that are very enlightened—saints like Krishnamurti and Ramana Maharshi, and even the Buddha, that did not have gurus...

SWAMIJI: Everybody had a guide. None did suddenly crop up from the ground. They had leaders, guides, whether you know them or not. Even Ramakrishna Paramahansa, the great saint of India, had a *guru*. Why should he have a *guru*? He is a master himself, and he was the *guru* of so many people; yet, he also had a *guru* for some good reason.

Visitor: Right.

SWAMIJI: Even Christ had a *guru*, and Krishna had a *guru*. They were great masters, and still they learned under some teacher. When you have attained almost a state of perfection, then, of course, there is no need for a *guru*; but who can say that one is in perfection? Everybody is on the path only, so it is better to have somebody who is superior. If you think that there is nobody superior to you in the whole world, then you do not require a *guru*; but, if you think that there are people in the world who are superior to you, then they will be your *guru*.

Visitor: Yes. I understand.

SWAMIJI: If you say that there is nobody superior to you, then you are the *guru* yourself. But, you cannot say that you are most the superior; how is it possible? You have to be a little humble. Respect for the elders is always good, and one day or the other, you will be benefited by that. Anybody can help you, under given conditions. There is no one who is incapable of rendering some service.

A mouse also saved a lion once. How can a mouse save a lion? Can you understand? One lion was going like this, and a mouse was moving. The mouse said, "Don't you come near me. I can help you one day, if the time comes."

The lion laughed. "You idiot, small thing, wanting to help me? What help can you give?" The lion laughed, but yet the mouse said, "No, one day, who knows? One day some occasion may arise when I can help you."

It so happened that one day the lion was caught in the net of a hunter. It was very difficult to get out of it. The lion struggled the whole day and could not break the net. The mouse came, "May I help you?"

"Oh, yes, if you can!" said the lion. The whole night this mouse worked. It went on nibbling the net in many places and loosened it. Then the lion tore it and came out, and the mouse ran away.

56

AFTER THE GURU HAS LEFT THE BODY

John: My problem is that I never felt sure in my heart that I'm in the right place. My guru, Paramahansa Yogananda, is not in the body, and I only meet representatives of his, and I have never felt really sure...

SWAMIJI: He was not in the body even when you saw him in the body. Even at that time, he was not in the body. People respect their parents, and hang a photograph of them on the wall of the house in reverence; but when that person departs from this body, the very thing whose photograph was hung on the wall is consigned to the earth or the cremation ground. Now, who is it that was revered actually? Was it that thing which was visible to the eyes and whose photograph was revered? Or was the person whom you revered something other than what you saw with your eyes?

If you say you consider that person as the very thing which you saw with your eyes, then you have no business to consign that person to the river, or the fire, or the earth, as if it has no meaning or value; but if you say that the person whom you revered is not the one whom you are seeing with the eyes, then your question is answered by yourself.

It is a perceptional difference, like the value of a currency note. A currency note is only a piece of paper whose value is less than half a penny, and you will call it a thousand dollars if you like. From where comes this value? When the substance that you are holding in your hand is not worth half a penny, how are you conceptually revering it as a thousand dollars? So the value is conceptual, perceptional, valuational,—not material, physical, visual. This applies to everything that we see in the world, including human beings and God Himself.

The visible is not the real; the invisible is the real. This requires a little time to think and appreciate. Usually we don't think in this fashion. We think in terms of sense organs, physical objects, tangible things, visible things, and we do not believe that the actual value of things is not in what we see, but in that which we think only.

The value of a currency note is in your thought. It is not the physical substance that has any value. You may have even a certificate from a bank. The signature of the manager of the bank is there as a certificate for deposit. All the money is in the bank only, not in your hand. You have only one signature of that man, and you are holding it as if the whole world is in your hand. It has no value except that you believe in your mind that it has a value.

All value is mental, psychological, ideational, based on consciousness. Finally, consciousness is the reality, not the visibility of a thing. You yourself are not the person sitting in front of me and talking to me. Neither of these two terms of relation in the conversation can be regarded as one body talking to another body,—nothing of the kind. It is not body talking to body, not body listening to body. It is a consciousness in you appreciating the manner in which my consciousness operates. It is a conversation between two terms of consciousness, and they can be perpetually there, even if the visibility thereof is not there. Do you understand the point?

John: So, I can assume that the master's consciousness is full. If I am unaware, the problem is here?

SWAMIJI: The difference is only that he is aware and

you are not aware, but the fact is the same. You are also some invisible reality, though you may not be aware of it.

John: So I should redouble effort at my sadhana?

SWAMIJI: Yes, yes. We try to do many good things in this world so that we may reap the fruits thereof in a better future. If no fruit will accrue from your good deeds, the good deeds will have no meaning. Now, when will you reap the fruits of your good deeds, knowing well that physical existence in this world is precarious? Nobody knows how long it will continue. Knowing very well the brittleness of physical existence, and comparing that condition with our hope of reaping good fruits of our good actions in the future, who is going to reap that fruit of good action? It is not this body. So, here is a demonstrable evidence before you that you are not this body.

When you say that you shall reap the fruits of your good actions, the body is not speaking. The body cannot say that, because it will not last to reap the fruit of those good deeds. It will not even go there, to the place where the fruits will be given to you. So, you are a spirit speaking, a consciousness that is speaking. It is consciousness saying that you shall do good things so that you shall have a good future, and it is a good future of the consciousness only, not of the physical body. So, the physical body has no value, finally. It is only a vehicle, and the rider of the vehicle is more important than the vehicle itself.

57

THE GURU-DISCIPLE RELATIONSHIP

Suzanne: This is a long question, so I am making it into two parts.

SWAMIJI: The answer will be short.

Suzanne: This question is for everybody, not only for me. It will be in the context of disciples,—not only seekers and devotees,—who are not in the physical proximity of the guru.

SWAMIJI: The disciple is not in the physical proximity of the *guru*?

Suzanne: Some are, but for those who are not, can the guru know what is happening?

SWAMIJI: What happened?

Suzanne: Anything very serious in his life, because he has total faith in the guru, which is an omnipresence.

SWAMIJI: In everybody's life something happens. There is no one in whose case something will not happen. So, what is your special question?

Suzanne: Suppose a disciple says, "I have faith. I am going and living by myself. I see my guru off and on; he sees me, he blesses me. The guru says, "Go. You don't need to be near me. Do whatever you have to do in life." So, the disciple believes that nothing really drastic will happen to him. But, still it happens. I understand, Swamiji, that everything can happen to anybody. . .

SWAMIJI: You mean to say that something that you call drastic should not happen to a person?

Suzanne: Can it be prevented by the guru? Is he aware that it is happening? My question is whether the guru is aware of it, or not.

SWAMIJI: The happenings in one's life are not the creation of the *guru*, nor is he responsible for it. Whatever happens to you is because of the impact created by whatever you thought and did in your previous life. Now, you want to say that the actions that you did in the previous life should not produce their effect?

Suzanne: No. Does the guru know? Is he aware that it is happening?

SWAMIJI: If he knows, in what way are you benefited by that?

Suzanne: I want to know if he knows.

SWAMIJI: Let him know. In what way are you concerned with that? You want him to stop the impact of the previous actions?

Suzanne: No, no. This is cause and effect. I understand. It is prarabdha karma.

SWAMIJI: If your heart is absolutely united with the soul of the *guru*, he will respond, and he will guide, and he may even mitigate certain adverse consequences of the impact of past *karmas*, but he cannot remove it. For instance, when a doctor performs a surgery, there is pain whenever a limb is cut off, but the pain is mitigated by an anesthesia. So, God or *guru*, whoever it is, may act as an anesthesia when some unpleasant experiences have to be passed through, but they cannot stop the experiences. These will have to be experienced. You will have to pay for whatever you have done.

Suzanne: Even death?

SWAMIJI: Death, of course, who can avoid it?

Suzanne: Sometimes it is avoided, Swamiji. We have

read in books by great souls that have pushed it away a bit.

SWAMIJI: Why are you against death?

Suzanne: I am not against it. It is not personally for me, Swamiji.

SWAMIJI: Do you want to live like an old lady for eternity?

Suzanne: No, Swamiji, I am already too old.

SWAMIJI: Then why did you say that death should not be there? Death is the process of the transformation of the whole personality into a new one, which is perhaps better than the present one. So, who can say that death is bad? The whole universe is undergoing a process of evolution, and evolution is nothing but the cessation of the previous condition, and the coming in of the new condition. Do you want the evolutionary process to stop completely?

Suzanne: No, it may be very good. But, all this is happening with, or without, the knowledge of the guru?

SWAMIJI: What you call death is the cessation of the earlier condition, creating a new condition which you call rebirth. It is neither good nor bad; it is a necessity. What is your point, finally?

Suzanne: My point is always the awareness of the guru.

SWAMIJI: If he is aware of what is happening to you, in what way are you benefited?

Suzanne: Then, why should we have a guru, if we are not benefited?

SWAMIJI: In fact, God Himself knows what is happening to you. Then, why do you want a *guru*? When God Himself is capable of knowing whatever happens to you, why do you want a smaller god?

Suzanne: There is no smaller god. There is only one God.

SWAMIJI: Then, you may call him the *guru*. So, there cannot be many *gurus* then. There is only one *guru*, and everybody is a disciple of one *guru* only.

Suzanne: Yes, but they don't think like that, Swamiji. Each one says they have their separate gurus. So, what is the point?

SWAMIJI: There is a *Guru* of *gurus* who will not die and vanish from your sight, because He is timeless, unconditioned by the process of time. Catch hold of him. Then all the *gurus* will immediately manifest themselves, and no problem will be there for you. Perhaps you are thinking that the *guru* is a human person. This is what you are thinking?

Suzanne: No. It starts like this. The contact is like this.

SWAMIJI: The *guru* is not the anatomical framework of a person that you are seeing with your eyes. It is the life that is operating through that frame of body; otherwise, what is the difference between a *guru* and a disciple? Both are anatomically the same, physiologically the same. They eat the same food, breathe the same breath, and have the same normal experiences; but there is a difference. The difference is that there is a light which inundates the *Guru's* personality, which is not so pointedly present in other people. The *Guru* is consciousness operating as a mentor or guarding angel.

You say sometimes that a great man is coming. When you say this, it does not mean that a great body is coming. It does not mean that. The greatness of a person does not lie in the length and breadth of the body of that person. It depends upon the consciousness that is operating inside. The greatness is the intensity of consciousness radiating in a person. When consciousness is clouded, and is not operating well, it looks like an ordinary creature moving.

If your heart is united with a thing, that thing will know what is happening to you. It may be the *guru*, or anything else; even a tree will respond to you, provided your heart is sunk in it.

Suzanne: Swamiji, it means that the awareness of the seeker or disciple has become the universe of consciousness also, though it may be of a different degree than the teacher?

SWAMIJI: Yes, right. If your heart is united with a thing, whatever it is, that thing will respond to you like a mother. The Ganga will speak to you, the mountains of the Himalayas will speak, the sun and the moon and the stars will speak. Everybody is your friend here. They are all *gurus* only.

58

LIVING THE TRUTH

Patrick: I want to discover what it means to live the truth.

SWAMIJI: When you are so clear in your mind as to what truth is, and your devotion to it is clear, why should there be so many questions? To be the truth is to live the truth. That's all. When you become the truth, you are supposed to be living the truth. So what is the problem about it? It is so clear. When the matter is clear to you, no question will arise further.

It is like asking how to be conscious that it is day-time now. Nobody will put such a question, because it is so clear. So when you are conscious that you are in truth, you have already lived the truth. That's all; the matter is closed. There is no question afterwards. Only if you have not entered it, you are still outside truth, the question arises as to how to live it.

Patrick: But is it possible for a person who has not had the experience of that which is beyond the mind to still live his life as a reflection of truth?

SWAMIJI: You can live conceptually, though you have not actually entered it. It is one of the stages. You can conceive it and live a mental conception of it, though you may not have actually entered it. It is a preparatory stage.

Patrick: There are many people who I feel have had the direct experience of who they are, but they are not fully established in that knowledge so they sometimes fall back to identifying with the emotions. So, they have the knowledge...

SWAMIJI: They cannot fall back if they have actually entered it. If the possibility of falling back is there, then they have not fully entered it. They have discovered it only conceptually, not actually.

Patrick: What do Self-realised people see?

SWAMIJI: Self-realised people do not see "others." The question of others does not arise. They will see one thing everywhere; the others are also included in that vision of the One. When you see the ocean, you have seen all the waters. There is no need of seeing different drops. The "other people" question will not arise, because they will be merged together with that Universal Being.

Himself, others, all will be inside that One Being so that the question of myself and yourself will not arise. The thought will be operating through the Universal Being. It won't operate through one person—neither through this person, nor that person. It will operate integrally through the Cosmic Being. That is how it works.

59

DEVOTION AND THE NATURE OF IGNORANCE

Patrick: Can devotion lead to discrimination as, for example, with the Gopis of Krishna?

SWAMIJI: Discrimination comes first, devotion and surrender afterwards. Without discrimination there can't be devotion. Devotion is only to that which is ultimately real, and how will you know what is real without discrimination? So discrimination precedes devotion. Unless you know what is real, how will you have devotion to it? The Gopies knew what was ultimately real; therefore, they had devotion to Krishna and considered Krishna as ultimately real. Otherwise, they would have hugged something else.

An American Visitor: Does the eradication of ignorance give birth to intuitive understanding or awakened knowledge, or does intuitive understanding itself need to be cultivated?

SWAMIJI: When ignorance is removed, there is nothing more to be done. Everything is clear, like daylight. Ignorance is like night; when it passes, you are in the daylight of enlightenment. There is nothing more to be done. After ignorance goes, there is no action. Everything is complete, because what you are seeking is enlightenment, and that is equivalent to the abolition of ignorance. So, ignorance goes, and there are no problems afterwards. It is ignorance that is the obstacle for everything.

When that goes, then all obstacles also go simultaneously.

Visitor: Can ignorance be eradicated by ceasing to respond in ignorant ways?

SWAMIJI: Ignorance cannot be removed by ignorance. It will be like a thief becoming a friend of another thief. Ignorance can be removed only by knowledge. Some people say there are degrees of ignorance: gross ignorance, like *tamas*; light ignorance like *rajas*; and transparent ignorance like *sattva*. So, the transparent ignorance, though it is also a kind of ignorance, may enable the seeker to get rid of the lower ignorances of the *rajasik* and *tamasik* types. So, from that point of view, you may say ignorance can remove ignorance.

Teachers and students are both human beings, yet the student differs from the teacher in the degree of his comprehension. Likewise, though there are stages of ignorance, the higher form of ignorance may help the seeker to eliminate the lower forms. When that function is performed, the higher ignorance also drops.

They generally give the example of a nut called "soap nut." It is a nut growing in a tree which is used for washing clothes in India. Even now it is available in the market. When you rub it, a froth comes out, just as froth comes from soap. This soap nut removes the dirt of the cloth, and afterwards settles down. Soap nut is also a kind of dirt because it is a sediment, but it does not stick to the cloth; it removes the dirt from the cloth, and then settles down. So likewise, the higher ignorance which is *sattvik* in nature can remove the lower one which is *rajasik* and *tamasik*, then itself settles down.

Sometimes when a thorn has gone into the foot, you remove that thorn with the help of another thorn, like a needle. Both are thorns only, but one thorn helps the removal of another thorn. So, likewise, one type of ignorance may help the removal of another type of ignorance. In that sense, you are right that ignorance can help ignorance.

60

WHEN GOD WANTS YOU

Visitor: About love of God?

SWAMIJI: It is true that you must love God. It is wonderful, of course, but it is not enough if you love God. It is necessary that God loves you. You want Him; it is very clear. But He also should want you; and when He wants you, then a miracle will take place. When you want Him, it is called *sadhana*, it is called *satsanga*, prayer, meditation, austerity, religion, Yoga, and so many things. But when He wants you, what do you call it? You cannot call it religion, meditation, and all that. God is not practicing religion and meditation, etc., when He wants you. So, what do you call that condition when He wants you? It is impossible to describe it.

Visitor: Realisation, freedom.

SWAMIJI: We cannot imagine what it would be, to be wanted by God Himself. The whole world will get concentrated upon you. Every leaf in the tree will want you; every tree will bend before you. The stars in the heavens will smile at you; the galaxies will pay homage to you. All these are mentioned in the scriptures. You will find all these wonderful things. Now it does not make any sense at all, but it will make sense. They say, the stars will roll under your feet. You will not understand what is the meaning of it all. The stars are so high, but afterwards you will find that they are under your feet only. You will be so big at that time.

It is good to wait for that time. When our heart

melts, this thing will take place, but it has not melted; it
is still hard, a little bit, and maintaining its independence.
It says, "I am also something." God does not want to
hear all these things, that you are also something, because
there is no "I" except He. He cannot tolerate any other
"I"; if you start saying "I," that is not fair before Him.
When this "I" goes, that "I" will take possession of all
these "I's."

Swami Sivananda had a little poem: "When shall I
be free? When I shall cease to be." So be happy. Have a
good journey in the train.

Visitor: Thank you.

61

DEGREES OF KARMA

Visitor: ...law of karma. Do we have a choice in our life, or is it predestined?

SWAMIJI: We have a choice, or?

Visitor: Or, our life is predestined----it means that we don't have choice, but what happens to us is a consequence of our past; or do we have a choice?

SWAMIJI: Whatever you have done in the past has two aspects: something which is good, charitable, noble, and pleasant; or, something which is detrimental, painful, harmful, etc. No one does only one kind of action. We are sometimes very good, very charitable, very kind, very honorable gentlemen; sometimes we are peevish, selfish, etc. These two aspects of *karma* produce two different types of reaction. That negative type of work that you have done, negative type of thought even, will push you in a direction over which you have no control. That is what you call the determining factor. But the other thing that you have done—good, noble, and pleasant deeds— that will illumine your mind, and provide you with a consciousness of personal effort in the right direction. That is why sometimes you feel that you are helpless, and sometimes you feel that you can do something.

When you are feeling that you are helpless, and nothing is under your control, everything is beyond you, the negative *karma* is working. When you feel it is not so bad, "I can do some good," the positive *karma* is working. So both these aspects are like two wings of the bird of your own total action.

Janie: Once one has the discrimination not to act or be moved by one's thoughts, to not act out of one's thoughts or, you know, be moved by them, would you say that it would be the end of karma?

SWAMIJI: End of *karma*?

Janie: When one is able to have that discrimination to not act out of one's thoughts?

SWAMIJI: It is not the end of karma. It is a step in the direction of ending *karma*. If the *karma* is totally ended, you would not be existing as a human being. But yet, it is a good sign that you are moving in the right direction.

Amir: Swamiji, what did you mean when you said that at the end of karma one would not exist as a human being?

SWAMIJI: It is the *karma* that makes you feel that you are existing as an individual personality. When the *karma* is lifted, you will melt into the cosmos and become Universal Existence. You will not be a person, Mr. so-and-so, afterwards. You will be a Universal Being. You will merge in God. It is like coming out of prison and being totally free.

Amir: But is it any different than my state?

SWAMIJI: State?

Amir: Is it any different than where I am now?

SWAMIJI: You will not be there at all. I told you that you will be like the river in the ocean. Does the river exist in the ocean, or does it not exist? What do you say?

Amir: It does not exist.

SWAMIJI: But it does exist; it has not vanished. So, you will be existing, and yet you will not be existing. You will be existing as a larger thing than the small thing you were earlier. Your dimension will increase into cosmic perspectives.

Amir: It is my experience that this state that you are talking about is right in front of my nose all the time.

SWAMIJI: Right in front?

Amir: It is right where I am.

SWAMIJI: Yes, you may say that.

Amir: And all I have to do is to recognise and accept the nature of reality as it is right now. There is nowhere to go, nothing more to experience.

SWAMIJI: It is perfectly so, but yet, at the same time, you have a consciousness that you are independently existing outside it.

Amir: I do not believe that idea.

SWAMIJI: If it is not there, you would not be speaking to me now. You will not speak to me, if that consciousness of personality were not there. It will be like the sky,—the sky is not speaking to me. You will not even know that you are existing, as the river does not know that it is existing when it has become the ocean, though it knows it exists, in a different sense. Otherwise, you will be maintaining your duality forever. You will be Mr. so-and-so for all times, looking at something as an external universality. That is not the aim of life. You will be seeing me merged into your consciousness, so that you will not have to speak to me afterwards. That is something difficult to comprehend, at present.

Michael: Swamiji, do you mean the end of taking birth altogether?

SWAMIJI: Taking birth?

Michael: Yes. Or, as in your book, you are talking about the guru is not a person, that he is something beyond.

SWAMIJI: The *guru* is a very wide dimension of consciousness appearing to be located through a person, like a high voltage current passing through a copper wire. The copper wire is only the visible thing before you, but it is charged with something which is far beyond the limitations of the copper wire. Some six thousand volts, ten thousand volts, may be passing through that. So, ten thousand volts of consciousness are passing through the divine personality, though the volts cannot be seen; you only see the copper wire. Such people we call super-men. And what did you ask?

Michael: In the guru there is still apparently an existing person.

SWAMIJI: Yes, yes, certainly!

Michael: But has karma ended, in that case?

SWAMIJI: His *karma* has not fully ended, but it is only very, very fractional and highly radiant, not like the binding *karma* of other people. Yes. His *karma* is like a mirror, but other people's *karma* is like a brick. *[laughter]*

Janie: Swamiji, are you saying that to exist in the human form, in the human body, a small degree of karma endures, or there is a small degree of karma?

SWAMIJI: There is a small degree of *karma*, but it is not a very binding thing, because it is radiant, like a mirror. You can see the whole Truth reflected in it, but you cannot see it reflected in the brick wall, so there is a great difference between super-men and ordinary men. They are incarnations, super-men, as you call them.

Richard: Swamiji, how is that the ocean can be aware of its own existence?

SWAMIJI: It is the ocean which is aware of its existence; correct. That is called God. God is the name that you give to the universal sea that is conscious of itself, but it is not a sea of water, it is a sea of consciousness.

62

THE AIM OF EDUCATION

Spanish Visitor: Swamiji, what is the final aim of education?

SWAMIJI: It is a process of drawing out the perfection that is already inherent in the human individual by gradual degrees. You said, "I am a total whole." You have a consciousness of total wholeness. This totality consciousness has various degrees. It is not an easy thing to understand what this total consciousness is. As a body, and mind, you feel that you are one total individual, isn't it?

Suppose you have got a family. You have got a wife, children, and all that. This family consisting of ten members is also a total whole. Though there are many people, the family is a total concept. It is an integrated consciousness of the harmony of many members into an organisation that you call a family.

The family is one individual. That is why there is harmony among members; one member will not act against the wish of another member, as one limb of the body will not act against the welfare of another limb. A family is one single individual. It is a social individual, not merely a biological individual. That is why you feel it is "my family." You identify yourself with the family, as if it is inseparable from you. So, the total consciousness has now expanded itself from the mere biological individuality to a family consciousness.

You are a man from Spain. The Spanish nationality also is one total whole. Do you understand me?

Spanish Visitor: Yes, Swamiji.

SWAMIJI: The consciousness of nationality of your country is one total perfection arising from you; but you are also a citizen of the international set-up, and so, the international concept also is one total whole. When you say that you belong to humanity, you begin to feel a totality of consciousness of a different type altogether. You belong to the entire earth; you are a citizen of this planet. That consciousness also is one total consciousness. You belong to the solar system, of which the earth is a planet; that also is a total consciousness. "Oh, I belong to the solar system!"; so big your mind becomes, even by thinking that. You feel a happiness that you are in a family of so many planets, and the sun is your father, the leader of the family. It is also a total concept. Solar systems are many in the universe, not one, and they also integrate into a larger total, and so on endlessly.

What do you mean by total consciousness, actually? There are degrees. It rises from one little individual to higher, higher, and higher things until you become identified with the whole space-time itself. You belong to the universe. The universe-consciousness is the final total consciousness.

If you can bring out these degrees of perfection gradually, stage by stage, in the minds of students, you are giving the right education to them; otherwise, you teach them mathematics, and physics, sociology and geography, all right. They have studied all these things, but they do not know the connection of one person with another person and so social conflict arises. There are wars taking place. One does not like another person really.

In this total consciousness, which I have explained to you in various degrees, there cannot be conflict of any kind, because everywhere there is a total, so how can there be conflict? There cannot be conflict with anybody, if this consciousness is in your mind always. Either you are in one level of consciousness, or in another level of consciousness; in whichever case, it is always a total. In total, there is no clash, just as your body does not fight with its own self,—the lung does not fight with the nose; the nose does not fight with the eyes. Likewise is the consciousness of perfection that you have to introduce in everybody. That art of teaching in this manner may be considered as the aim of education, finally.

You may teach mathematics or physics; it is quite all right, but the aim is something else. It is not only to get a job that you become a physics professor. You study physics and become a physics professor; what happens afterwards? You earn a salary, and have a comfortable life. This is not education.

Education is not meant for a job and a comfortable life. This may be there incidentally, but the aim is perfection. What perfection is, I told you in various degrees. In every level, in every stage, you are in the state of perfection. If this can be inculcated into the minds of students through proper educational curriculum, that is perfect education.

I cannot tell you too much, but something I have told you which is important.

Spanish Visitor: All knowledge should be together?

SWAMIJI: All arts and sciences are branches of a single knowledge. They have to be together, naturally. You are the son of some father, you are the father of some children; you are the boss of some subordinates, you are the subordinate of some boss; you are the husband of a wife, you are the brother of another person. Do you think all these aspects are capable of harmonising in one individual, or are they all totally different?

These so-called irreconcilable things that I mentioned just now are reconcilable in one personality. You

can be a father and a son at the same time. Are they not
contradictory, that you are a father and son at the same
time? You can be a husband and a brother at the same
time. How is it possible? They are two different things. If
all these so-called self-contradictory aspects can be combined into a single whole in one person, all knowledge
can be combined into one knowledge, which is another
way of repeating the same thing that I told you in the
morning, in answer to your question of what education is.
In that process which I described to you as education,
every science, every psychology, is included. Nothing can
be outside it. The knowledge of the True Self includes
every other knowledge.

63

THE BALANCE OF NATURE

Spanish Visitor: There is so much suffering, and struggle; a war is going on right now because of egoism, power, pride...

SWAMIJI: You see, sometimes you sneeze, sometimes you have pain the stomach, sometimes you have fever; are these good things or bad things? These things are not called good things, but why do they happen, if they are not good? Why do people vomit sometimes? Why do these things happen?

The reason why these things happen is also the reason why the other things happen, to which you made reference. It is a cosmic dislocation making internal adjustments. These things, sneezing, stomachache, fever, etc., are internal adjustments of the body to maintain its balance. It passes through certain peculiar painful adjustments for the purpose of maintaining a balance of health. Otherwise, unnecessarily, why should you vomit and all that? No purpose is served. Nature maintains a kind of balance where certain extremes take place, which maintain the balance.

When you eat too much, you will have a loose motion. Now, it is not a bad thing that is happening, though it is certainly not a happy thing. It is necessary for the maintenance of the health of the body. You have done some extreme thing by overeating. You have walked in the rain, which is an extreme thing that you have done, so you got sneezing and fever. You have not slept properly, because you travelled too much in the railway train for days together,

Mild dislocations are set right by mild adjustments. Serious dislocations may lead to surgical operations. Then, destruction, flood, earthquake, war, and wholesale wiping out of humanity in certain parts also can take place, as when some extreme illness has crept into the system, some limb of the body may have to be severed by amputation. It is not a bad thing, because it is necessary for maintaining the balance of your system. It is a painful thing, but it is a necessary thing, also.

You have to see as Nature sees, not as one person sees. A limb that is severed by amputation may not like to be amputated, but you must not see it from the point of view of the limb only. You must see from the point of view of the whole organism; then, you will see the necessity for it, though it is a very unpleasant thing. So, unpleasant things are not always unnecessary things.

We cannot have a cosmic eye, and we cannot think as Nature thinks. The total eye of Nature alone can see the total need within its constitution, which includes people like us. We are also a part of Nature only. So, when it does something for maintaining its own internal constitutional balance, and it does it for its own purpose, which is the well-being of the whole, we, as isolated individuals, who cannot think as Nature as a total thinks, find that some odd thing is taking place; it looks like it is not very good.

Nature never does a bad thing. There is no such thing as a bad thing for Nature. It looks unpleasant, because we are outside Nature, psychologically. If we are one with Nature, we will see nothing improper taking place. We are looking at things by standing outside nature. That is why we cannot see things properly and impartially.

American Visitor: War and hunger and these things have been happening since the beginning of time, and you said something about Nature taking its course. Could you clarify that for me, on how Nature affects?

SWAMIJI: I have already told this, and again you are asking the same question. Which point is not clear to you? We are parts of Nature. Every one of us is a part of Nature. Do you understand? And every part is supposed to be in harmony with the whole. A part should not be in disharmony with the whole; otherwise, the whole will take action against the part, and set it right by doing something, which is what I mentioned in some detail, and that something is the thing that you see with your eyes.

We are in disharmony with Nature, disharmonious with God Himself. We are asserting our individuality too much, which Nature abhors. No limb of the body can assert independence totally out of harmony with the organism; then, pain will start, aches and all sorts of illness will arise. That illness is rectified by Nature's medical activity; the medical activity may be bitter medicine, or it may be a surgical action, which it does, as all these events that you see in the world taking place. It can be a thunder, it can be a flood, it can be anything; it can do whatever it likes for its purpose.

In the same way as you do not complain against anything that is happening within yourself, you will not complain against anything happening in the world, if you are one with the total whole. You do not go on complaining against yourself. You know the reason for it. You do not complain, you simply see that it is rectified. Similarly, you will not make complaints against anything if you are one with Nature, and if you can think through the mind of Nature and see it with the eye of Nature. Now, we are not able to do that; we are thinking individually, so we do

not understand what is happening. The lower whole has
to be sacrificed for the higher whole.

64

THREE KINDS OF MEDITATION

Spanish Visitor: How can I practise meditation on Cosmic Consciousness?

SWAMIJI: What are you conscious of, at that time? That thing is the object of your meditation. You have no particular object. You are conscious of this earth, the sky, time-space, and stars, etc.; you are conscious of the entire atmosphere. Can you adjust your mind in such a way that you are conscious of all these things at the same time,— not one after the other, but simultaneously? Cosmic consciousness initially begins with simultaneous concentration on all things.

Again, I come to the analogy of the limbs of the body. You have many limbs of the body, and you are conscious of them, simultaneously. You do not think, "Today I have a nose, tomorrow I have an ear"; you do not think like that. At once, you are conscious of all the limbs of the body. That is called total consciousness. In a similar manner, if you can be conscious of all things conceivable—the entire world, space-time and objects, not one after the other, but simultaneously—if you can do this exercise, that would be an attempt on your part to become transcendentally conscious. This is one kind of meditation.

I am not saying that everybody should do only this. This is one way. But in the beginning, this kind of abstract concentration may be found a little difficult. That is why they suggest concentration on a deity, and I wanted to know what your deity is. You seem to suggest that you repeat the *mantra* of *Om namah sivaya*. The meaning of the *mantra* is prostration to the great deity Siva. Can you think of Lord Siva, his features, his characteristics, his knowledge, his power?

Spanish Visitor: Yes, Swamiji.

SWAMIJI: Can you concentrate on that figure?

Spanish Visitor: The mind comes and goes. I cannot keep it in focus.

SWAMIJI: The mind comes and goes because it wants something other than what you are thinking of in meditation. It says, "I want another thing." Now, you put a question to yourself. You tell the mind: "When you have decided that a deity like Lord Siva is final, and whatever you want, you can have from that deity, why are you going elsewhere? Do you believe that Lord Siva cannot give you all things? If you do not believe that this is capable of blessing you with everything, then why do you concentrate on that?"

The mind is playing a dual trick. On the one hand, it says this is the object, and if I meditate on that, I will get everything; but subtlely it says, "No, it will not give me everything; I want to go to the marketplace." So, it is playing a game with you by telling you two things at the same time. If you are sure that this will not bring any blessing to you, why should you meditate on that? But you are feeling it is not like that: "It will certainly bless me." You will perhaps get everything that you want through meditation on this deity. But another subconscious voice says, "No, no. You should not concentrate like that. You go to the shop and eat some delicacies." It will say like that.

You have to act like a teacher. You are a schoolmaster. You know how to handle students, and the mind is a student; you tell it, "You are a stupid thing. Why are you

running about here and there when you can get all things
in the supermarket here? Lord Siva is a supermarket;
everything is there. Why do you go to some little shop?
What is the purpose?"

Tell the mind again and again, "You are stupid! Why
are you running here and there? Don't you know that
everything you want can be had with Him? Not only that,
everything that you cannot even imagine in your mind,
all things you can get here. An ocean of blessings will
come. Don't go!" Even verbally, you can tell like that.
Not merely thinking, even by words, tell the mind,
"Don't go anywhere! You are getting everything here!"
Don't you speak like that to your students in a school?
"This is good for you. Don't be like that. Study!"

Like a father talking to a little baby, you talk to your
mind: "Don't be foolish; don't go here and there. You
will get nothing by going here and there. You are only
losing your energy and wasting time. All that you want
you can have in one place. Therefore, identify yourself
with and meditate on that, and receive blessings from
that." If you think it is Lord Siva, all right, go on with it.

For the time being, I suggest that you can adopt this
method, and a higher thing also I mentioned to you,—
Cosmic Consciousness. And, in that little book that I
gave you in the morning, these small suggestions are
mentioned: meditation on the external, meditation on the
internal, and meditation on the Universal. There are three
stages of meditation.

Now, what I have mentioned to you on Lord Siva is
a kind of externalised meditation,—conceiving God as
something placed before you as a cosmic externalised
presentation. That is one kind of meditation in the path of
devotion, or *bhakti*, as they call it.

The other thing is internal, the purely psychological
contemplation, as we have it in the Buddhist methods, for

instance. The meditations in Buddhism are purely psychological. They do not suggest any god, deity, or any such thing. Perhaps you are aware of some techniques in Buddhism; and in Hinduism also, there are techniques of this type. Observing the breath, observing the mind, observing the thoughts, and conducting the thought in different parts of the body, etc., are internal meditations. And the highest is Universal meditation.

In the beginning, you must start with external meditation only. You need not go into internal meditation suddenly. The meditation on Lord Siva is all right for you. You carry on with that method. Slowly, you can rise higher.

Spanish Visitor: Swamiji, the other type of meditation is watching the thoughts or observing the thoughts without identifying with them?

SWAMIJI: That is one method. You can choose whichever method you like. Sometimes, you can adopt all the three methods, alternately: sometimes praying to Lord Siva, sometimes analysing the mind inside, sometimes thinking cosmically. All the three methods are good; you can combine them, if you can do it.

When you do office work or any other kind of work, this should be the background of your thought throughout the day. Then only it will get settled. Actually, you have no other occupation. This is the main occupation; all occupations get merged into this. All that you want through any other work, occupation, etc., will be given to you through this. It is the main object, the main purpose of life. Unity with Reality is the main objective. The very purpose of life is this. Because we are unable to achieve it, we are going here and there in search of jobs and all that. We do not require jobs afterwards; Nature itself will give you whatever you want. But we are unable to do that in the beginning, so we have to do some work, also, some service, together with the attempt at meditation. When meditation deepens, you can lessen your activities, and take to meditation more and more.

65

THE FIRST THOUGHT AND THE GREAT THOUGHT

*Visitor: The most difficult moment in the whole day,
like my conditioning, my fears, or whatever, comes up
very strongly after waking up. Then, I get up and begin
the day, and it goes away. And I have been talking to people, and I have seen that for many people, it is the same.
I was wondering if it has to do with what happens in
dreams, or the unconscious processes. I do not know, but
I just find that day after day, when I wake up. . .*

SWAMIJI: What is the first thought, generally, that occurs when you wake up in the morning? The moment you
wake up, what do you think first, usually?

Visitor: The first thought? I do not know.

SWAMIJI: You should observe it.

Visitor: Yes. I have to observe it.

SWAMIJI: Tomorrow morning, you observe it—when
you wake up, suddenly, what do you think?

Visitor: Yes.

SWAMIJI: The first and the last thought of the day.
Both are important. And the last thought is very important in many other ways, for unthought-of reasons. Do
you know why the last thought is important?

Visitor: Why is it?

SWAMIJI: Suppose one goes to bed, and does not
wake up in the morning; the future will be determined by
the last thought. If any hodgepodge thought was the last

thought, the future will be accordingly something not very pleasant. And who can guarantee that there will be a real waking in the morning? Is there a guarantee?

Visitor: No.

SWAMIJI: Then how can one be so foolhardy as not to be careful about the last thought? So, here comes the importance of the last thought,—some trouble can be there in the next birth.

He who is last shall be first in heaven, and he who is first may be the last one. If nobody wants you, there will be somebody who will want you. If everybody starts wanting you here, then the prize you have got is here itself, so, don't expect any further prize. When everything goes, all things shall come. If all things have to come, everything should go, also. These are all mystical truths.

When everything is renounced, then everything will come also at the same time. If there is a vacuum, the entire air of the space will rush into that place. "Empty thyself and I shall fill thee," the great master said. But if you are already full with something, the question of filling does not arise.

It is the small person who wants to pretend that he is great, and wants appurtenances. Any demonstration of one's importance is not necessary if the person is really important. Royal paraphernalia is used for demonstrating one's greatness. You can be a pauper in the eyes of people, and you may be one of the greatest people in the world.

66

SADHANA CAN BE DONE ANYWHERE

Visitor: Swamiji, how can I find the best place to do my sadhana?

SWAMIJI: I can stay anywhere. I can stay under a tree, or I can stay in the city also. I won't say that I can stay only in this place. Whether it is the market place, a shop, a tree, or a temple, it makes no difference to me. Anywhere I can stay. I won't complain that it is a bad place and all that. I have no bad place. I have only to find a place for breathing, and eating a little food, and that is there everywhere in the world. What does it matter in which country it is?

Your problem is not in the country, it is in your mind; and wherever you go, even in heaven, you carry your mind. There can be hell even in heaven, because you carry the hell there. This is a kind of distraction of the mind. The mind is so tricky that it doesn't want you to progress. So, it selects circumstances, conditions; finally life goes away in this talk only. Practically, you do nothing. You go on selecting places, and the whole life you do only that. It is like thinking only of the plate, and eating no food afterwards. These are all secondary matters, which have no connection with spirituality. You could stay in any country, anyplace. What is the problem?

People cannot help you, the country cannot help you. You have to help yourself with your higher reason. There are troublemakers even in heaven. It doesn't mean there is only milk and honey. Everyone thinks that in heaven there is no problem. But you ask Indra and other people if there is a problem or not! So many times he was thrown out. How is Indra happy?

Swami Sivanandaji Maharaj has taught us that you can be happy anywhere, under any condition, because God has created the whole world. He has not created India, Italy, Germany, etc. There is no such thing. The earth is only a ball of mud, which is the same everywhere. Any place is equally good, so you can stay anywhere. Why do you create problems unnecessarily? We have created these differences of countries, languages, etc. We are living on a ball of mud, which is called earth, and crawling over it like insects.

I can sit in a railway station and meditate. The noise of the train will not disturb me. I will not say that it is a hopeless place. I will make friendship with the railway train. What is wrong? It is also my friend. You must be a little broad-minded, and a little common sense must be used; otherwise, what happens is that we become old, and our time goes away in these discussions, and nothing substantial comes out.

67

RENUNCIATION AND TRANSFORMATION

Visitor: What place does renunciation have in the holy life,—in this meditation that you have been speaking about?

SWAMIJI: What is your question?

Visitor: What place does renunciation have in the meditative process of realising one's true Self?

SWAMIJI: Can you tell me what your idea of renunciation is? What does it mean, actually?

Visitor: To be more interested in realising what is true, and one's true Self, than anything else in life.

SWAMIJI: No. If you are interested in realising your Self, you are saying that you are going to renounce something. Isn't it?

Visitor: I think that is the result of being more interested in it.

SWAMIJI: What are you going to renounce? What are the things that you would like to renounce for this purpose?

Visitor: It might be old ways of being, old ways of thinking, old ways of interacting with people, old ways of understanding things.

SWAMIJI: That is all right. But, actually, renunciation means renunciation of all the desires that are connected with the world of perception. Have you desires connected with this world? If they can be renounced, you have attained perfection. Old ways of thinking, and other things you mentioned to me just now,—actually, the old way of thinking is the way of desiring things in the world.

Visitor: Yes.

SWAMIJI: And, if that can be overcome, and if you desire the Self only, and desire nothing external to the Self, you have renounced, really. Renunciation is not abandoning objects of the world, persons and things,— but the longing for them. Now, many people are seated here. Can you say, "I have renounced them"? The question does not arise, because you have no connection with them at all. Therefore, the question of renunciation, also, does not arise. Like that, if you have no concern with anything in the world, then the question of renunciation, also, will not arise.

Visitor: Yes.

SWAMIJI: If you have got concern with something, then the idea of renunciation, or not renunciation, arises. You are concerned with the Self, as you understand it correctly. And if there is nothing else that can interest you, then you have renounced perfectly, and you have done the best thing in the world. That is my answer.

Visitor: Thank you.

Visitor: I have another question, Swamiji, about transformation—how does transformation take place in time?

SWAMIJI: What kind of transformation?

Visitor: Of the personality, of the old way of being, the old way of seeing things, and understanding things to the new way of being more interested in the Self.

SWAMIJI: Transformation is actually a state of consciousness. When you are aware of something, consciousness envelops that thing, and it takes the shape of that particular thing, whether it is a human being, or any particular object of the world. And, you are transformed at that time into the form of the object which you are thinking in your mind. But, if the object does not exist for you, as you have concluded just now—they are not matters of concern for you,—you have nothing to do with anything in the world, and then the consciousness transforms itself into its own true nature.

Now, we are empirically conscious, sensorially aware, and filled with object consciousness. We are seeing this world; we are looking at the buildings, we are seeing the wall, and so many people around us. There, in that condition of perception of things, a psychological transformation takes place. The mind assumes the shape of that which it cognises; then, you are able to see that such a thing exists. As molten lead cast into a crucible takes the shape of that crucible, the mind takes the shape of any object which it cognises, or perceives through the sense organs.

This is called bondage to the objects. If you are not concerned with anything,—you are seeing so many people here, but your mind is not transformed into the shape of these people, because the mind has no concern with them,—it is a blank looking and seeing, without any emotional connection. If that emotional connection with things is withdrawn, and your concern is centralised in the Pure Self, you undergo a metaphysical transformation, as they call it,—a transcendental transformation— transformation into a form of God Himself, I should say. Instead of your consciousness taking the shape of a thing that it cognises outside, in the form of objects, etc., the centralised consciousness, with no concern external in space and time, gets modified into the form of the Transcendent Being, which is God-consciousness. That is the transformation that you are expecting, which will take place automatically, if you are freed from object-consciousness, or any kind of desire-consciousness. That is what you are expecting in your spiritual transforming process.

The Self almost loses contact with itself, and moves outside in the form of objects of sense, when it desires anything. That is an unnatural condition of the mind. The senses have to be withdrawn from such perceptional activity, and consciousness has to rest in itself. The resting of the consciousness in its own self, which is Universality of Being, is the highest Yoga or meditation. There is nothing more to be done afterwards. That is the final goal.

British Visitor: In your book The Realisation of the Absolute *there is one part where you say that if a person does not realise himself, then Nature, in some way, takes revenge. And it made it sound like Nature has some sort of purpose, or some sort of reason. I just wondered if you could explain that.*

SWAMIJI: Nature does not take revenge, but it will constrain the person to the laws of Nature, to which we are all subject, so to say. The consciousness of finitude, fear of death, sense of insecurity, and a feeling of dissatisfaction with everything—these are the ways in which Nature will react upon the person who has not realised the Self.

Self-realisation means the experience of the Universal Eternal Being, where Nature does not stand outside it. Inasmuch as it is universal, there is no one to control it. There is no one to restrict it; inasmuch as it is everywhere, it cannot die, also. It cannot be born; it is perfectly free, and ultimately absolute. This is how we describe the state of supreme realisation, called by various names like Self-realisation, God-realisation, the realisation of the Absolute,—where One alone is, and there is nothing external to limit you in any manner whatsoever.

That is ultimate freedom, the aim of life, for which

you have to struggle hard in deep meditational process. Deep meditation is necessary. You have to spend practically all your time in contemplation on this supreme completeness, the Total Whole, what you call the Absolute, where everything is, which is All-in-All, which is inseparable from your own existence.

This meditation is the primary duty of every person, and when that duty is discharged, everything is fulfilled, and you become perfect in every sense of the term. This is the thing for which we have to struggle and strive, day in and day out, in all our activities, in all our doings. Whatever our performances be in this life, they all have to get streamlined in the direction of this great meditative process on the Absolute. This is the duty of all.

68

FEAR OF LOSING THE WORLD

SWAMIJI: Sometimes it looks like a very pleasant, smooth, honeyed path. Sometimes it looks like an uplifted thunderbolt. In the Upanishads, there is a statement which makes out that God is like an uplifted thunderbolt. Everybody dreads Him. The sun and moon dread Him; the gods dread Him. Everybody dreads this uplifted thunderbolt. That is one aspect of justice. God is justice.

Justice is fearsome, because what justice will do to you, you do not know; so, naturally, you dread justice. But, at the same time, you have a sense of protection from justice. If justice is not there, you will not be protected. So, you have a sense of security and satisfaction that there is justice, but you dread it also, because it may do anything. Your understanding of justice is not so clear; therefore, you have a dual feeling towards it.

Every person born in the world has to pass through these stages of movement, from the three-dimensional world of space and time, to the transcendental Godhead. What sorts of troubles and pains you will have to undergo internally, you cannot know now. You will have to know it only when you actually encounter it. It is a fear sometimes that some important thing, very delicious, delicate, and worthwhile will be lost. The world is being lost. The world is a good thing; we see the world is so nice. We cannot say that it is an unpleasant thing. But, we seem to be giving a goodbye to it, for the sake of something of which we have no idea. This is our fear.

"For what am I searching? All the goods of the world I threw away into the sea, and then afterwards, I am searching for some hazy, vague, unthinkable something, calling it enlightenment, calling it God." Sometimes these fears will grip the soul. It is only in the initial stages that there is enthusiasm; afterwards, there will be a reversion, sometimes. The consciousness will give a kick and say, "Go back to the world. I cannot go with this. It is not possible for me."

The ocean will push the river some miles, sometimes, and the river becomes salty. You must have observed this, in some cases; several miles of the mouth of the river may be salt water because of the force of the ocean, which gives a kick to the river.

But, there are some rivers which are so powerful that they push the sea also two hundred miles. In South America, there is one river called the Amazon. They say it is so forceful that two hundred miles of sea water has become sweet water, by the force.

So, you need not be a little stream that is made salty by the power of the unknown. You can be pushing yourself forward. Why are you diffident? The trouble is, we are accustomed to a very happy, pleasant life of the sense organs in this world. We see beautiful things; we eat beautiful things; we hear beautiful things; we touch beautiful things; we smell beautiful things. This is the world. The world is made up of five things: beautiful seeing, beautiful smelling, beautiful hearing, beautiful tasting, beautiful touching. Minus these, there is no world. Now, you want to withdraw yourself from these beautiful things; then, what happens to you? All the beautiful things go. If all the beautiful things go, what remains? This is the fear.

But actually, what you call beauty in this world is not beauty. It is a distortion, and the senses are misguiding you into the wrong belief that you are seeing nice, tasty, delicious things in the world. The real beauty is elsewhere, which is the origin of your personality, the archetype, as they call it. Your real being is reflected through your mind, which looks like this so-and-so sitting here. So, we are all reflections of our own selves, really. The originals are somewhere else. If the reflections are so attractive, what would be the nature of the originals? Thus, tell your mind, "Do not be afraid. I am going to gain some better thing than what I have here in this world."

But, when you are in a psychological impasse of this kind, the only solution is to go to a *guru*. Independently, one cannot tread this path. It is not possible. One day or other you will see a dark wall in front of you, or a black curtain, and you will not know how to go. At that time, when you are not able to move forward, go to your teacher and say, "I have this trouble. I am in distress, what do you say?" At that time, whatever the *guru* says is your solution.

Every student must have a *guru*. Totally independent marching is not possible. You cannot even pilot an airplane of your own accord without training under some *guru*; otherwise, somewhere wrong you will go. For everything a *guru* is necessary. A teacher is absolutely essential, especially in this path where the future is totally unknown to us. We are passing through some track, of which we have no idea at all, and we do not know what is ahead of us. And so, we have to be guarded by the caution of the *guru* only, and when you have got a competent *guru*, you should have no problems.

It is not that every day you should go to the *guru* and put questions, but whenever you have a difficulty which is genuine, poignant, and eating your vitals practically, and you are in distress, at that time only you can tell him that this is the difficulty.

Sometimes, you have to be a little lenient to yourself. Very hard you should not be on always. Do not punish yourself too much. You see, spiritual discipline is not torture; otherwise, if you torture yourself too much, there will be a reaction from your mind and body, and you will get nothing afterwards. Very carefully, you have to tread. Neither you should be over-indulgent in things, nor should you be extreme to the breaking point. Both things must be avoided.

That *via media*, the golden mean, is sometimes missed in our enthusiasm, and then only we get into sickness, whether it is internal or external. That is why, to guard ourselves from any kind of extreme behavior, a teacher is necessary, who will be teaching you what is proper. A *guru* is necessary. You go to meet the *guru*.

Visitor: What you said about justice,—I am not sure exactly what you meant, but to me it meant when you go into the Unknown, the justice is just the Truth that you have to face, right? I am not sure. And, you said it will be justice, but that is where you find the security, also. So, do you mean that?

SWAMIJI: Justice is a source of security, and also a source of fear.

Visitor: Right.

SWAMIJI: You know why it is so. It acts in both ways. It can act either way; therefore, you fear it and also you like it. You cannot exist without it, and, also you do not want to be interfered with by it, too much.

Visitor: It is the same as the truth, then? The truth is painful, and yet it does liberate.

SWAMIJI: Yes, it is painful, and yet liberates. Right. It is painful to the bound individual, because it does not want to free itself from bondage, since bondage itself has been taken as a necessary joy. We are in a state of bondage, but we do not think that it is worth throwing it down in one second, like that. We have got our own belongings, including this body. They are a source of bondage, but we would not like to throw them away. Bondage also becomes part and parcel of our existence. For people living in prison for fifty years, that becomes a natural way of living; when they come out, it will be a little odd thing, for some time. So, whatever is there to which we get habituated, that looks normal to us, though it is not actually normal.

There are people who are permanently sick. They are never all right. Always there is some temperature, some stomachache, some lack of appetite for the whole day, and for months together, and that becomes a normal way of thinking. They do not know what health is. That is the manner of our involvement in things. That is why we dread separation from the world of involvements, because that has become something very real and normal for us.

Now, the other thing which is really there, and which is supremely normal, has been always a kind of thought and abstraction for us. Concrete contact with it has not been practicable. We concretely, substantially come in contact with objects which are seen by the sense organs, but we cannot physically contact that which we are contemplating as the Ultimate Reality. It remains mostly as a kind of thought, and we are not able to convince ourselves fully that what we have only in thought is as good as what we can physically contact.

So many kinds of psychologically engendered fears harass us. We cannot get out of these things without practical guidance from a *guru*.

69

THE SEVEN STAGES OF ENLIGHTENMENT

SWAMIJI: I was thinking about enlightenment, just before you came here. Enlightenment is like sunrise, I felt within myself that in the morning, the sun rises, but the sun suddenly does not jump up to the top.

Andrew: It rises slowly.

SWAMIJI: It is pitch dark in the night, as if there is no hope of any light. That is the state of ignorance.

Andrew: Yes.

SWAMIJI: Nobody can imagine that there can be any such thing as light when it is pitch dark, like coal. Later on what happens, slightly, the sky assumes a grey colour.

Andrew: The dawn.

SWAMIJI: Slowly it becomes grey color. After that, it becomes a little pinkish, then slightly whitish, and then you will see the great Man rising slowly in the east.

Like that, is enlightenment. I was just now thinking about it in my mind. In the beginning, it is all like idiocy, all darkness. There are people who are working on the roads carrying bricks, and cutting wood in the forest, and living their livelihood. What do they think in their mind?

Andrew: Survival.

SWAMIJI: Survival,—that is all. It is complete darkness, as far as enlightenment is concerned.

Andrew: That is right.

SWAMIJI: Then, a day comes in the life of a person when one wishes to do a good thing and not a bad thing.

In the animal condition of human life, the idea of doing the proper thing, and avoiding the improper thing, does not arise. The day comes when, "After all, I must do some good thing."

Many people come here to the Ashram, leaving their homes, leaving their jobs, and giving resignation to their occupations. "Why have you come?" "I just want to do some good service." This is the first stage of enlightenment, says the *Yoga Vasishtha*, a great scripture of India. That first stage is called *subheccha* in Sanskrit. *Subha* means good; *subheccha* means desire to do good.

The next stage is, how to do good. The desire to do good is there, but what is good? You go on cogitating and thinking what exactly good is. This is the state next to the mere desire to do good, which is called the state of investigating. It is cogitation, thinking oneself, "What is actually the good thing? What am I searching for? What do I want?" This stage is called *vicharana*.

The third stage is called *tanumanasi,* the thinning out of the mind. The mind is fat with egoism, with desires of every kind. In the *Yoga Vasishtha* there is a verse in Sanskrit: By accumulation of wealth, by greed for pleasures and attachment to this body, the ego becomes fat. They say the body can be fat; but the ego, also, can be fat.

There are people with stout egos. When the mind starts thinking, "What is the proper thing for me to do?" it begins concentrating on one thing only, wanting the proper thing. Because it is concentrating on one thing only, the distractions caused by the earlier movements of thought in various other directions gradually cease.

Andrew: Subsides.

SWAMIJI: It subsides. It becomes thin, thread-like, as it were. The mind is like a film that covers the consciousness of the Self. When it is very thick and dark, the reflection of Self-consciousness is prevented completely. When it is thin, it becomes perspicacious, as a light can properly reflect itself through a clean glass, but it will not be reflected in a thick brick. So, in this condition of thinness of the mind, called *tanumanasi* state, it is about to detach itself from all earlier occupations concerned with sense objects. Up to these three stages, the enlightenment has not started yet. It is only a preparatory stage,—a stage of kindergarten.

It is in the fourth stage that one feels a flash, as if there is a lightning. The *sattva guna,* the *sattva* quality of the mind, manifests itself in the fourth state. In that condition, when one beholds flashes of lightning, not from the sky but from within, one is designated as *brahmavid*—one who knows Brahman. But, he is still on the portals, only at the gateway to the palace of Brahman. He has not entered it. This stage is called *Sattvapatti*, attainment of high purity.

Then, in the fifth state, the consciousness of externality melts down into the consciousness of universality. Now I see the world. I see people, I see space-time, sun, moon and stars. I see them because they are apparently outside me. Suppose the sun, moon and stars and all people are studded within my own body; I will see nothing outside me. The consciousness of the external existence of things, including space and time, ceases. It is the stage called *asamsakti*,—total detachment from particularity, externality, causality, etc.

Then, comes the next higher stage, which is the sixth one,—*padarthabhavana,* or non-material apprehension. Quantum physicists tell us that matter is light. It is not a dull, stone-like substance that this earth is. It is inherently light itself. In this sixth stage, matter sheds its materiality, solidity, hardness, externality, weight, and dimension, and there is a flood of radiance everywhere, as if the whole universe is one sun.

When one single sun rises in the east, we can see how much light is there. Here, in this enlightenment, the entire space becomes sun. What would be the radiance? What would be the light? This is sometimes identified with what Patanjali calls, in his *sutras*, *savikalpa samadhi*,—a penultimate state of union with the Absolute.

In the last state, which is called *turiya*, there is none to behold this radiance. The beholder becomes the radiance itself. The radiance beholds the radiance; the sun sees the sun, and there is only the sun. The entire space-time complex that you call as existent, as the causative factor of the universe, becomes one mass of indescribable radiance, not of physical light, electrical light, nor even sunlight, but consciousness-light. In that last stage, which is the seventh, nobody is there to behold it, because the beholder has become the very thing which is to be beheld. This is the Absolute-Experience.

Andrew: It is dissolution.

SWAMIJI: Here is the pinnacle of enlightenment, and you will not know what happens to you at that time. People ask questions, "What happens after enlightenment?" Nobody will be there to ask a question like that. No person will be existing at that time. Yet, it is said in the scriptures that the body of such a person may continue to exist for some time. It does not mean that he will die immediately.

The belief is that in this state of total absorption in consciousness-light, a person physically cannot live for more than two weeks, sometimes three weeks. The body will be shed then.

There was one person in Maharashtra who attained this kind of state. Nobody knew his name. He was living in a place called Akalkot, so people used to call him Akalkot Swami. He would not speak, but people around him knew that he was a great master. He would not utter one word; he would not ask for anything. Day and night he was like that, alone to himself.

One poor man, knowing that this is a great person, wanted some blessing. Generally, no blessing is given; he would not speak at all. The poor man had to have his daughter married, but he had no funds. He went and prostrated himself before the great master of the seventh stage that I am describing, and asked for his blessing.

The Swami pointed to something, the skull of a dead man. A marriage is supposed to be a holy act, and such an inauspicious thing he is trying to give? The man felt disgusted, but because of his faith in the great master, he tied the skull in a rag, and went to his house, and threw it in the rear veranda. He borrowed money and had the marriage performed. After a month or so, when the wife was sweeping the veranda, she hit this bundle and it burst into little shining pieces.

There was no skull there. They were all little, shining stones,—so much! He took one to the shop in the market and asked, "Is this stone of any value?"

"From where did you get it?" the shopkeeper asked. "This costs a hundred thousand rupees."

The man's heart broke. He went back to the old saint and prostrated himself. "The skull has become a reservoir of gems!" he said, but this great master would not speak one word.

This is some of the ways in which great masters of the seventh stage behave. Their attitude nobody can understand. There was one Swami like that, living on the other side of the Ganga many years back, in the time of Swami Sivananda, looking like a crazy person. He would not wear any cloth, also. He would go to the market. If he sees baskets of sweets, he would lift them and throw them in the road, and go away. Again, he would go to another shop, and throw the whole thing to the ground. Afterwards, they say, the business of those shops multiplied a hundredfold. Then, people used to run to him: "Please throw, please throw!" He would not listen. He would go away unconcerned.

Great masters, like Shirdi Sai Baba, Sri Ramakrishna Paramahamsa, this Akalkot Swami, and many others are there of that kind, who were not human beings. As I mentioned, they say that the body will not last very long because the *prarabdha*, which keeps the body intact for some time, gets exhausted by the work that it has completed, and then it has no work to perform. Consciousness is shrouded in this body, and when consciousness bursts forth, the body cannot stand.

It is also mentioned in the *Yoga Vasishtha* that people of this type can be counted on the fingers. They will not be a multitude of people. You will not find them everywhere moving on the road. Very humorously it says that the weight of these people, the earth cannot bear. The earth cannot suffer the weight of these people. It is a humorous way of putting it. Very few will be there of this kind.

Suka Maharishi, Vyasa's great son, a little boy of sixteen years old, was one with all the trees, mountains, and everything. He was just going naked, without consciousness of the body. When Vyasa, his father, called, "Suka, my son! Where are you?" the trees in the forest everywhere started vibrating, "I am here."

There is another story about this great Suka. There was a king called Yudhisthira known in the Mahabharata—a very virtuous man, who did a lot of charity. He won the Mahabharata battle. Do you know the story of Mahabharata?

Andrew: A little bit.

SWAMIJI: Oh, it is worth reading. Indian culture cannot be known unless you read the Mahabharata.

Andrew: This is the second time you have told me that.

SWAMIJI: And, after he was crowned king, he had a desire to feed millions of people, as a gesture of his greatness as emperor, and he also wanted to know how many people had eaten. He asked great Vyasa, "Can you have some method contrived so that I might know how many have eaten?" Vyasa hung a bell with his *mantra.* He said, "When one thousand people eat, it will ring once. You can count the number of times it rings, and imagine that so many thousands have eaten."

After all the people had eaten and gone away, the bell started ringing continuously; non-stop it rang. "What is this? Is something wrong with the bell?" Yudhisthira said.

Vyasa said, "My bell cannot do wrong. Some tremendous mystery is there behind it. Once only it will ring when a thousand people eat. You find out if anybody else is eating."

He went looking around and found this little boy Suka, looking unkempt, sitting with a dog, which was licking the leaves, the remains of the people who had eaten, and he was eating one grain. When he ate one grain, the bell started ringing.

The king ran to Vyasa, "Some poor boy is standing there, and he is eating one grain, and immediately it rings as if one thousand people have eaten. Who is that boy?"

Vyasa said, "He is my son. He is the whole universe himself. If one grain goes into his stomach, millions have been fed."

Yudhisthira wept. "I feel ashamed. I never knew that

such a person exists, and I am boasting that I have fed millions of people." He fell prostrate before that boy, but Suka was unaware.

These are stories of the enlightened people who have pierced through the cosmos and made it their own,—not merely made it their own, they themselves are the cosmos. The Upanishad says the universe is his,—nay, he himself is the universe. What more can we say about enlightenment? It is worth thinking deeply.

Andrew: Thank you.

SWAMIJI: It is worth thinking on this matter, and one day we all shall have it. And let the bell ring.

70

THE BLESSINGS OF SWAMI SIVANANDA

Janie: Swamiji, I was wondering if you would be able to tell us something about when you met your own Master, Sivananda.

SWAMIJI: What do you want to know?

Janie: I was curious to hear if in the meeting with him, that you recognised what you had always known.

SWAMIJI: Oh, to meet him was like meeting a giant. Do you know what a giant is? So, I met a giant who will stun anybody who goes near him. But that stunning was also a kind of teaching, and a reception. When you go out from your cave, or a room, into the hot sun, you will receive a stunning welcome from the sun, and the sun's power is so much that you really will be stunned. You will not be able to tolerate it for long time. What do you say?

Visitors: Yes.

SWAMIJI: It was something like that. So it took days and months for me to get adjusted to that atmosphere of the towering personality. I do not know what you are wanting me to say. I am saying something. It was not easy to adjust oneself, in many ways. We had to change the diet that we eat, change the way of living, change the pattern of our rooms, and all that—less comfort—and change the way of thinking, also, which is the worst thing; it is very difficult.

You would be thinking one way in your home, normally, and think in a totally different way, as you are in the Ashram. It is centered in a new world of new laws, new regulations, in which the mind will find it hard to accommodate itself immediately and it will be a suffering for some time. It will be suffering for months; even the physical suffering the body cannot tolerate. Climatic conditions also, they are new here. It is very hot, very cold, and sometimes very rainy, and all that. You have to adjust yourself to the climatic conditions, also.

But, with all those difficulties, people like us⁻here were very happy. You would be wondering how a man with sufferings of this kind can be happy. It is because those difficulties are something like the pains you feel during surgical operations, and are you not happy at that time? You are happy that you are going to live a healthy life afterwards. That happiness goes in harmony with the suffering and agony of undergoing the surgical operation; otherwise who will undergo the suffering? So, with all the pains of this medical treatment, there is also a simultaneous happiness that you are under this protection of good physician that cancels all the pain and makes you feel very positive, hopeful, and secure. This is what we felt.

All those people, who were here at that time when I came here, some 50 years back, are not here today. These people whom you are seeing in the Ashram are latecomers. Those people, out of them, only two or three are here now. All others that you see here, many of them have not seen Swami Sivananda.

Persons like me, one among the two or three as I have said, feel very blessed that we lived under his umbrella, and basked in the warmth of that brilliant sun. Here is the answer to your question. What else can I tell you? We basked in his sun of glory

Janie: Did you discuss what was going on for you

*with the others, the people who were also going through
the same thing?*

SWAMIJI: Yes, I am telling you, these people are not
here now.

Janie: At that time.

SWAMIJI: Oh, you will be wondering that here, in
those days, discussions were not allowed. We will not
talk; we will not talk to anybody. There is no need to talk
to others, because there is no subject to discuss with
them. We cannot talk to Swami Sivananda, because he
was too frightening. We had no occasion to say anything;
so we would only be doing the work which was allotted
to us, and no talk. We would talk to ourselves only.

In those days, the total population of this Ashram
was less than twenty, and only about half a dozen
rooms,—not like this as today. So, nobody can talk; there
is nothing to talk about. We were all under the stunning
influence of that great master, and a stunned person cannot speak. [*laughter*] It was a great, wonderful thing.

You cannot find such a person in this world now.
Such persons are rare, and I don't know how many are
there like that person in the world. Such great people
have vanished. We cannot find them. They were super-
men,—not men. He was physically also tall, and very
charitable, large-hearted, good natured, smiling, positive,
and always saying "Wonderful, yes, good, good." He will
not say, "bad" and all that. Everything is good, fine, nice.
He will always finally conclude by saying it is all right.
It gives you some courage, to hear those words: "It will
be all right." How it will be all right, he will not say, and
it really becomes all right after some time. Yes.
[*laughter*] Now he has become the universal immanence,
not a particular person, so we feel his presence even now.

You people like to go to *gurus* and sit with them, but
we used to run away from him. If he comes that way, we

would go the other way. [*laughter*] Don't you think that disciples flock around the *gurus*? But we were not like that. We will run away—as far away from him—if we don't see him for three days, we were very happy. [*laughter*] Yes, really, if we see him coming that way, we will go the other way. We never encounter him on the way. So, that was a different kind of *guru* altogether.

The difference between our situation and his situation was so much that we could not stand before him. That is the reason why we ran away; and also, we were afraid as to what he will tell. He may say anything, and it would be very surprising. We do not want to hear surprising things, so we do not want to see him at all.

He may even say suddenly, "For three days, do not eat." We would not expect that thing from him. And why is he saying like that? We will be shocked. What is the matter? "Hey,—from tomorrow, three days you don't eat!" What? A shock?

If we go scantily dressed in cold winter, he will say, "This is foolish renunciation. You are torturing your body and falling sick afterwards. This is the body given by God as a temple of worship, and you are tormenting it under the impression that you are a great ascetic. Put on a woolen shawl," he will say.

Afterwards we would put it on, and go on like that. It goes on, for two or three months we go on putting on the shawl; then, afterwards, one day, he would say, "Look at this man, so much attached to this shawl! [*laughter*] Even when it is warm, and the shawl is not necessary, he is clinging to it. Hey! This attachment is very bad,—even to a blanket!" he would say. You see, we never wore it. On his insistence, we put it on. Now he is criticising because we put it on. How do you stand before that Swami? You don't know what he will say.

These things he says are very unpalatable, but they

are great instructions,—that you may not go to extremes, either this way or that way. Spiritual life is not an extreme of avoiding or getting. It is a balance that you have to maintain between two things. Neither you should cling to the body, nor should you torture it. That is the mean that you have to maintain,—the golden mean, and he was insisting on it.

People go to extremes. They go on doing *japa* always, and no work will be done, so he says, "You will become very lethargic afterwards. Do some work." If you do only work, he will say, "You are attached to the work. Do some *japa*, also." That is, every day he will prick you like this, giving one instruction or the other, and it was not easy for people to get on like that, when they could not understand him properly. Many ran away; they could not stay. And some, by God's grace, stuck, and those who stuck, I should say, were in many ways blessed—many ways.

Visitor: Swamiji, was there discussion with him?

SWAMIJI: We had no occasion to discuss. We were under the spell of his presence, and, when you are under a spell, you will not speak. We had a great satisfaction among ourselves that we are under the protection of him, and a satisfied person does not speak much. And, also, all of us were of the same category. It is not one superior, another inferior, and all that, and so one cannot communicate any wisdom to the other, as if he is superior to the other. All are all on par with each other, so what will they communicate among themselves? And, also, we were very busy, hardworking; the whole day we had to work. If we had any real difficulty, we can, of course, mention it to Swami Sivananda himself. Normally, we do not place before him any problem; but if it is very stringent, of an emergent nature, then, of course, we tell, and he will say that it will be all right. His answer is simple: "It will be all right." That is all,—and, it somehow becomes all right, afterwards. How it becomes all right, you cannot say. His word itself is a recipe. The presence itself is a teaching. He need not have to go on saying anything. It is not necessary. Some of the greatest people never say anything. They simply keep quiet, and you see them, have *darshan*, and go back. That is enough. He would not encourage people to question, and ask, and all that. He said, "Don't ask anything. You see what I am doing, and that is itself the teaching." Sometimes, we used to say, "Swamiji, we want some instructions, and some lessons from you." He says, "No, no. Don't say anything. You don't ask questions. You see what I am doing. That itself is the teaching. How I live, and what I do from morning to evening you observe, and that is the teaching."

Swami Sivananda never went out anywhere. He stuck to this place, from beginning to end. He had a little cottage down on the Ganga and he was staying there. He never changed his house; he never changed his cottage. He never wanted a better building, or any such thing. A little dungeon-like room, with not much ventilation, and even that building does not belong to this Ashram! It belongs to somebody else. And in that, he was staying. He had his own Ashram, and so he could shift, but he would not. "This is all right. Ganga is everything. All is well." His blessings on us all are always with us, ever.

APPENDIX

MARRIAGE: WHAT DOES IT MEAN?

Scientists are accustomed to the well-known phenomenon known as the "Big Bang," an occurrence which is regarded as the origin of creation of the universe. The meaning attributed to this phenomenon is that the universe was originally a single Cosmic Atom, as it were, known in Sanskrit terminology as *Brahmanda*, which split into two parts by a bang, an instantaneous separation of itself into two parts, representing what may be called the Cosmic Subject and the Cosmic Object. The *Brihadaranyaka Upanishad* has already proclaimed that there was one Universal Self which projected Itself as a subjective side and an objective side of Itself, the Cosmic Positive and the Cosmic Negative. The intriguing secret behind the relationship of the two Cosmic parts seems to be that there is on the one hand the duality of the positive and the negative and there is on the other hand the correlativity of the positive and the negative, since the two phases are actually the two types of the phenomenal occurrence in the otherwise unitary indivisible original existence.

Sage Yajnavalkya says that each unit of life is actually like a split "pea," in which one cannot easily say whether the pea is one or two things joined together. Also, the very idea of a bi-polar existence implies the interference of space and time, and even if it is accepted that the apparent two-fold life is an appearance of the original one life, the idea of "another" cannot arise unless there is some medium through which it looks as if it is there, just as one person can look like two persons when one beholds oneself through the medium of a mirror. Such a possibility involves the existence of space and time which are the most elusive things everywhere in creation. No one can understand what these actually mean since these are involved in the process of thinking itself, and no one can also deny that they do exist.

The *Brihadaranyaka Upanishad* goes on to say that the two Cosmic parts are comparable to husband and wife, in which context, the one part rushes towards the other part to come in contact with it while the other part wishes to avoid the contact since such a contact is not possible as the so-called "other" really cannot stand apart from that which seeks the contact. Humorously, through an analogy, the Upanishad says that the wife aspect ran away to escape the husband aspect coming in contact with it since an attempt at such a contact looked meaningless and also abortive. The Upanishad goes further and says that the bi-polar wholeness reduces itself to lesser and lesser "wholes," from gods in heaven down through humans, animals, plants and trees and even the lowest of creatures like insects, thus making out that this dual pull is present everywhere in creation from the highest to the lowest of created elements.

At the human level this principle of bi-polar existence takes an interesting turn, since in the human being there is an element of the instincts of the lower species and at the same time a reason which reflects the characteristics of transcendental existence. While in the earlier stages of evolution mentioned, the process of bi-polar existence appears more or less as a spontaneous feature, at the human level it becomes slightly complicated due to the reason and the instinct clashing with each other almost everyday of one's life, causing a lot of misery. As the human being is a unit in human society, the laws framed by society condition the activities of a person, while the instinctive impulses come from the other levels of life insist that they should have an upper hand over all things, and when the instincts are strong enough they can rebel against social norms, much to the chagrin of the individual, as is well-known in human history. In order to obviate this problem of conflict between individual and society, people in a common agreement among themselves have instituted a system called marriage.

Now, what exactly is marriage? It is quite clear that it is a form of legalisation of the inherent instinct of the bi-polar existence asserting itself and then a check upon any uncontrolled ravaging activity of the instinct. The point is that a person cannot live totally isolated from society since existence itself would be difficult without cooperation from others. Inasmuch as this instinct is present in every person and everyone would like to manifest it as much as possible, there would be difficulty in such a behaviour since everyone else also would like to do the same thing. This goes to say that the institution of marriage is a process of granting limited freedom to the operation of the instinct permitting it to operate within the circle of social norms, with due respect for the welfare of everyone equally.

However, with all this that has been said above, a question will arise as to why is there such an attraction between the male and the female. Philosophically, to answer this question in the light of what has been detailed above, the explanation would be the struggle of the two parts of the one whole to unite themselves into a single unit of existence. But as two things cannot become one, the sexual demand fails to fulfil its purpose ending in exasperation, disillusionment and a distrust in the meaning of life itself. The other aspect is the much neglected side of the phenomenon, namely, Nature's intention to multiply the species. Everyone knows the power of Nature and no one can resist it. The would-be entrant's push towards this world, which we call the coming of a child into existence, is the process of an integral impulse since the child is a whole being, as whole as either the father or the mother. The pressure of the would-be individual, being very strong, compels the male and the female to seek each other with great vehemence, to such an extent that the male and the female elements would even wish to die if this impulse is not going to be gratified, forgetting thereby that they are only serving the injunctions of Nature, though Nature has cleverly put them under an illusion that what they do is for their own personal benefit. Since everything is destroyed by Time, there is a fear that one's existence would be terminated one day, and to escape from the grief of this possibility, the biological impulse wishes to reproduce itself as a child, a son or a daughter, which become a replica of the parents, whom they hug as themselves, as if the child is inseparable from the parents. Considering the fact that no one can go against the injunctions of Nature, sexual life permitted by marriage should be regarded as reasonable and unavoidable, but considering the welfare of the individual himself or herself, it brings no such benefit, ending in depletion of energy, slowly tending towards old age and physical extinction. It looks that the whole drama of creation is a "hide and seek" affair of the truths of existence where everyone does something helplessly under the impression that it is done voluntarily for one's own assumed immortal satisfaction, while the fact is that the entire exercise is a hypnotised person's supposed voluntary enterprise, though commanded by the hypnotist's will.